Redressing Institutional Abuse of Children

Also by Kathleen Daly

GENDER, CRIME, AND PUNISHMENT (*1994*)

UNDER THE GUN: Weapons, Crime, and Violence in America (*with Wright, J. and Rossi, P., 1983*)

Redressing Institutional Abuse of Children

Kathleen Daly
Professor of Criminology and Criminal Justice, Griffith University, Australia

palgrave
macmillan

First published 2014 by
PALGRAVE MACMILLAN

Palgrave Macmillan in the UK is an imprint of Macmillan Publishers Limited, registered in England, company number 785998, of Houndmills, Basingstoke, Hampshire RG21 6XS.

Palgrave Macmillan in the US is a division of St Martin's Press LLC, 175 Fifth Avenue, New York, NY 10010.

Palgrave Macmillan is the global academic imprint of the above companies and has companies and representatives throughout the world.

ISBN: 978–1–137–41434–2

This book is printed on paper suitable for recycling and made from fully managed and sustained forest sources. Logging, pulping and manufacturing processes are expected to conform to the environmental regulations of the country of origin.

A catalogue record for this book is available from the British Library.

A catalog record for this book is available from the Library of Congress.

Contents

List of Tables

Acknowledgements

If it takes a village to raise a child, it has taken several villages to write this book.

My enthusiastic and loyal research assistants were pivotal to the success of the project. Gitana Proietti-Scifoni and Anne-Marie Tripp worked in 2010–12, and Gitana returned in 2013; Rhyl Armstrong, 2012–14; Dannielle Wade, 2012–14; and Victoria Meyer, 2013–14. Thank you for your research memos and analysis, tracking down information, creating numerous spreadsheets and datasets, and for your patience and perseverance. And just in the nick of time, Dr Robyn Holder arrived at Griffith to work with me and provided invaluable insight and critique in reading the final draft of the book.

I relied on many people in Canada, Australia, and elsewhere who helped me understand the cases and provided key information. I list them alphabetically, ordered by the 19 Canadian and Australia cases.

For the Canadian cases:

- Geoff Budden, Budden Morris Law Offices; Jackie Hillier, Centre for Newfoundland Studies, Memorial University of Newfoundland (*Mount Cashel*).
- Bill Blakeney, Blakeney, Henneberry, Murphy & Galligan Barristers and Solicitors; Bruce Henry and Joannie Levasseur, Archives des Jesuits au Canada; Donald C. McLean, retired lawyer and former legal counsel for the Jesuit Fathers of Upper Canada; Marion Mussell, Recorder; Father Winston Rye, Jesuits of Canada (*George Epoch*).
- Ann Hoffman and Ben Hoffman, Recorder (*St John's and St Joseph's*).
- Justice Duncan Beveridge, Nova Scotia Court of Appeal; Sonia Dubinsky, *Grandview* survivor; Bruce Feldthusen, University of Ottawa; Reg Graycar, formerly of University of Sydney; Deborah Leach, Ontario Ministry of Children and Youth Services; Ana Kapralos, Ontario Ministry of Attorney General; Seetal Sunga, Department of Justice Canada; Wanda vanderStoop, Vtape, Toronto; Susan Vella, Rochon/Genova Law Firm; Jane Wangmann, University of Technology, Sydney (*Grandview*).
- Fred Kaufman, former justice, Québec Court of Appeal; Crystal McGraw, Nova Scotia Department of Justice (*Nova Scotia Institutions*).

- Tony Fenn, Department of Justice Canada; Chris Kenopic, The Canadian Hearing Society; Sanda Rodgers, formerly of University of Ottawa and adjudicator for *Grandview* and external assessor for *Ontario Schools for the Deaf* (*Ontario Schools for the Deaf*).
- Lupin Battersby, Simon Fraser University; Rodney Hunt, Simon Fraser University; Lisa Lee, British Columbia Ministry of Justice; Jane Morley, lawyer and mediator; Anne Sheane, Anne Sheane Law Corporation; Rebecca Storey, Provincial Deaf & Hard of Hearing Services (*Jericho Hill*).
- Norm Bosse, New Brunswick Child and Youth Advocate; James Lockyer, University of Moncton; Faye Morehouse, New Brunswick Department of Public Safety; Bernard Richard, formerly New Brunswick Ombudsman and Child and Youth Advocate (*New Brunswick Institutions*).
- Jon Faulds, Field Law, Edmonton; Jana Grekul, University of Alberta (*Alberta Sterilization*).
- Pierrette Brie, Ministère de l'Emploi et de la Solidarité sociale; Marc Lurin and Louise Proulx, Secretariat for the 2007 National Reconciliation Program (*Duplessis Orphans*).
- Denis Bouthillette, Aboriginal Affairs and Northern Development Canada; John Trueman, Indian Residential Schools Adjudication Secretariat (*Indian Residential Schools*).

For the Australian cases:

- Rory Whitelaw, Department of Aboriginal Affairs (*Stolen Generations*).
- At the Forde Foundation Trust: Keara Forde; at Griffith University: Leneen Forde, Chancellor, and Ian O'Connor, Vice-Chancellor; at Lotus Place: Lachlan Douglas; at Queensland Department of Communities, Child Safety and Disability Services: Margaret Allison, former Director General; John Bottesini, Grace Bromley, Desrae Cameron, Yvette Lynch, and Heidi Mathieson (*Queensland Institutions*).
- Mervyn Humphreys and Ian Thwaites, Child Migrant Trust; Cameron Lawnton, Manager, Clontarf Aboriginal College Campus; Bob Taylor, former resident of Bindoon (*Child Migrants*).
- Helen Bodycomb, artist; Stella Conroy, Families Australia/Alliance for Forgotten Australians; Charles Gibson, UnitingCare Victoria and Tasmania; Joanna Penglase, historian and co-founder of Care Leavers of Australia; Cheryl Rickard, Rockhampton Regional Library; Shurlee Swain, Australian Catholic University (*Forgotten Australians*).

- Jeremy Harbottle, Tasmania Department of Health and Human Services (*Tasmanian Institutions*).
- Michael O'Connell, South Australia Commissioner for Victims' Rights; Martin Penhale and Margaret Ribarich, South Australia Attorney General's Department (*South Australian Institutions*).
- Marilyn Rock, Western Australia Department for Communities (*Redress WA*).

For providing insight and analysis on institutional abuse and redress outside Canada and Australia, I thank Catrien Bijleveld and Henk Elffers, both of the Netherlands Institute for the Study of Crime and Law Enforcement (the Netherlands); Jenny Johnstone, University of Newcastle (England); Timothy Lytton, Albany Law School (United States); Ingunn Studsrød, University of Stavanger (Norway); Jasmine Thompson, Ministry of Justice (New Zealand); and Stephen Winter, University of Auckland (New Zealand).

Others were instrumental in bringing the research forward. My thanks to Judy Cashmore for the invitation to present at the Historical Sex Abuse Forum, University Sydney Law School, May 2013; Tony Waters and David Kerr for the invitation to speak at the Victims of Crime National Conference, Adelaide, September 2013; Mark Finnane, Amanda Kaladelfos, and Yorick Smaal for organizing the Griffith University Interdisciplinary Workshop on Child Sexual Abuse, Brisbane, October 2013; and Trish Malins and Claudia Pitts at the Australian Royal Commission into Institutional Responses to Child Sexual Abuse. My thanks to Australian researchers and advocates: Jodi Death, Queensland University of Technology; and John and Nicola Ellis, Ellis Legal, Lawyers & Advocates.

At Griffith University, my appreciation to the library staff for locating hard-to-find documents: Margaret Bremmer, Cherie Basile, Urmila Charan, Ian Hobcroft, and Jana Rutledge; and securing and expediting inter-library loan requests: Sandra Kalms and Elspeth Wilson.

Colleagues at Griffith who helped me shape the structure of the book are Philip Stenning, Mark Finnane, and Olivera Simić. Philip was especially helpful in answering my many questions about Canadian history, law, and politics. Other colleagues were important in calculating the financial outcome data (Matthew Manning) and de-coding the Queensland State Library catalogue and having spirited discussions on the project (Yorick Smaal). I am indebted to Janet Ransley, Head of School, Criminology and Criminal Justice (CCJ), for her support, advice, and release time to write the book, and to the School of CCJ and the Arts, Education, and Law (AEL) Group for academic study leave in 2013. Support from two Australian Research Council Grants (2008–11; 2013–15) and bridging funds in 2012 from the Key Centre for Ethics, Law, Justice and Governance (Key Centre) ensured continuity in the project. I am grateful also to Janet Ransley and Paul Mazerolle (Pro-Vice-Chancellor, AEL) for providing matching funds to support research staff on my current ARC grant. Key Centre facilities, together with financial and staff support, have been essential to sustaining the project. Over the course of the project, three Key Centre managers – Kellie Hinchy, Noël Kumar, and Victoria Meyer – were instrumental in hiring and supporting members of the research team, preparing contracts, and reviewing the project's financials. The enthusiasm and support of my colleague and the Key Centre's former Director, Ross Homel (2012–13), fostered a positive and productive atmosphere; and Acting Director Tina Murphy and Director Anna Stewart have continued in the same spirit.

At Palgrave Macmillan, my appreciation to Senior Commissioning Editor, Julia Willan, for seeing the value of the project and encouraging me to complete it by a set date, and to Harriet Barker for cheery and helpful editorial advice. For supplying the book's cover photograph, I thank Peter Lindeman, Fairfax Media; and for legal review, Rhiannon Campbell, Griffith Office for Research, and Brad Eaton, Griffith Legal Services Unit.

Friends and colleagues who are mainstays are Elena Marchetti, Heather Nancarrow, my feminist reading group colleagues (Francesca Bartlett, Karen Crawley, Heather Douglas, Rachael Field, Zoe Rathus, Olivera Simić), Chris Hancock, Andrew Goldsmith, and Philip Stenning.

I dedicate this book to the memory of my mother, Claire, and to my brother, Paul, who died in a total institution.

Brisbane
July 2014

Note on the Cover

A record check by the Child Migrant Trust reveals that the cover photograph was taken in November 1947 as the children were disembarking the SS Ormonde in Sydney. Like other photographs, it depicts 'boys and girls with bright-eyed, hopeful faces', not knowing their fate (Margaret Humphreys, *Empty Cradles*, 1994, p. 53).

The photograph was acquired by Fairfax Syndication in 1989; it was first published in *The Age* in 1998, and subsequently, in other media.

Introduction: Setting the Context

Redress for institutional abuse of children is a new field of knowledge, spawned by a spate of inquiries and redress schemes in the 1980s and 1990s, and a cascade in the first two decades of the 21st century. When I began this research in 2010, I wanted to learn more about the responses to Canadian and Australian cases of historical institutional abuse. In time, my interests grew. I wanted to understand why institutional abuse emerged as a social problem and what adult survivors' memories of institutions were. Institutions for children include orphanages, homes, farm schools, training schools, hostels, facilities for those with mental and physical disabilities, and youth detention.

This book is the first to consolidate responses by Australian and Canadian Governments (and in some cases, churches and religious orders) to historical institutional abuse, and to situate current responses in historical perspective. My analysis is of 19 major cases: eleven in Canada and eight in Australia. They range in size and scope: from abuse in one to five institutions (for example, *Mount Cashel, Grandview, St John's and St Joseph's* in Canada) to the impact of country-wide policies of removing children from families (*Indian Residential Schools* in Canada; *Stolen Generations* and *Child Migrants* in Australia) and placing them in homes, residential schools, and reserves. As I show in chapter 4, the institutions and policies in the 19 cases were established, on average, in 1900, and complaints of abuse to the police or other authorities were lodged, on average, in 1959. However, it was not until 1996, on average, that authorities began to respond to complaints, 37 years later.

Key questions arise. Why, after many decades of knowing about child maltreatment did authorities begin to take it seriously in the 1980s and 1990s? What were their responses? What justice mechanisms were used, and what were the outcomes? What do the responses tell us about redress?

Chapter 1 opens with the story of *Mount Cashel*, the first case of historical institutional abuse of children in Canada. Chapter 2 encapsulates all the cases, comparing and analysing their elements; and chapter 3 examines the enablers of institutional abuse, survivors' and care leavers' memories of institutional life, and its impact. Chapter 4 puts institutional abuse in historical context by sketching earlier inquiries and investigations from the mid-19th century, the rise of the social problem of institutional abuse in the 1980s, and the elements that sparked an official response. In chapters 5 to 7, I describe and analyze the major justice mechanisms used – criminal prosecution, civil litigation, public inquiries, and redress schemes – with a focus on redress scheme processes and outcomes, and survivors' experiences with them.

My research draws upon, but departs from previous research in several ways. First, I do not focus on how and why members of the clergy (or others in similar roles) use their occupational role or organizational power to abuse children in community-based settings (for example, Terry et al., 2011). Second, I do not solely consider public inquiries, as others have (for example, Sköld, 2013) because inquiries are just one type of justice mechanism. Third, I analyze many cases in two countries, not the more typical focus on one institution or case; this approach permits an analysis of patterns and variation.

The social problem of institutional abuse of children is not self-evident. My analysis centres on historical abuse in residential and out-of-home care, not community-based institutions (the latter includes organizations in the public, private, voluntary, and faith-based sectors that provide educational, sporting, recreational, cultural, and other activities for children). However, since 2000, some have argued for widening the term 'institutional' to include non-family community-based contexts of victimization. The inclusion of these settings is a consequence, in part, of the decreasing reliance on large residential care facilities for children in Australia, Canada, the United Kingdom, and other affluent nations (although the reverse is occurring elsewhere in the world due to poverty and displacement; see Csáky, 2009). It is also a consequence of an increased focus on *sexual* victimization of children in non-family settings. Thus, today, the social problem of institutional abuse of children is constructed in at least three ways: *sexual abuse* of children by adults in a range of residential care and community-based settings; *physical, sexual, or emotional abuse* of children by adults (or their peers) in residential and out-of-home care (the latter includes foster care and group homes); and most broadly, *the conditions of life* in the 'dehumanising institutional environment' of residential care (Penglase, 2005, p. 48).

Joanna Penglase, who grew up in a state Home (which she capitalizes to distinguish it from a real home), argues that greater attention must be paid to the conditions of life in institutions. Her argument deserves consideration, although with some exceptions, legal responses to institutional abuse have centred on physical or sexual acts and their consequences. Penglase makes these points. First, growing up in an institution 'is *in itself* a traumatic and damaging experience *for any child*, regardless of whether or not that child has been "abused"' (pp. 59–60, emphasis in original). She believes that when attention is directed to 'abuse alone, we lose sight of the appalling bleakness of the life in which that abuse occurred' (p. 59). Second, media stories of abuse, whether in residential care or community-based settings, have focused almost entirely on sexual abuse of children by adults, often clergy or members of religious orders. As such, a tendency is to individualize the problem as one of a few 'bad apples' and to ignore a broader social and political context in which adults have power over children, including an ability to render children's experiences invisible. Third, she argues that too much attention has been paid to why adults have abused children, with comparatively less concern for the subjectivities of the children themselves. She invites us to 'put ourselves in the shoes of these children and ask, "What would it be like to be treated as if I were not a human being with the same feelings as other human beings? What would it be like to live in that sterile and loveless institutional environment?"' She identifies several blind spots: not seeing the greyness of institutional life, the character of adult-child power relations, and the world from a child's perspective. To these, I would add church-state power relations (McAlinden, 2013), gender and sexuality (Keenan, 2012), and post-colonial relations (Jung, 2011). Social structural relations and children's worldviews do not typically feature in the media frame of celebrated cases and 'sex scandals' of institutional abuse.

This book aims to make a contribution to the field in three ways. First, I seek to create an authoritative record of the history of institutional abuse, how it came to public attention, and what the responses and outcomes were in the 19 cases. By authoritative I mean a complete and accurate record, including, for example, when the institutions were opened and closed (or the time span of policies or legislation), the events that gave rise to a sustained response, and what the actual outcomes were. Of the 19 cases, 14 had redress schemes; and one had two schemes. Of a total of 15 redress schemes, two had complete reports on processes and outcomes. Several more had reflective reports on process, but were otherwise incomplete. Data on the numbers applying for financial payments, the percentage validated, and the amounts paid were lacking in most cases. In the Canadian cases, outcomes were still evolving when significant research was published by Kaufman (2002), the last government-commissioned review for eight of the eleven Canadian cases. For Australia, except for a Senate Report (2010), there is no analysis of the nature and quality of government or church responses; and like the Canadian cases, outcome data were not readily available and had to be sought from a range of sources.

Second, I offer a systematic understanding of the cases. To do so, I wrote a detailed synopsis of each case, drawing on primary and second sources (the 'case study'). I then created variables that tapped the history and demographics of the cases, the justice mechanisms used, redress scheme elements and outcomes, and presence and preservation of survivors' voices in official responses and in other media such as books, television, and film. Thus, in my analysis, I am able to move between the detail in individual cases and the variables across the cases. A significant contribution is an analysis of outcomes: the money logic used in redress schemes and the range and average in financial payments; services and benefits; and symbolic and preservation outcomes (apologies, monuments, commemorative activities, oral history projects, among others).

Third, I put forward and test a more robust theoretical framework to assess redress, from a victim's perspective. Much has been written on survivors' memories of abuse, the cruelty of institutional regimes, and their continuing impact into adulthood. However, less is known about survivors' experiences and aspirations in seeking justice. When analyzing justice responses, scholars have drawn from restorative justice, therapeutic jurisprudence, and transitional justice. I take a different tack by using the Sexual Victimization and Justice Matrix and its construct of 'victims' justice interests' (Daly, 2014). The matrix captures a large set of victimization-offending contexts (individual, organizational-occupational, institutional, and collective) in developing and developed countries at peace, conflict, or post-conflict. Each cell in the matrix identifies typical victim-offender relationships, the problems victims face in seeking justice, and the justice mechanisms available. The research reported here centres on one cell in the matrix, institutional abuse in developed countries at peace. I examine the problems that child victims (or family and community members) faced when reporting offences to authorities and what happened when they did. The justice mechanisms utilized were criminal prosecution, civil litigation, public inquiries, and redress schemes. I analyze these, with a focus on redress schemes, and to a lesser degree, large civil suits and public inquiries, to determine how well they met victims' justice interests of participation, voice, validation, vindication, and offender accountability. These five justice interests are large concepts that required modification when applied to the available empirical evidence in the 19 cases. However, my proposed analytic framework offers a significant advantage in assessing and comparing justice mechanisms from victims' and survivors' perspectives.

Since the mid-19th century, many inquiries and investigations of the conditions of care in institutions for children have been conducted. However, the first to focus on 'institutional abuse', as a named social problem, was in 1979, with hearings before the United States Senate Sub-Committee on Child and Human Development. Other early inquiries were established in the 1980s in England and Wales, Northern Ireland, and Canada, and in the 1990s, in England and Wales, Canada, and Australia. A significant turning point in the history of responses to institutional abuse of children occurred in the 1990s when a number of Canadian cases established redress schemes. Since 2000, many more national inquiries, redress schemes, and related responses to historical institutional abuse have been launched or completed in Australia, Belgium, Canada, Denmark, England and Wales, Finland, Germany, Iceland, Ireland, the Netherlands, New Zealand, Norway, Scotland, Sweden, and the United States. In addition, in 2012 and 2013, two large inquiries were launched: one in Northern Ireland (Inquiry into Historical Institutional Abuse) and another in Australia (Royal Commission into Institutional Responses to Child Sexual Abuse).

Current national inquiries, such as the Northern Ireland Inquiry and the Australian Royal Commission, will enable adult survivors to tell their story of victimization in institutional contexts, although this has occurred in many previous inquiries. Each story will, of course, be unique to that person and victimization context. At the same time, we may expect that it will resemble the thousands of other stories that have been told already to authorities, inquiry and commission members, tribunal members, recorders, researchers, and interviewers for oral history projects, as well as those published by victims and survivors themselves. The stories emerging from the recent Australian and Northern Ireland inquiries will show a similar 'truth' as those that have been told in the past. The only difference, and it is not insignificant, is that it may be the first time a survivor is telling his or her own story to an authority and being listened to and believed. However, many survivor groups are now pressing for greater recognition: they want more than the opportunity to tell their stories, to receive apologies, or to participate in commemorative activities. They are seeking redress. This text documents the landscape of redress for institutional abuse in Canada and Australia. It provides a comprehensive and accessible resource for the political and policy debates that lie ahead.

Part I

The Problem

1
Discovering Institutional Abuse

Mount Cashel beginnings

On Monday, 13 February 1989, St John's radio host Bill Rowe received a call to his morning talk show program, 'Open Line'.[1] It was from Steve Neary, a colleague of Rowe's during their years together in politics. On air, Neary said that in a 1979 inquiry, testimony was given of a cover-up in 1975 when the police investigated sexual and physical abuse of residents at Mount Cashel, a school for boys in St John's, Newfoundland. Interviewed later, Neary said he had no idea that his phone call 'was going to set up such a chain reaction. In my wildest imagination, I did not think there were such goings-on…at Mount Cashel…I was completely shocked, the same as everybody else in Newfoundland' (Harris, 1990, p. 262).

That day, Katherine Caddigan, who had listened to the show, rang Associate Deputy Attorney General of Newfoundland and Labrador, Robert Hyslop. She demanded that a public inquiry be conducted of cover-ups in the 1975 Mount Cashel investigation. Hyslop recalled that he had 'heard rumours' about the school, but thought they were confined to 'strapping of children' for which charges had not been laid. He told Caddigan that it was 'long in the past' and he was unable to do anything about it. Another listener was to have a more decisive impact, the wife of the Honourable John Mahoney of the Newfoundland Court of Appeal.

The next day Hyslop received a phone call from Mahoney, who asked whether Hyslop could verify the allegations of a cover-up at Mount Cashel, which his wife had heard on the radio. Hyslop recalled that Mahoney asked him, 'was there anything sexual involved?' (Harris, 1990, p. 263). Hyslop said that he thought the allegations concerned 'over-zealous strapping' but was unsure because he had not seen the police reports. According to Hyslop, 'as a result of [the judge's] query and my inability to provide detailed answers to him, I decided to investigate further' (Hughes, 1991, p. 184).

According to Hughes, 'Hyslop then engaged in a flurry of activity with momentous consequences' (p. 179). He requested police reports, written in the mid-70s, related to alleged abuse by the Christian Brothers at Mount Cashel. Upon reading a report dated 18 December 1975, he learned of 'sexual abuse by at least three brothers on a horrifying scale...the amount and type of which boggles the mind' (pp. 180–1). However, the report had subsequently been altered in March 1976; it contained fewer references to sexual abuse, although some witness statements remained. Hyslop showed the material to others that day, including the Director of Public Prosecutions, a staff member in the Special Prosecutions Unit, and the Deputy Minister. They then met with the Minister of Justice, advising her that there 'were strong indications of sexual abuse charges, including confessions having been given by at least two brothers'; further, they concluded that the offences 'were not statute barred and...we should re-open the investigation'. The Minister concurred, and Hyslop 'phoned the Chief of Police on the afternoon of February 14, 1989, and advised him to re-open the matter and that a letter would follow' (p. 185). In his letter to the Chief, Hyslop said:

> It is clear in my mind that at least one person committed over 100 individual indecent acts on at least 15 boys. *Having discovered this horrifying fact on February 14, 1989*, what cause of action is open to us? (reproduced in Hughes, 1991, p. 182; emphasis added)

Believing that 'we cannot...let this lie fallow' (p. 182–3), Hyslop asked:

> Where are these offenders? Who else is at risk? Who else has been molested by these people? Where are the victims of the crimes that these people perpetrated? Will they give evidence? Who ordered this investigation [be] terminated and why? (p. 183)

He concluded by stressing 'the need for urgent action on this file'.

This is the start of *Mount Cashel*, which was a turning point in Canada's history of responding to institutional abuse of children.[2] Although Canada was among the earliest countries to respond, other jurisdictions were beginning to take allegations of institutional abuse seriously. In related developments in the United States and Ireland, sexual abuse by Catholic clergy in community and residential settings became the subject of intense media attention, civil litigation, and criminal prosecution (beginning in 1984 in the United States and 1994 in Ireland; see respectively, Lytton, 2008; and Keenan, 2012).[3] The 1980s was a turning point in how state and church authorities decided to respond to a problem that had been known to exist for many decades.

Mount Cashel was among the earliest cases, but not the earliest, with criminal prosecution and convictions of adults (in this case, Christian Brothers) for sexually abusing children (in this case, boys) in their care. In December 1982, David Burton (a brother) pleaded guilty and was sentenced to serve 4 months for sexually abusing a boy on many occasions over a year at Mount Cashel. On appeal, his sentence was reduced to time served (12 days). A year before, in 1981, three care workers in Northern Ireland – William McGrath, Raymond Semple, and Joseph Mains – were convicted of sexual offences against 11 boys in their care, from 1960 to 1980, in the Kincora Boys' Home in East Belfast. Their sentences were 4 years (McGrath and Semple) and 6 years (Mains). Belfast police were aware of what was occurring in the boys' home in the 1970s, 6 years before they arrested the men in 1980 (Dorman and O'Cleirigh, 2013).

Like the Kincora case, the cases in this study have a longer history and an earlier starting point. In *Mount Cashel*, there were police investigations of sexual and physical abuse in 1975 conducted by Detective Robert Hillier. Although two Christian Brothers had admitted to sexually abusing boys at the time, no charges were laid. A 'deal' had been struck between the police and Department of Justice, under pressure from the Christian Brothers, to halt the investigation. In 1979, during an inquiry into a suspicious fire, a copy of Hillier's 1975 report had been leaked to the media, but the story had no momentum. In 1982, there were more investigations at the school, this time of older boys who had sexually victimized younger boys, but these were not pursued because the police did not want to lay charges against the residents.

In 1988, James Hickey, a priest in the Archdiocese of St John's, was convicted of sexual assaults against teenage boys, which he had committed over 17 years. Highly publicized, Hickey's case brought forward allegations against five other priests, who had been serving in the Archdiocese and two, who had been 'living in a lay state within the Archdiocese' (Winter, 1990, p. 1). The offending did not occur at Mount Cashel, but in the priests' residences.[4] However, these cases contributed to a general awareness of the problem, particularly for boys who had been former residents at Mount Cashel and who had reported their experiences of abuse to the police in 1975. One of them was Shane Earle.

When Earle heard that the Mount Cashel investigations were re-opened, he decided to go to the police. It was 16 February 1989, late in the evening when he gave his statement, which detailed abuse from the age of 6 when he first entered Mount Cashel in 1973, to age 19, when he left in 1986.[5] Harris (1990, p. 270) reports that when Earle gave his statement, he was 'weeping uncontrollably at times'; and when recounting the cover-up in 1975, he told the detectives that he and other boys felt a sense of betrayal, that society 'had shut the door on us, and society didn't really care about what happened to the kids at Mount Cashel' (p. 270). Shane Earle was the first *Mount Cashel* survivor to give a statement to the police.

Publisher and editor-in-chief of the St John's weekly, *The Sunday Express*, Michael Harris was following developments when the investigation re-opened; and on 12 March 1989, his strongly worded editorial called for an inquiry into 'the deal' between the Christian Brothers and Department of Justice. Earle read it, and later said to the Hughes inquiry that 'finally somebody knows what they're talking about, finally someone's not talking in circles any more' (Harris, 1990, p. 272). Earle talked with Harris about having his story published in the newspaper; and after considering the consequences, he decided to write about what had happened, which was published in two parts on 19 and 26 March 1989. Harris reports that it 'went off like a bomb' (p. 274). Now there was a human face to *Mount Cashel*: that of a 6-year-old boy being sexually abused by a Christian Brother. What was Shane Earle looking for? In part 2 of his *Sunday Express* story, he said,

> I'm just looking for a lot of answers. Why this went on? Why nothing was said? Why there was no counselling? And why there was no guidance? Mount Cashel was supposed to be a place for boys. But it turned out to be hell on earth. (p. 275)

In 1989, Earle appeared on the Oprah Winfrey show, where he said he lit a fire in the basement of Mount Cashel, hoping that the building would burn down (Weisblott, 2011).

On 14 April 1989, the province announced the establishment of a Royal Commission of Inquiry into the Response of the Newfoundland Criminal Justice System to Complaints, chaired by the Honourable Samuel Hughes, a former member of the Ontario Court of Appeal. It was the first inquiry into institutional abuse of children and its handling by state authorities in Canada, and among the earliest of its kind.[6] Three weeks later, in response to the James Hickey case and others of clergy abuse in the St John's Archdiocese, Archbishop Alphonsus Penney established a Special Commission of Enquiry into Sexual Abuse of Children by Members of the Clergy, chaired by the Honourable Gordon Winter, former Lieutenant Governor of the province.[7]

During 1989–90, the Hughes inquiry and police investigations were occurring at the same time. This created 'a sense of incompletion [in] the proceedings ... of dire and unfinished business' (Harris, 1990, p. 366) because none of those alleged to have committed offences was called to answer questions at the inquiry. (This would come later with prosecutions and convictions in the 1990s.) A total of 31 former Mount Cashel residents participated in the inquiry. Some were later interviewed by the Institute for Human Resources Development (IHRD) (1998), who reported that they 'found it an extremely distressing process' and that Hughes 'was not sensitive to [their] needs, cutting them off or not allowing them to say what they wanted' (pp. 72–3). Rather than televised hearings, which 'made it into a circus' (p. 15) and 'put them on display' (p. 72), some would have preferred to speak more privately with Hughes. On 31 May 1991, Hughes submitted his two-volume report to the government; it was released nearly a year later, on 24 April 1992, after the first set of trials concluded. Hughes said that the police should have laid charges in 1975, and he inferred that a Department of Justice official had a 'consultation' with the assistant or police chief to cease the investigation (Hughes, 1991, p. 209). He recommended several approaches to recompensing victims, but these were not taken up by government officials; rather, victims would have to prove their case in court.

Shane Earle, who filed a law suit in 1989, settled for an undisclosed sum with the Christian Brothers and the province in 1995. Shane's brother settled soon after. Two major civil settlements were reached in 1996 and 2004, each taking 7 to 8 years; and on 23 May 2013, a third major settlement was announced.

Ripple effects

Mount Cashel was important in the evolution of responses to institutional abuse of children: not only was it the first response in Canada, the Hughes inquiry was watched on television by many.[8] It was also the subject of a two-part television series, first aired in Australia in 1993, *The Boys of St Vincent*. There are several examples of the ripple effects and connections of *Mount Cashel* to the other cases.

One is its relationship to *St John's and St Joseph's* (Ontario). David McCann, who would become the leader of a victims' advocacy group, Helpline, learned about the Hughes inquiry when watching the television news. He followed the inquiry closely, having himself been abused at St Joseph's School. At the time, he told his mother about it, and she relayed it to a probation officer; however, it was 'either rejected or ignored' (Henton and McCann, 1995, p. 91). On 4 November 1989, McCann rang the Hughes Commission office; and although it was nearly midnight, Counsel David Day was in the office and answered the phone. McCann asked him whether the inquiry could address abuse incidents that occurred outside Newfoundland, making reference not only to his experiences, but also to those of 'other boys, his chums, [who were] mistreated at St Joseph's' (p. 91). David Day said, no, he could not, but that McCann should tell the police or a lawyer in Ontario. McCann decided instead to call a journalist, and in time, he met journalist Darcy Henton, who began to investigate McCann's claims. Henton visited the Archives of Ontario and came across a notation to an inquiry into St Joseph's School in 1960, and he decided to file a Freedom of Information request for the documents. Months later, in March 1990, he received documents that detailed internal investigations of sexual and physical abuse during 1958–60, none of which had been reported to the police. His efforts would ultimately lead to the government re-opening the case in 1990. At the close of his book with Henton, McCann says 'to the boys in Newfoundland: thank you for your courage and for leading the way' (p. 298).

A second is the relationship of *Mount Cashel* to *Child Migrants*, one of the Australian cases. For background, the British and Australian Governments established a policy in 1912 to transport 'immigrants of good sound British stock' to Australia (Child Migrants Trust, 2013). (Children were also sent to other Commonwealth countries, including Canada, New Zealand, and Rhodesia [Zimbabwe]). About 7,000 children were sent to Australia, and about half, to Western Australia. In Alan Gill's book on Child Migrants, he reports that when *The Boys of St Vincent* aired in Australia in August 1993 (and again in June 1996), audiences noted 'its marked similarity to alleged events at Western Australian orphanages run by the Christian Brothers' (Gill, 1997, p. 516). He said that a former Child Migrant rang him 'as the [television] credits were rolling', and told him, 'it's like history repeating itself. I know it was in Canada, but I could swear it was Bindoon. I felt I was there' (Gill, 1997, p. 519).

This strong sense of connection between experiences of abuse in Western Australia (Bindoon was a receiving institution for *Child Migrants*),

Newfoundland (*Mount Cashel*), and Ontario (*St John's and St Joseph's*) can be been traced to how the Christian Brothers ran these institutions and others under their control. However, the commonalities run deeper: when reading across the cases, survivors' stories of abuse are remarkably similar. *Mount Cashel* and *Child Migrants* show that while the reasons that children were placed in institutions differed (British children were sent to Australian institutions as a result of a policy between two governments, and Mount Cashel boys were state wards or voluntarily placed by parents), once in an institution, children's experiences were similar. This comes from living in a total institution.

Total institutions

Erving Goffman (1961) created the concept of 'total institution' after spending a year in the mid-1950s as a fieldworker in the St Elizabeth's Hospital (Washington, DC), an institution for those diagnosed with mental illnesses. Goffman assumed the role of hospital inmate, 'pass[ing] the day with patients, avoiding sociable contact with the staff…to learn about the social world of the hospital inmate' (p. ix). He did not sleep in the wards, but the management knew what he was doing and provided him access to all parts of the hospital. Goffman's aim was to convey inmates' perspectives of the 'daily round of petty contingencies to which they are subject' (p. x). His gift was to lift the empirical specificity of one institution to a larger theorization of the character of 'total institutions', the treatment of 'inmates', and the transformation of 'the self' when an individual moves between a 'home world and the institutional world' (p. 65). He defined a total institution as

> a place of residence and work where a large number of like-situated individuals, cut off from the wider society…, together lead an enclosed, formally administered round of life. Prisons serve as a clear example, providing we appreciate that what is prison-like about prisons is found in institutions whose members have broken no laws. (p. xiii)

Goffman conceptualized total institutions as having elements found in other social settings, but to a much more intense degree. In total institutions, three spheres of life – sleeping, playing, and work – are 'conducted in the same place and under the same authority…in the company of a large batch of others…and tightly scheduled' (p. 6). He recognized that other settings such as 'farm families may have all their major spheres of life in the same fenced-in area' (p. 6), but they are not subject to batch living or regimentation. He concluded that 'the total institution is a social hybrid, part residential community, part formal organization' (p. 12). He gave examples of inmates' experiences in many types of total institutions, but with the exception of youth detention facilities and boarding schools, none of his examples were of residential facilities for children. His omission is telling, but not surprising.

When Goffman was writing in the 1950s, there was little public awareness of abusive regimes in institutions *for children*. These were largely invisible places, where children of poor or 'unfit' parents or unmarried mothers were sent; some had been taken away from parents who loved them, and others, who abused them; still other children had mental or physical disabilities. As Ferguson (2007, p. 137) suggests with respect to the Irish industrial school system, in place from 1869 to the early 1970s, 'a striking feature ... was the unquestioned and apparently *unquestionable moral authority of the care providers*' (p. 137, emphasis added), who were both lay and members of religious orders. Care providers 'put significant effort into concealing the children's bruises and other injuries to the outside world ... and created the false impression of adequate care' (p. 128). In this closed institutional context, 'abuse thrived because it was so well hidden by those who knew they were doing wrong' (p. 137). This began to change in the 1980s.

Child abuse, institutional child abuse, and historical institutional abuse

The victimization of children is as old as recorded human history (Tomison, 2001), but the words now used to describe it – physical abuse, sexual abuse, and institutional abuse – are new. I shall be using these terms throughout my analysis, with the recognition of their recent vintage. Up until the 1980s, physical abuse in institutions was termed 'cruelty', 'mistreatment', or 'harsh discipline'; but as Rollinson (2006, p. 22) suggests, 'care must be taken in how the term [abuse] is used retrospectively'. In Chapter 4, I analyse why institutional abuse of children emerged as a social problem in the 1980s. Here, I briefly sketch child abuse and institutional abuse as concepts.

Parton (1979) traces the 'discovery'[9] of child *physical* abuse to a paediatric radiologist in the United States, whose research in the mid-1940s identified traumas to the skull and leg. The radiologist's findings were confirmed by others in the 1950s. A significant breakthrough occurred in the United States in 1962 with an article by Kempe et al. (1962) on 'the battered child syndrome', a 'condition in young children who have received physical abuse ... from a parent or guardian' (p. 105). According to Parton, the article was important not only for identifying a medical condition, but also for its 'firm emotive level' (p. 436), which urged that when diagnosed, doctors should report cases to the police and welfare authorities. The next step in the history of the term was 'concept diffusion' – of seeing child physical abuse as widespread – which began in the late 1960s and early 1970s.

The 'discovery' of child *sexual* abuse began in the 1970s. Among the earliest uses of 'child sexual abuse' as a term in published research was by Vincent de Francis (1969) and David Gil (1970), who distinguished 'child sexual abuse' from 'physical child abuse'. In the early 1970s, second-wave feminism brought sexual victimization of children and women to public attention, although child-saving workers in the 19th century were well aware of the problem (Gordon, 1988). The next step – of seeing child sexual abuse as widespread – began in the 1970s and continued into the 1980s. Like child physical abuse, attention centred on intra-familial sexual abuse.

'Institutional abuse' of children was a concept coined by David Gil (1975), who viewed it as situated between the familial and societal levels of child abuse. Gil's value-based definition of child abuse was not solely concerned with bones or bodies. He defined child abuse as 'inflicted gaps in children's circumstances that prevent actualization of inherent potential' (p. 346); this included not only 'abusive interactions' (acts of abuse), but also 'abusive conditions' and policies (p. 347). With this definition, a large array of settings and policies was identified as contributing to child abuse: 'day care centers, schools, courts, child care agencies, welfare departments, and correctional and other residential care settings', where, Gil argued, 'legally sanctioned abuse' occurred (p. 347). Likewise, Garrett (1979, p. 62) said that 'physical and sexual maltreatment represent the most dramatic forms of abuse, are the simplest to define and verify, and have come to symbolize the issue', but other forms should be included: 'emotional and intellectual damage', caused by a lack of providing children opportunities for growth, and 'social damage and labelling', by institutionalization itself or by being labelled 'mentally retarded or emotionally disturbed' (pp. 62–3). As the editor of the proceedings of the first National Conference on the Institutional Maltreatment of Children, held in 1977 in the United States, Garrett represented the views of his colleagues and the expansive mood of the times.

Broad conceptualizations of institutional abuse began to narrow when the United States Government funded pilot projects on institutional child abuse in the late 1970s. One of the first surveyed abuse in residential and out-of-home care facilities in San Francisco, including '...long-term shelters, detention homes,...group homes, foster homes, and juvenile shelters' (E. Gil and Baxter, 1979, p. 693). A significant finding was the denial of abuse by the administrators of care facilities. Some had 'remembered "vague rumours" of a particular staff member physically or sexually abusing a child', but none believed that 'abusive behaviour' by their staff toward children 'was a potential or existing problem' (p. 694). It would take another decade before institutional abuse was recognized as a social problem.[10]

Gil's (1975) definition of institutional abuse, which included any type of institution for children and all types of 'abusive conditions' and policies, was too radical to have staying power.[11] As the term evolved in the 1980s, institutional abuse of children continued to be defined as that occurring in residential and out-of-home care, including foster and group homes (Powers et al., 1990). Then, a change occurred. In 2000, the 'institutional' in institutional child abuse began to expand; and for some, the abuse in 'abuse' contracted. Gallagher (2000, p. 797) proposed that institutions should include not only residential settings and foster care, but also community-based organizations such as 'schools, clubs for children, and child minders' homes'. While Gallagher's definition of institutional expanded, he restricted 'abuse' to sexual abuse of children by 'an adult who works with him or her' in a variety of paid or unpaid capacities (p. 797). Gallagher was principally concerned with child protection, and as such, he was interested to find better ways to identify and intervene in any non-family context where *contemporary abuse* of children might occur. Alongside his proposed re-definition of institutional abuse, another new term has emerged: 'historical institutional abuse'.

It is unclear who coined the concept of historical institutional abuse and when it was first introduced. In 2000, the term was used by the Law Commission of Canada (LCC), who defined it as 'institutional child abuse that took place many years ago' (LCC, 2000, p. 6). The LCC report said that 'we must come to terms *with history* and deal with the wrongs committed', but at the same time 'scrutinise the situation of children *currently in care* outside their homes' (p. 7, emphasis added). However, as research on and responses to institutional abuse of children have evolved, what is considered 'past' and 'present' institutional abuse often differs. In general, if the focus is on *historical* institutional abuse, there is a wide understanding of 'abuse' that is physical, sexual, emotional, and in some instances, cultural; and the types of institutions considered are 'total' or segregated from the mainstream. By comparison, if the focus is on *contemporary* institutional abuse, there may be a broad understanding of institutions that includes residential facilities and any organized activity outside the family home, but attention centres on sexual abuse. Thus, the literature on historical institutional abuse deals with residential institutions for children in the past, and with adult survivors seeking recognition and redress; whereas that on contemporary institutional abuse is concerned with mapping the prevalence of sexual abuse in a wide variety of settings and identifying modes of intervention and prevention. Adding more complexity (and definitional confusion),[12] institutional abuse of children, as a term, may refer to both historical and contemporary abuse. To illustrate, the Ireland's Ryan Commission to Inquire into Child Abuse (2009) and its Residential Institutions Redress Board, and Northern Ireland's Inquiry into Historical Institutional Abuse are responses to historical institutional abuse (both physical and sexual). However, Australia's Royal Commission into Institutional Responses to Child Sexual Abuse is concerned with historical and contemporary institutional abuse, but as the name of the Commission suggests, it is sexual abuse only. I have taken some time to clarify terms because the field of institutional abuse can be confusing for anyone new to it. In addition, my aims are to reclaim Goffman and to ask why child sexual abuse has assumed a privileged status.

Reclaiming Goffman

In the last several decades, some have argued that Goffman's concept of total institutions is overdrawn and less relevant because some total institutions are 'not-so-total'. Farrington (1992) puts forward this argument, having in mind prisons in the United States; and he says there are 'points of interpenetration' between those inside and outside its walls. Likewise, in her analysis of adults with mental illness, Perring (1992, p. 127) suggests that there are 'broader patterns of movement between [a total institution] and the wider community'. However, neither author considers institutions for children. Movement between a residential care facility and the wider community was not unusual for children in residential care: some attended school away from the residential facility (as occurred in at Mount Cashel from the late 1960s); others visited or took trips with family members or relatives; and others were invited to Sunday lunch by community members. Thus, the experience of residential care could be 'total' and 'not-so-total'. Wolfe et al. (2002) argue that Goffman is less relevant today because he does not consider community-based institutions; however, if one is interested in historical institutional abuse, their argument is less compelling.

In my view, the concept of total institution is as fresh and relevant today as it was when Goffman first presented it.[13] It helps to explain the enablers of institutional abuse and the difficulties victims have (and have had) in reporting it to authorities. It also helps to conceptualize a range of institutional contexts, some of which are more encompassing and closed off ('more total') than others. The more closed off an institution is, the more hidden the abuse, and the less likely an individual is able to report or escape. Furthermore, as Ferguson (2007, p. 137–8) suggests, although changes to residential care occurred in affluent nations in the 1970s and 1980s, 'the construction of ... looked after children as ... "moral dirt" lingers', a consequence of the 'painfully low status of children in care'. Thus, when analysts focus largely on sexual abuse in community-based institutions, I fear a loss of interest in children who are among the most vulnerable and least visible in society, those in residential care.[14]

Why is sexual abuse privileged?

Drawing from Penglase (2005, pp. 105–18), the common experiences of Australian children in residential care were 'feeling fear on a daily basis', being stripped of a sense of self and identity, living with strict controls and regimentation, having to eat poor food and going hungry, suffering extreme corporal punishment, and being subject to 'sexual use' by adults for their own gratification. I develop several points that Penglase makes on sexual use and abuse.

First, 'sexual use' by adults may be more accurate than 'sexual abuse' because 'children in institutions *were used* by adults for their own sexual gratification. They were commodities' (p. 144, emphasis added). Another aspect of adult's sexual use was that 'older children would victimize younger ones, passing the abuse down the line' (p. 145). Second, 'sexual abuse is always highlighted as if it is the "worst" abuse.... What gets lost is that children were violated in every sense in an institution, and being used sexually was just one of those violations' (p. 145). Penglase argues that viewing sexual abuse as the 'worst' abuse 'is an adult-centred perspective, focusing on the criminality and "unnaturalness" of the physical act itself'.

The latter point is crucial to understanding both the contemporary and historical institutional abuse of children. Institutional abuse emerged as a social problem in the 1980s at Mount Cashel School and elsewhere because it was *sexual* abuse, often by adult men of boys; and at Mount

Cashel, it was by members of religious orders. Recall Justice Mahoney's question to Robert Hyslop: 'was there anything sexual involved?' We may wonder, why was (and is) 'sexual activity' of greater concern than mere 'physical strappings'?[15] The reasons may seem self-evident to some: the 'unnaturalness' of same-sex sexual coercion of children by adults. However, from a child's perspective in residential care, it may be less so. Penglase quotes from a male adult survivor, who had been in Queensland farm home in the 1950s:

> Naturally, there was also sexual abuse. It took place in the showers, mostly. Sometimes it was the warders who did it, other times, it was the bigger, older boys who abused the smaller, younger ones. Oddly enough though, *in a place so full of brutality, sexual abuse did not rank as highly as the other forms of abuse,* such as mental and emotional torture, lack of adequate clothing, shortage of food, and the strings of punishment that never seemed to end.... That sexual abuse was the least of our worries should tell you how bad things really were. (Penglase, 2005, pp. 142–3, emphasis added)

Penglase may be right to say that the assumption of 'sexual abuse' as being the worst form of abuse may be an 'adult-centred' concern. Here, we may wonder why some desire to broaden contemporary institutional abuse to include community-based settings, but then limit the wrongs to sexual abuse by adults of children, as Gallagher (2000) does, and as do the terms of reference for the Australian Royal Commission into Institutional Responses to Child Sexual Abuse. Why has this occurred? Why are some wrongs against children wrong, but not others? Or why are some wrongs thought to be 'more wrong' than others?

Discovering abuse: a wrap up

Mount Cashel reveals the key elements in the 'discovery' of historical institutional abuse. The discovery is of *sexual* abuse by adults of children in their care, not 'mere physical strappings', which might have been more acceptable. Furthermore, it is sex-specific: adult men are abusing boys, a 'horrifying' fact. Sustained media attention focuses not only on the abuse, but also a history of failed investigations and alleged cover-ups by the police in the past, perhaps in collusion with church authorities. Care leavers and survivors give public stories of abuse, which encourages others to come forward and creates public concern for and sympathy with children who had lived in residential care. A cultural platform is built around survivors' stories of institutional life (or policies that led to their institutionalization), which transcends particular locales and gives greater credibility and observability to historical institutional abuse as a social problem. As more cases come to public attention, allegations are made against both male and female lay and religious workers, and by male and female survivors.

Once discovered and identified, the responses to institutional abuse vary. *Mount Cashel* is similar to other cases in my sample in that there were police investigations and criminal prosecutions, and civil suits were filed. However, it is unusual in that in addition to the Hughes public inquiry, the only other justice mechanism was major civil settlements. Fourteen of the 19 cases had redress schemes, which were either negotiated between lawyers for the plaintiffs and government (or church) or government-stipulated. The schemes varied in the degree to which victim advocacy groups participated in their design, the specific elements in the redress scheme, how they were implemented, and what the outcomes were. However, it is premature to speak of similarities and differences without first understanding the history and character of each case. That is the subject of the next chapter.

2
The Cases

Each case is a bundle of thousands of people (and at times, hundreds of thousands): as *victim/survivors*, their family members (past and present), and friends; as alleged *individual offenders* (who are recalled, reported, prosecuted, convicted, or acquitted), their family members past (and present), and friends; or *organizational offenders* (government, church, and other organizations)[1]; and as *front-line observers and responders* (citizens with information, staff working at the institutions, police officers, journalists, prosecutors, judges, social workers, counsellors, government staff, church staff, and many more). A wider circle has watched television series or documentaries, visited museums, and participated in oral history projects or in political demonstrations for change. Each case also has a long history, whether of the establishment of a policy or institution; and each has a local meaning and significance, which outsiders may not fully appreciate. Each incorporates many organizations and political–economic interests, which have intersected with the lives of children and their families. Of this vast pool of information, I sketch the historical elements of each case and those aspects most germane to understanding redress.

Country and case selection

For country selection, Canada and Australia are among the first countries to hold public inquiries and create redress schemes in response to historical institutional abuse. The countries are similar in many ways. Indigenous populations were colonized and killed by the British and other colonial powers during the 17th and 18th centuries, and subject to forcible assimilation policies from the late 19th century to the latter part of the 20th century. As 'settler democracies', both nations today confront a legacy of political disenfranchisement of and discrimination against Indigenous and Aboriginal peoples. The countries have similar social and legal histories and took the same approach to developing institutions for children, with oversight by state authorities but day-to-day running of the facilities by church and charitable organizations. In the contemporary era, both have state or provincial governments, with strong national-level political structures. Geographically, both have large land masses, with both dispersed and highly concentrated populations. The countries are often the subject of comparative analysis because of their many similarities.

For case selection, the criteria for inclusion were historical cases of physical or sexual abuse of children in residential care,[2] which had public inquiries, major civil litigation, or redress schemes. The cut-off time for inclusion was mid-year 2010.

The Canadian cases were initially identified in reviews by Bessner (1998) and Shea (1999a), who conducted research for the Law Commission of Canada (LCC) (2000), and in Kaufman's (2002, chapter XVI) review. One requires explanation: *George Epoch*. Epoch, a priest and member of the Jesuit Fathers of Upper Canada, sexually abused over 120 children. The case concentrates on the period of Epoch's offending, from 1969 to 1983, when he was a pastor at Wikwemikong (a Jesuit mission) and St Mary's Church (a diocese that includes Cape Croker and Saugeen), which are three First Nations communities in Ontario. The abuse occurred mainly in the Cape Croker rectory, a small house that sat behind the church. Epoch's *modus operandi* was similar to that of other priests (or adults acting in 'caring' or teaching roles), who groom children with money, alcohol, and cigarettes. However, the children lived with their families, and Epoch's home was not a 'total institution' in the Goffman sense. Rather, according to the First Nations Recorder, it was 'a hangout for the "guys"', who protected it from view by adults in their community (Mussell, 1995, p. 5). I included it because the abuse occurred in *symbolically closed communities*; and like other cases, it had a redress scheme.

Since mid-year 2010 in Canada, two other cases of institutional abuse of children have emerged. One is the Huronia Regional Centre (originally Orillia Asylum for Idiots), established in 1876 in Ontario for children with mental disabilities. A class action was certified (that is, approved by the court to go forward) in July 2010, and the case was settled in September 2013, with a structured settlement of payments, an apology, and memorial. It was the first Canadian class action suit against a government-sponsored psychiatric facility, and others are in the pipeline. The second is the Nova Scotia Home for Coloured Children, which opened in 1921 in Dartmouth. The Home was subject to court action, and it settled for $5 million in 2013 with former residents. A class action by former residents against the province was filed and certified in December 2013, and a tentative settlement was reached in June 2014.

The eight Australian cases were all those as of mid-year 2010. Since then, others have emerged or concluded. In Western Australia, an inquiry into abuse in country hostels for children began in 2011; and in 2012, a redress scheme was announced. Two major state inquiries on child abuse in religious organizations (Victoria) and state care (Queensland) were concluded in 2013; and another on police investigations of child sexual abuse in a Catholic Diocese (New South Wales) was concluded in May 2014. The Australian Royal Commission into Institutional Responses to Child Sexual Abuse, which includes Commonwealth, state, and territory jurisdictions, began in January 2013. With a proposed 2-year extension, it will likely run to December 2017.

Case types and overview

My analysis reveals different types of institutional abuse cases. These can be conceptualized as a core with two concentric rings. Common to all cases, at their 'core', is a failure of authorities to protect and care for children. Of the 19 cases, 12 are 'core' cases in that this was the sole basis for response. In addition, five are 'core-plus' cases. In these, policy or practice wrongs were committed against certain groups of children ('core-plus-one' cases), or such policy or practice wrongs against children were embedded in a more general discrimination against a political minority group ('core-plus-two' cases). In the core-plus cases, allegations of (and convictions for) institutional abuse are relevant, but secondary to the policy or practice wrongs. Two cases are redress scheme-only: one was state-level redress for a core-plus-two wrong (*Tasmanian Stolen Generations*) and the second was state-level redress for physical or sexual abuse for any child in state care (*Redress WA*). As discussed in Chapter 4, the core-plus cases moved in the public arena in different ways than the core cases, and they have a large cultural platform.

Appendix 1 gives a snapshot of the cases. Reading it, from left to right, column (1) shows the case number (CA1 to CA11, AU1 to AU8) and if the case continues (that is, litigation continues, a redress scheme remains open, or benefits and services continue). Column (2) gives a short case name and the type of case (core, core-plus-one, and core-plus-two). Columns (3) and (4) show the complete name, associated institutions, when they opened and closed, and location. The types of institutions are listed in column (5). Here we see that in Australia, five cases included foster placements;[3] and in Canada, three cases were composed entirely of institutions for children with physical or mental disabilities. Column (6) shows more sources of variability. Most cases concerned sexual and physical abuse (some also included neglect), but four dealt with sexual abuse only. Although abuse by staff was the focus in most cases, abuse by residents was included or not explicitly excluded in ten cases (when no information is given, peer abuse is not relevant to the case, not known, or highly unlikely). The institutions held a wide range of groups of children in residential care, including wards of the state, voluntary placements, those with disabilities, and those adjudicated delinquent or sentenced for crime. Columns (7) and (8) give the numbers of institutions and children affected. For cases with significant civil litigation (that is, 70 or more plaintiffs in civil settlements), the numbers are shown in column (8).

Differences are evident in the Canadian and Australian cases: almost all the Canadian cases are of one to five institutions in one province, whereas all the Australian cases have a high number of institutions state- or country-wide. For the Canadian cases, those with the largest number of institutions are *Duplessis Orphans* (at least 26) and *Indian Residential Schools* (139 eligible schools). In the Australian cases for which the number of institutions is known, the range is 52 to 334. For numbers affected, the largest Australian case is *Forgotten Australians*, with an estimated 500,000 children, and the largest Canadian case is *Indian Residential Schools*, with an estimated 150,000 children. An encapsulation of each case follows, ordered by country and then by core and core-plus cases. I sketch the historical background to the case, how the problem of abuse (or policy/practice wrong) emerged, and the response. It is a barebones sketch, with more layers to the story given in Chapters 3 to 7 and Appendices 2 to 6.

Canadian core cases

The eight Canadian core cases are *Mount Cashel*, *George Epoch*, *St John's and St Joseph's*, *Grandview*, *Nova Scotia Institutions*, *Ontario Schools for the Deaf*, *Jericho Hill*, and *New Brunswick Institutions*.

Mount Cashel, Newfoundland and Labrador (CA1)

Mount Cashel Orphanage was established in 1892 in the family home of Archbishop Howley in St John's. With increasing numbers of children, a larger facility was built in 1898 on the property, which Howley bequeathed to the local Catholic Archdiocese. For many years, Mount Cashel was a residential facility for boys who were homeless or whose parents placed them voluntarily. The Christian Brothers of Ireland managed the orphanage and taught the boys. From 1966, Mount Cashel received children referred by the Department of Social Services, as wards of the state. Up to the late 1960s, it was a 'self-contained institution with schooling, recreation, and daily care' all taking place on its grounds (Hughes, 1991, p. 10). This changed when the brothers taught at schools in town during the day, and the boys attended school in town, returning to the residence for lunch and in the evening (p. 8). In 1969, it was renamed Mount Cashel Boys' Home and Training School, and the province funded the school's operations; however, from the early 1950s, the government had taken an interest in how the school was run (pp. 8–9).

In 1975, the police investigated allegations of sexual and physical abuse and took statements from 25 Mount Cashel boys. Detective Hillier was ordered to re-write his December 1975 report to remove references to sexual abuse. He edited it, but included the boys' statements. When ordered to submit a second report in March 1976, he produced one with less detail, although it contained some of the boys' testimonies. During the 1975 investigation, two brothers (Ralph and English) admitted to sexually abusing the boys, but no charges were laid, and they were ordered to leave Newfoundland. Three others were implicated (Kenny, Burke, and Short). In February 1989, public attention was drawn to Mount Cashel with a phone call to a radio program, suggesting a cover-up by police and justice authorities. Pressure was put on the government by a local paper, with articles appearing in March by the publisher and a former resident, Shane Earle. The government re-opened the 1975 investigation, and in April 1989, announced the establishment of a Royal Commission of Inquiry. From 1982 to 2004, 18 individuals were charged (17 brothers and one civilian). Of these, 15 were convicted and sentenced (14 brothers and one civilian), two were acquitted, and one outcome is not known.[4] Among those convicted were Ralph, English, Kenny, and Burke.

Mount Cashel closed in June 1990; and in 1992 the building was razed. The land was sold to Sobeys Inc., a large food retailer, who in 1998 built a $20 million supermarket and a small housing development on the site. From 1995 to 2013, about 209 former residents received payouts from individual and group civil settlements. The Christian Brothers issued an apology, but the government did not. Litigation continues.

George Epoch, Ontario (CA2)

Epoch was a pastor in Wikwemikong in 1959–60, 1969–71, and 1983–86. During 1971–83, he lived in Cape Croker and would travel from there to Saugeen. Cape Croker and Saugeen are First Nations communities, which together form the Chippewas of Saugeen Ojibway Territory, located on the Bruce Peninsula about 250 kilometers (155 miles) north of Toronto. Across the strait on the eastern side of Manitoulin Island is Wikwemikong, a First Nations community. Epoch died on 1 October 1986 and was buried in Wikwemikong because residents requested he be buried in their community rather than the Jesuit cemetery. His offending mainly occurred in his Cape Croker rectory, and to a lesser degree, Saugeen and Wikwemikong.[5]

Epoch's rectory in Cape Croker was a small house that sat behind the church. According to Marion Mussell, a First Nations woman and Recorder for the survivors (1995, pp. 5–6):

> It was a curious place filled with bric-a-brac and odds and ends enough to delight the eyes and curiosity of any child. The walls were filled with pictures of children and their artwork.... From the ceilings hung mobiles and gadgets with moving parts to engage the visual senses... These odds and ends proved enough enticement for children to want to be in his place... It was intended to be a haven, a warm welcoming trap for children.

Mussell says 'it is curious that no one ever considered how peculiar it was for a grown man to decorate his home as Father did.... No one ever openly questioned it [or] suspected it was a home of so much victimization' (pp. 5–6). Epoch's collection of odds and ends that he bought at flea markets was 'seen as a reflection of his amiable eccentricity' (p. 6). The male survivors said the rectory 'was a place where they were welcomed and could spend time and do whatever they wanted' (p. 5). However, it came at the price of sexual abuse. In addition to sexually assaulting children in the rectory, he did so in his van, on camping trips, and in the church. His victims were mainly male (80 per cent) and 7 to 16 years old (p. 4).

The first complaint of abuse was made in June 1985 to Father Frank McGee, who was visiting Cape Croker. On two occasions, a survivor in his 20s gave the information to McGee in confidence, saying he did not want to see Epoch confronted. The Jesuits conducted an internal investigation in 1985, but McGee did not report the complaint to the police until April 1990, 4 years after Epoch's death. More allegations of abuse were made in 1991–92, and the Jesuits' investigations concluded there was a history of abuse by Epoch. A sincere apology was given by the Jesuit Provincial Superior in August 1992; and in addition, the Jesuits began an informal response, Appropriate Assistance, to provide 'concrete support to those who needed it' (p. 15). Cash payments were made to 40 Epoch victims in 1993–94, and other funds were spent for counselling, education, and creation of healing centres in Cape Croker. However, 'the numbers were getting too large, and the cost, too expensive' (p. 15); thus, another response was required.

A negotiated agreement was forged from meetings with a small group of victims and the Jesuits; formalized in 1993, it was ratified in October 1994. During the year leading up to ratification, Mussell (1995, p.10) says that in Cape Croker, 'the situation became more politically intense and the community more divided…The Band Council opted not to be an active participant…The Council withdrew…' It had been assumed that 40 people would ratify the agreement, but this grew to 97 by the deadline. Like other agreements in Ontario (*St John's and St Joseph's* and *Grandview*), the agreement in *George Epoch* had a financial payment, access to benefits in an Opportunity Fund, and services.

Most adult survivors were still living in the communities. When increasing numbers of survivors came forward in the 1990s, an escalation of tensions and divisions occurred. In Cape Croker, residents 'would not find common ground on which to work as a community' (Mussell, 1995, p. 11). In Saugeen, an initially positive response to survivors gave way to 'negative attitudes,…and victims became targets of verbal abuse about their victimization and were marginalized in the community.…Some of Epoch's survivors left their community…no longer feeling supported or welcomed…because they were seen to have benefitted from their victimization' (p. 12). There were 83 validated claimants, but the total number of survivors is at least 124 when including others who participated in civil settlements.

St John's and St Joseph's, Ontario (CA3)

These two institutions were training schools for boys: St John's was located in Uxbridge (north of Toronto); and St Joseph's, in Alfred (east of Ottawa, on the border with Québec). Both were operated by the Brothers of the Christian Schools under the supervision of the Ontario Government. St John's opened in 1895 in Toronto, relocated to Uxbridge in 1957, and closed in 1977.[6] St Joseph's opened in 1933 in Alfred and closed in 1973.[7]

Department authorities were concerned with the brothers' use of corporal punishment, as early as 1940 (Hoffman, 1996, p. 80). The earliest complaints to the police were in 1957, but the police did not pursue them; instead, they were treated as internal matters between church and government authorities. In 1990, all of this changed. *Toronto Star* reporter, Darcy Henton, obtained access to Ontario Government records by a freedom of information request; and in 1990, he began to publish stories of survivors' experiences.

Former residents came forward with allegations of abuse, inspired in part by what had occurred in Mount Cashel School, and in part, by the news stories of survivors. Aware of Henton's Freedom of Information request, department officials sought the same documents; their inquiries led to the start of police investigations in February 1990. Charges began to be laid in April 1991. Over the next decade, 34 individuals were charged (33 brothers and one civilian). Of these, 16 were convicted and sentenced (15 brothers and one civilian), and six were acquitted. For nine, the charges were withdrawn or dismissed (five) or the proceedings were stayed (four); and for three, the outcome is not known.[8]

In 1990, an association of former students, Helpline, was formed; it originally had 250 to 280 members.[9] The group considered several options, but decided that a negotiated agreement was optimal. It entered into discussions with the Ontario Government, the Toronto Christian Brothers (which had run St John's), the Ottawa Christian Brothers (which had run St Joseph's), and the Archdioceses of Toronto and Ottawa. The Toronto Christian Brothers eventually pulled out. Negotiations began in early 1991; after 20 months, an agreement was reached in August 1992 and subsequently ratified by 95 per cent of Helpline members.

The redress scheme had a financial payment, benefits and services, and other outcomes. Over time, there were three groups of claimants; information is available for the first two groups of 580 validated claimants, but none is available for the third group of 430 applicants. The case is remembered by some as path breaking by taking a more victim-centred approach to negotiating a redress scheme. However, Henton and McCann (1995) give a mixed picture, noting that many problems arose in the implementation of the agreement. Apologies were given by the government and the Archdioceses of Toronto and Ottawa.

Grandview, Ontario (CA4)

The Ontario Training School for Girls – Galt,[10] was opened in 1933. The institution changed its name to the Grandview Training School for Girls in March 1967. It closed in 1976, when allegations emerged of physical and sexual abuse of the residents. Grandview housed orphans, those from 'broken' and disadvantaged families, and court-adjudicated delinquents.

Following the 1976 complaints of abuse, an investigation was undertaken. Although sources are not clear, it was likely a departmental, not police investigation. No legal action resulted. In 1991, two former students told their psychologist in separate counselling sessions of being abused at Grandview School. The psychologist asked each woman whether she wished to meet the other; and he offered support if they chose to make their experiences public. The two subsequently appeared on television, asking other Grandview women to contact authorities. Police investigations began in mid-1991; five cases were prosecuted, and by 1998, two resulted in convictions. The Grandview Survivor's Support Group (GSSG) began meeting in 1991–92 to share their stories and investigate options for seeking redress; it grew to over 200 members. Negotiations between the GSSG and Ontario Government commenced in 1993 and continued for 10 months. In February 1994, an agreement was put to a vote and ratified by the GSSG; it was subsequently approved by the government in June 1994.

The agreement was unusual in having a high level of survivor participation in designing the elements, including the oral hearing process. A total of 329 women participated, a high proportion of whom were validated (I estimate the same validation rate as *St John's and St Joseph's* for an estimated 320 validated claimants); but the precise number is not given in any source. The agreement had a financial payment, benefits and services, and other outcomes. The government apologized in 1999. Of all the Canadian cases, *Grandview*'s redress scheme is among the most favourably evaluated by the LCC (2000).

Nova Scotia Institutions (CA5)

This case has three provincial institutions (with Waterville added in 1988), but it is difficult to keep them straight because each had name changes and population shifts. I use the most recent name for the institution, but the dates span the entire period of the institution, even when it was relocated to another site. The institutions are Shelburne Youth Centre (hereafter Shelburne), 1865–2004; Nova Scotia School for Girls (hereafter NSSG), 1914–85, in Truro; and Nova Scotia Youth Training School (hereafter YTS), 1929–97, in Bible Hill. During the timeframe of abuse, Shelburne accommodated boys adjudicated delinquent; from 1985, girls and boys; and from 1988, girls only.[11] NSSG accommodated girls serving sentences (up to 1985), and YTS accommodated girls and boys with mild to moderate mental disabilities. Two other facilities were initially part of the case (Sydney Children's Training Centre, 1969-end year unknown and Dartmouth Children's Training Centre, 1969–97), but an independent investigation found no evidence of abuse in them.

Three counsellors who had worked at Shelbourne and NSSG were prosecuted, convicted, and sentenced in 1992–93 for sexual offences against residents: George Moss, Douglas Hollett, and Patrick MacDougall. All had a history of previous complaints against them during the 1960s or 1970s, for which no action was taken (Kaufman, 2002, pp. 24–33).[12] Complainants in the cases filed civil actions in 1993 and 1994. The province considered several options: litigate each claim, settle each claim, group the claims together and settle, or devise a negotiated agreement (termed by participants an 'ADR process', the acronym referring to alternative dispute resolution). Province officials had in mind a process similar to that in *St John's and St Joseph's* and *Grandview*. In November 1994, it announced a 'three-pronged response': an audit of two facilities (November 1994 to March 1995), an independent investigation (December 1994 to June 1995), and a redress scheme (May 1996 to 2000 when the program closed). The audit by Viki Samuels-Stewart reviewed conditions of detained youth in Shelburne and Waterville. The investigation, chaired by the Honourable Stuart G. Stratton, was of alleged abuse in the institutions from 1956 to the mid-1970s. The findings of the audit and investigation led to perceptions of 'widespread systemic abuse' (Kaufman, 2002, p. 105).

The redress scheme (termed by participants the 'compensation program') was based on a Memorandum of Understanding (MOU), which went through three phases: the original MOU (May to November 1996), the amended MOU (December 1996 to October 1997), and the Guidelines (from 6 November 1997 to the end of the program). It had a financial payment and benefits. The changes in program implementation were caused by a high number of unanticipated claimants and concerns of claimant fraud; thus, validation procedures tightened over time. In addition, there was no due process provision for current employees who were alleged to have committed abuse. This set the stage for significant conflict.[13] In 1999, the Honourable Fred Kaufman was appointed to conduct a review of the government's handling of the case. At the program's conclusion, there were 1,101 validated claimants. This case is significant because allegations of abuse were made against currently employed government workers, which had not been anticipated at the start of the redress scheme. The government issued an apology when the redress scheme was first announced in May 1996.

Ontario Schools for the Deaf (CA6)

Three institutions for the Deaf[14] were originally part of this case: E.C. Drury, located in Milton, established in 1963; Robarts School for the Hearing Handicapped, located in London, established in 1973; and Sir James Whitney School for the Deaf (formerly Ontario Institution for the Education of the Deaf and Dumb, established 1870, renamed Ontario School for the Deaf in 1913, and given its current name in 1974), located in Belleville. All the institutions still operate. As the case evolved, it appears that only former Sir James Whitney students participated in a negotiated redress scheme.

In 1991, former residents of Drury and Robarts reported sexual abuse to the police. Gerald Hall, a former teacher at Drury and Robarts was convicted of sexual offences in 1993, which he committed at Drury in 1970–73 and Robarts in 1973–84. In 1992, students from Sir James Whitney came forward alleging abuse. According to Shea (1999b), five staff members from this school were charged: two were convicted in 1993 (surnames Baker and Webb) and a third in 1996 (surname Bradshaw); one was acquitted, and the outcome could not be determined for the fifth. Different dates are reported for the timeframe of abuse at Sir James Whitney. Shea (1999a, p. 44) says 1940 to 1980; and a newspaper article, which cites a Belleville police inspector, says 1955 to 1985 (*Toronto Star*, 1992).

After the 1991 reports to the police, the Ontario Ministry of Education initiated a Review of Student Care at the Provincial Schools for the Deaf and Blind and Demonstration Schools (Herbert, 1991). Former students of Sir James Whitney initiated meetings with two government departments to negotiate a response to their own and others' allegations of physical and sexual abuse. These negotiations, aided by a lawyer, appear to have started in 1993; it took 4 years for a negotiated agreement (termed by participants 'the ADR Project') to be finalized. The application process began in May 1998 and ended by April 2000. The agreement had a financial payment and benefits. After 86 claims were validated by the project coordinator, a former *Grandview* adjudicator decided the payment levels for each claim, using the *Grandview* template as a guide. The government made no apology.

Jericho Hill, British Columbia (CA7)

Jericho Hill Provincial School (1922–93) was run by the British Columbia Ministry of Education. Opened in 1922 in Vancouver as the British Columbia School for the Deaf and the Blind, it was renamed Jericho Hill

School in 1955, with a new school built in 1962. The school's male and female students were 5 to 20 years old. In 1993, the school moved to Burnaby, and its residential component moved there in 1997, to an area called Victory Hill. Abuse claims spanned 1950 to 1992.

Sources give somewhat different details about early allegations of abuse. I rely on the British Columbia Ombudsman's report (1993, pp. 12–27) and Special Counsel Berger's report (1995, pp. 9–11) to depict events. In 1982, a male student told a psychologist that 'he had been sexually abused by a female child care counsellor, and that he and other students were encouraged or even forced to have sex among themselves' (Berger, 1995, p. 1). Interviews were conducted with 12 boys, ten of whom reported being abused by three counsellors (one female and two male) and by other students, and who admitted that they had sexually abused girls as young as 7 years old. In 1983, another allegation was made against one of the counsellors. The Vancouver city police investigated, but no charges were laid; the three counsellors left the school.

In 1987, one of the 1982 complainants, now a former student, again raised allegations of abuse against the female counsellor, and again reported that boys sexually abused girls 'to prove they were not homosexual' (Berger, 1995, p. 10). The Ministry re-opened its investigation in 1987 and interviewed 35 students. A children's officer, Roberta Hughes, 'identified a pervasive culture at the residence that required students to submit to a sexual rite of passage if they were to successfully cohabit with their peers'; she said there were 23 offending students 'who should not return to the residence' (p. 11). The Vancouver city police investigated, but no charges were laid. The identified offenders were not removed from the school because the administrators were concerned 'they would have nowhere to go' (p. 11). By 1987, 44 children had been identified by other students as abuse victims, and they 'disclosed almost nightly sexual activity in the dormitory' (British Columbia Ombudsman, 1993, pp. 23–4). The Ombudsman's office initiated a complaint to the Ministry of Education in 1987; officials said that changes would be made, and the Ombudsman took it no further.

News stories in 1991 prompted the Attorney General to re-open investigations, which led to the Jericho Hill Intervention Project, a protocol devised in 1991 to investigate disclosures and provide counselling. More news stories appeared in 1992 about abuse at the school, which generated calls from parents and advocates of former students, as well as students themselves. The Ombudsman's office re-opened an investigation. Its 1993 report concluded that 'people in positions of trust and in positions of power knew reports had been made and did nothing', and it recommended that students who had disclosed abuse in 1982 be offered 'appropriate compensation and an apology' (p. 39). In June 1993, the Attorney General appointed Thomas Berger as Special Counsel to consider the 'extent and severity of sexual abuse' at the school, 'the province's responsibility' for it, and 'remedies' (Berger, 1995, p. 1). Berger found that sexual abuse had occurred at the school from as early as 1956, but it was 'most prolific...from 1978 to 1987', and that the government had been aware of it since 1982. He recommended that the province accept responsibility (but not liability) for sexual abuse of students, and outlined the basis for a redress scheme. The government created the Jericho Individual Compensation Program (JICP), which provided a financial payment, benefits, and services. JICP began in 1996 and finalized its last case in 2001.

In 1997, a law suit was filed by Anne Sheane, on behalf of 'about a dozen' Jericho Hill students (Gidney, 2004).[15] As the case was making its way through the courts, the JICP was underway. In November 1999, the JICP was temporarily suspended for 3 months, when the British Columbia Court of Appeal certified the class action. The JICP was re-instated in February 2000. When the JICP concluded in February 2001, there were 359 validated claimants; and when the lawsuit was settled in April 2004, it had 350 class members. Of these, about half (175) had received a payment from the JICP. The *Jericho Hill Class Action* resulted in a significant package of financial payments, benefits, and services.

In 1995, Spencer Gallagher (who had been a dentist at the school) was convicted at trial on three of seven counts of indecent assault (the offences were alleged to have been committed between 1954 and 1966 against male students). Gallagher was sentenced to serve one year (Surviving the past, 2013). In June 1995, when Berger's report was tabled and the JICP was announced, the Attorney General for the province issued a statement of regret. In May 2004, the Premier, on behalf of the province, expressed regret for the abuse.

New Brunswick Institutions (CA8)

Three facilities were part of this case: two for male youth adjudicated delinquent or awaiting foster care placement, and one for male and female children with mental disabilities or wards of the state. The first two were the Boys' Industrial Home at Saint John, which opened in 1893 and closed in 1962, when staff and students were relocated to the New Brunswick Training School (NBTS) at Kingsclear, north of Fredricton, 1962–98. The third was Dr William F. Roberts Hospital School, which has an unknown start date, but closed in 1985. As the case evolved, attention focused on abuse occurring at NBTS, although residents of the two other facilities were eligible for the redress scheme.

The Fredricton Police Force began investigating allegations of abuse at NBTS in 1985, when a NBTS counsellor reported that a staff member, Karl Toft, had sexually assaulted three boys. Toft was transferred, but no further legal action was taken. The same NBTS counsellor again reported his concerns about Toft in 1990, but this time he had gained the attention of 'a senior news reporter and the provincial Attorney General' (Commission for Public Complaints [CPC] Against the Royal Canadian Mounted Police [RCMP], 2007, summary, p. 3), who asked the RCMP to investigate. Their investigations focused on Toft, but widened to include other former NBTS employees and an RCMP officer. In December 1992, Toft pleaded guilty to 34 counts of sexual assault and was sentenced to serve 13 years.[16]

On the day that Toft was sentenced, the government announced a commission of inquiry to investigate allegations of abuse at the three facilities, chaired by the Honourable Richard L. Miller. It took some time for Miller to formally commence hearings because other alleged offences by Toft and three former employees were under investigation by the RCMP.[17] Miller's (1995) report found evidence of sexual abuse complaints as early 1961 and 1962; and he said it was 'unforgivable' that for so long, 'not a single person in the Justice Department...ever instigated a serious investigation...' (p. 91). He proposed a 'program of compensation' (p. 153) for sexual abuse; and in 1995, lawyers for the government and victims negotiated a redress scheme, which had a financial payment and benefits. There were 345 validated claimants.[18] The government did not issue a public apology.

A major investigation by the CPC began in 2004. It examined the RCMP's investigations of alleged physical and sexual abuse of residents at NBTS at Kingsclear, specifically that 'the RCMP engaged in activities designed to cover up...alleged criminal conduct' (CPC, 2007, p. 1). It concluded that while there was 'no substantiated evidence' of a cover-up by RCMP members, there were 'inadequacies' in its investigations that were 'serious enough to create the perception of a cover-up' (p. 6).

Canadian core-plus cases

The core-plus cases are *Alberta Sterilization* and *Duplessis Orphans* (core-plus-one) and *Indian Residential Schools* (core-plus-two). In core-plus-one cases, a policy wrong was committed against children; and in core-plus-two, the policy wrong committed against children was part of a more general discrimination against a group of people.[19]

Alberta Sterilization (CA9)

Four hospitals and training schools in Alberta were the 'feeder schools' in the involuntary sexual sterilization of children and adults with mental disabilities. They were Alberta Hospital (Ponoka), Provincial Training School in Red Deer (PTS) (termed by some, the Michener Institute), Alberta Hospital (Oliver), and Deerhome in Red Deer. These institutions presented 99 per cent of cases to the Eugenics Board (others came from travelling mental health clinics that visited small towns and rural areas). Teens and young adults were disproportionately represented in approvals and sterilizations, as were females and First Nations people (Grekul et al., 2004).

The *Sexual Sterilization Act* was introduced in Alberta in 1928, revised in 1937 and 1942, and repealed in 1972. During its 44-year period, the Eugenics Board approved 4,739 individuals for sterilization; 2,834 were carried out.[20] The *Act* was strongly influenced by eugenics theories of the day. In its initial version, the Board was authorized to approve requests for sexual sterilization of individuals with mental disabilities, who were about to be discharged from a mental hospital (*Sexual Sterilization Act 1928*, s4). The Board's decisions had to be unanimous, and an individual had to give consent, 'unless they were mentally incapable', in which case, 'the consent of a next of kin had to be obtained' (Grekul et al., 2004, p. 361). Gaining consent proved to be a problem for the Board. The *Act* was amended in 1937 to expedite the process. If an individual was 'deemed to be "mentally defective", their consent was no longer required before sterilization could take place' (p. 363). At this time and without legislative support, the Board introduced another reason for sterilization, 'incapable of intelligent parenthood' (p. 363). This widened the application of the *Act* considerably.[21] A 1942 amendment widened the scope further to include those 'with syphilis, epilepsy, ... and Huntington's Chorea, [although] consent of the patient was still required' (pp. 363–4). The expedited methods of consent and a broader application to include anyone in a mental institution translated to high numbers of people who were involuntarily sterilized. Although this case centres on involuntary sterilization, interviews of former residents (almost all of whom had been in PTS, Red Deer) suggest that police were aware of physical and other abuse. Specifically, some said that 'they told police about beatings and other abuse after being picked up for escaping from the institution', but the police took them back to the school without investigating their complaints (Institute for Human Resource Development [IHRD], 1998, p. 105).

In January 1996, Leilani Muir successfully sued the province for wrongful sterilization and wrongful confinement at PTS in Red Deer.

She was awarded $740,780 in damages and $230,000 in legal costs (*Muir v Alberta*, 1996). This opened a floodgate of litigation for involuntary sterilization. In 1998, 'approximately 700 individuals [had] filed claims against the province' (Alberta Government, 1998b); the number swelled to about 900 by October 1999. The cases were finalized in four major civil settlements during 1998 and 1999. When the last settlement was announced, the government issued a statement of regret.

Duplessis Orphans, Québec **(CA10)**

This case includes nurseries, orphanages, industrial schools, and psychiatric institutions in Québec that received children as wards of the state. In addition to farm schools, the case includes at least 26 institutions. From 1930 to 1965,[22] Québec was able to obtain federal funding for housing thousands of children by falsely classifying them as psychiatric patients or as mentally retarded. This practice emerged because funding was provided to institutions by child group: the 'smallest allowance was for orphans, followed by sick children, the mentally retarded, and lastly, the insane'. An institution 'could obtain nearly twice the amount per child, and sometimes more, depending on how children were classified and where they were placed' (Québec Ombudsman, 1997, p. 6). In addition, in psychiatric hospitals, the daily allowance was based on the number of beds occupied; thus, many hospitals increased admissions and kept patients hospitalized as long as possible to maximize revenue. Such practices led to maltreatment and misclassification of children as mentally deficient.[23] Those falsely declared mentally ill were subject to 'electroshock therapy, lobotomies, prolonged solitary confinement, ice baths, chaining, force feeding, strait jackets,...and chemical restraints' (p. 15). They were 'often neglected, and abused physically and sexually' (IHRD, 1998, p. 94). As the Québec Ombudsman (1997, p. 15) suggests, 'the situation [was] an endless circle':

> From orphans, the children went on to become mentally deficient, i.e., 'not adoptable'. They were *subsequently classified – and in some cases became – mentally ill*, a label of legal and social inferiority that has remained with them long into adulthood. Everything was set in place to maintain a long period of institutional dependence. (emphasis added)

The children became known as the *Duplessis Orphans*, after Maurice Duplessis, who was Québec's Premier in 1936–39 and 1944–59. In 1997, it was estimated there were 5,000 orphans, with 3,500 still alive (p. 2).[24] The Québec Government and Catholic religious orders, who ran the institutions, colluded in the benefits that arose from taking advantage of a federal policy.

The *Duplessis Orphans* first came to public attention in 1961 with the book, *Les fous crient au secours* (*The Crazy People Cry Out for Help*). The book led to an inquiry of conditions in psychiatric hospitals throughout Québec, resulting in the Bédard Report (1962), which documented practices of misdiagnosing children as mentally ill or retarded and their wrongful placement in psychiatric hospitals. The Comité des Orphelins et Orphelines Institutionnalisés de Duplessis (COOID) began advocating on behalf of the *Duplessis Orphans* in 1991.[25] During the 1990s, COOID and a team of lawyers and social scientists attempted to bring forward a class action, but failed. Police investigations in the early 1990s involved 'some 30 institutions, 240 complainants, and 341 suspects' (Québec Ombudsman, 1997, p. 20); but in 1995, the Attorney General announced that no charges would be laid. (There was one successful prosecution, but it was privately initiated). In 1995, the Minister of Justice 'announced that the case of the Duplessis Orphans was closed' (IHRD, 1998, p. 97).

COOID brought their case to the Québec Ombudsman in 1996. In his 1997 report, the Ombudsman said that the Duplessis Orphans 'believe themselves to be the victims of a hostile and inaccessible legal system ... [and] the government, the medical establishment, and the religious orders ... have also fallen victim to the limits of the legal system' (Québec Ombudsman, 1997, p. 33). He proposed a financial payment, public apologies to victims, and other benefits and services (pp. 36, 42–3). The first government-stipulated redress scheme ran from 2001 to 2002; a second began in 2007 and remains open as of this writing. Each had (and has) a financial payment only. As of September 2013, there were 4,493 validated claimants in the two schemes. The government apologized in 2001.

Indian Residential Schools **(CA11)**

This nation-wide case includes 139 industrial, boarding, and residential schools that were under the authority of the Canadian Government from 1867 to 1996. From federation in 1867, the schools were largely government-funded, but church-run. In 1883, they were explicitly established to forcibly assimilate Aboriginal children into mainstream society. They sought to eliminate the intellectual, cultural, and spiritual influences of children's parents and communities, that is, 'to take the

Indian out of the child' (Jung, 2011, p. 224). They are called Indian Residential Schools.[26]

There were two types of residential schools: smaller, church-run boarding schools, which were located on or near reserves, and industrial schools, which were established to 'prepare older students for assimilation into Euro-Canadian society' (Truth and Reconciliation Commission [TRC], 2012, p. 6) and located away from the reserves. A third type, day schools, which operated on the reserves, were the most prevalent. The TRC (2012) says that up to 1883, 'there was not a residential school system, but a series of individual church-led initiatives to which the federal government provided grants' (p. 6). In 1883, the Canadian Government began to build schools, using the industrial school model, which had been recommended by Davin (1879). The aim was 'to civilize and Christianize' Aboriginal children[27] by separating them from their families and communities. The schools existed in all provinces and territories except Prince Edward Island, New Brunswick, and Newfoundland and Labrador.

Under the *Indian Act 1894* and subsequent legislation, the government could require attendance of Aboriginal children in residential schools. Some parents placed their children in the schools voluntarily, believing that it would provide them a good education and better opportunities, but other children were removed by coercion and without parental consent. As summed up by the Royal Commission on Aboriginal Peoples [RCAP] (1996, Vol. 1, p. 353),[28] the 'persistently woeful condition of the school system and the too often substandard care of children' could be traced to

> ...the government's and church's unrelieved underfunding of the system, the method of financing individual schools, the failure of the department to exercise oversight and control of the schools, and the failure of the department and the churches to ensure proper treatment of the children by staff.

From an Aboriginal perspective, 'the most damaging part of residential schools...was that children were taught that their culture was not worth preserving', and that it was inferior and 'primitive' compared to that of other Canadians (Cold Lake First Nations, 2013, p. 10). When the last residential school, the Gordon Residential School in Saskatchewan, was closed in 1996, an estimated 150,000 Aboriginal children had been removed from their homes and communities (Jung, 2011, p. 223).

The first complaints of sexual abuse in residential schools, which resulted in criminal prosecution and conviction, were of Derek Clarke in 1988, Harold McIntee in 1989, and Claude Frappier in 1990. Drawing from Bessner (1998) and Shea (1999b), 24 individuals were charged from 1988 to 1998. Of these, 20 were convicted and sentenced, two were acquitted, and in two, the charges were dismissed or withdrawn.[29] These figures may underestimate prosecution activity.[30] Civil litigation ensued, with the government receiving its first civil claim in 1988 (Russell affidavit, 2006, paragraph 8). In May 2005, when Frank Iacobucci was appointed federal representative to negotiate a settlement, there were 13,500 individual claims and an additional 11 class actions (Iacobucci affidavit, 2006, paragraph 6).

In the 1990s, several developments brought the parties to the negotiation table. In 1990, Aboriginal leader Phil Fontaine appeared on CBC television and spoke in radio interviews in October and November, disclosing his experience of sexual abuse in a residential school (Fontaine, 1990a, 1990b). Other survivors came forward. As one area of investigation, the RCAP (1991–96) analyzed the history and consequences of the residential school system, and it recommended a public inquiry. Exploratory dialogues from 1998 to 2003 were not able to keep pace with rising litigation, and by 2005, the class action claims had strong momentum. On 8 May 2006, the Canadian Government, legal representatives for survivors of the residential school system, the Assembly of First Nations, Inuit representatives, and many church organizations entered into the Indian Residential School Settlement Agreement (IRSSA), the largest out-of-court settlement in Canadian history. Finalized by court decisions in 2006 and 2007, the IRSSA took effect in September 2007, with a significant package of financial payments, benefits, services, and other outcomes. The financial payment numbers have not been finalized. As of 31 December 2013, the number of validated claimants for a level 1 payment was 79,179, of which a smaller number have sought level 2 payments. There were government and church apologies.

Australian core cases

Three Australian core cases are *Queensland Institutions*, *Tasmanian Institutions*, and *South Australian Institutions*. Because these cases are statewide, I cannot detail the relevant criminal prosecutions and convictions. *Forgotten Australians* is difficult to classify; although I consider it a core case, it sailed in the slipstream of two other Commonwealth inquiries (both of which were core-plus cases); thus, I describe it in that section.

Queensland Institutions (AU2)

This case includes all institutions that housed children in Queensland, run by government and non-government organizations from 1911 to 1999, a total of 159 facilities. Included were orphanages, youth detention centres, children's homes, family group homes, and industrial schools. Excluded were foster care placements and institutions for children with disabilities or with acute or chronic health problems (Forde, 1999, p. 1). A separate inquiry was conducted for children in foster care (Butler, 2004).

Queensland's policies of child welfare and juvenile justice emerged in the 1860s and 1870s, with legislation for the care and protection of children; the state's first orphanage was established in 1865 (Forde, 1999, pp. 31–3). By 1880, 77 per cent of children in state care were in an orphanage (p. 33). However, with critiques of the orphanage system in the late 19th century, fostering became the preferred policy, and the share of children in state care who lived in institutions dropped to 40 per cent in 1900 (pp. 33–7); from 1900 to 1960, it ranged from 10 to 22 per cent. By the 1930s, many problems were evident in residential facilities: overcrowding, poor sanitary conditions, too few staff, and inadequate resources to supply proper bedding, food, clothing, and health care for the children. There was excessive discipline, coupled with limited education and recreation (Forde, 1999, p. 63–86). Residential facilities decreased in size during the 1960s to 1980s, but this did not necessarily result in positive outcomes (p. 97).

In the late 1980s and throughout the 1990s, media attention and public discussion began to centre on physical and sexual abuse of children in state care. There were allegations that a girl had been raped while in a detention facility, general concerns with paedophilia and cover-ups in police investigations, and allegations of sexual abuse at St Joseph's Orphanage in Neerkol (west of Rockhampton). When the Broken Rites national hotline for clergy abuse victims was established in Australia in 1993 and a Queensland child abuse hotline in 1996, the early and frequent callers were former Neerkol residents. Their allegations of rape and sexual assault against Reginald Durham, who had been a chaplain at St Joseph's, were investigated. Durham was charged in 1997 and convicted in 1999. Former residents also settled civil claims in 1999.

In 1998, the government established a commission of inquiry, chaired by Leneen Forde. It ran from August 1998 to May 1999; its report recommended that some form of compensation be established. The government initially rejected the idea, but 8 years later, in May 2007, a government-stipulated redress scheme was announced. It had financial payments and services (counselling). The financial payments had two levels: the number of validated claimants for level 1 was 7,453; and of this group, a smaller number applied for a level 2 payment. The Forde Foundation Trust, which was created in 2000 and is still operating as of this writing, provides small grants to registered claimants for household goods, dental, and other items. There were government and church apologies.

Tasmanian Institutions (AU5)

This case includes all residential institutions for children in Tasmania: government-operated receiving homes (later known as family group homes), government-operated institutions and detention centres, and approved children's homes run by churches and voluntary organizations, under the *Infants' Welfare Act 1935* or the *Child Welfare Act 1960.* Also included were foster placements (Tasmanian Ombudsman, 2004, pp. 14–25). In phase 1 of the redress scheme, 21 eligible institutions were named (pp. 15–16); and in phase 2, the number increased to 38 (Tasmanian Ombudsman, 2006, pp. 4–5).

The Tasmanian Ombudsman's (2004) report lists 21 cases of rape, sexual assault, or sexual abuse that had been lodged with departmental or police authorities from the 1940s to the 1990s. None of the complaints resulted in a conviction (forward, p. 6 document view). A 'lack of corroborating evidence' was the reason often given (pp. 63–5).

On 11 July 2003, a television program, *Stateline*, aired an interview with Walter Tusyn, who said he was sexually abused while in state care. This prompted an independent review of claims of abuse, which was undertaken by the Tasmanian Ombudsman. The review was announced on the same night the *Stateline* program aired; and at the end of the program, it was announced that a telephone hotline was available. It was open for 6 weeks, after which calls were taken by the Ombudsman's office (Tasmanian Ombudsman, 2004, p. 1).

The Ombudsman's review began on 14 July 2003. Six weeks later, the Tasmanian Premier announced that an *ex gratia* payment of up to $60,000 would be offered. The redress scheme ran for nearly 10 years: from July 2003 to 15 February 2013. The maximum payment amount decreased over time (from $60,000 in phases 1 to 3 to $35,000 in phase 4). The scheme had financial payments and benefits. As of September 2013, there were 1,836 validated claimants in four phases of the scheme. After the scheme closed in 2013, a benefits program was announced for those who had not yet sought an *ex gratia* payment. The government apologized in 2005.

South Australian Institutions **(AU6)**

This case includes 56 institutions (19 state and 37 other types, including secure care) as well as foster or family care placements. It centres on sexual abuse by both staff and residents.

Concerns with abuse of children in state care were gaining attention in South Australia during the 1980s and 1990s (Mullighan, 2008a, p. 351). In 2003, a review of South Australia's child protection policies was undertaken. The Layton Report (2003) recommended ways to address child sexual, physical, and emotional abuse. Early in 2003, allegations of sexual abuse of children came to public attention. A television program, *Today Tonight,* aired a segment naming a victim and perpetrator and suggesting systemic sexual abuse of children in state care (South Australia [SA] House of Assembly, 19 February 2003, p. 2312). In June 2003, the Anglican Church announced it was conducting an inquiry into child sexual abuse by officials in their church. When the church released its report, the government called for the Archbishop to resign (SA Legislative Council, 30 June 2004, p. 1901). In October 2003, *Today Tonight* aired another program about child sexual abuse in which '...startling revelations...about government cover-ups, shredding of government documents and less than satisfactory investigation by the Catholic Church' were made (SA House of Assembly, 22 October 2003, p. 572).

In February 2003, the opposition party called for an inquiry. The government resisted the idea for over a year, until June 2004, when it announced an inquiry. In November 2004, an inquiry was established, chaired by the Honourable Edward (Ted) Mullighan. It had two components: one with hearings in cities and towns, and a second, in the geographically remote Aboriginal area of the Anangu Pitjantjatjara Yankunytjatjara (APY) Lands. Mullighan (2008a, 2008b) produced a report for each. In the first, he recommended that the state investigate other redress programs. In 2010, a redress scheme (*ex gratia* payment) for abuse in state care was established as part of the Victims of Crime Fund; as of 30 July 2014, there were 91 validated claimants. Many have also sought redress by civil litigation. The government apologized in 2008.

Australian core-plus cases

Two core-plus cases are *Stolen Generations* (core-plus-two) and *Child Migrants* (core-plus-one). *Forgotten Australians,* while not a core-plus case, was the third in the trilogy of Commonwealth public inquiries on historical abuse of children in Australia.

Stolen Generations (AU1)

Indigenous children (Aboriginal and Torres Strait Islander) were removed from their families under different state and territory legislation. In the 19th century, the emphasis was on policies of protection-segregation, and this merged and blended in the 20th century with an emphasis on assimilation. Children were placed in foster or adoptive families, or sent to orphanages, settlements, missions, or training institutions. 'Stolen Generations' is the name[31] given to cohorts of children, who were forcibly removed from their families, using legislation established to 'absorb' or 'assimilate' Indigenous people into white society. Drawing from Manne (2001, p. 27), 'no reliable generalization about the nature of these removals can be made'. Specifically,

> ... Many were first generation, so-called 'half-castes', ... others were children of mixed descent who lived on Aboriginal settlements or on the outskirts of the country towns, especially in New South Wales, Victoria and the southern areas of South and Western Australia (p. 27) ... In Queensland it was common to remove whole families or even communities to missions or reserves ... Some lost all contact with their families ... Some maintained regular contact ... (p. 28)

Early policies of segregation began in the first half of the 19th century, as early as the 1830s in Tasmania. These policies were combined with those for 'protection', when state governments established segregated reserves and assigned responsibility for the care and welfare of Indigenous people to a Chief Protector or an Aboriginal Protection Board. By 1911 all jurisdictions (except Tasmania) had protectionist legislation which granted a Chief Protector extensive power over Indigenous people.

By the late 19th century, 'although the full descent Indigenous population was declining, the mixed descent population was increasing' (Human Rights and Equal Opportunity Commission [HREOC], 1997, p. 24). State and territory governments' policies then shifted to 'merging' more light-skinned or 'white-appearing' Indigenous people into mainstream society, with the expectation that Indigenous people would disappear by 'absorption' (p. 24). Child removal practices were essential to this task. In 1937, a national approach to assimilation was discussed at the inaugural Commonwealth-State Native Welfare Conference. After the conference concluded, governments' assimilation legislation became more aggressive: previous policies of merging were a 'passive process of pushing Indigenous people into the non-Indigenous community and denying them assistance', but from 1940, assimilation policies became a 'highly intensive process, necessitating constant surveillance of people's lives, judged according to non-Indigenous standards' (p. 27). Assimilation policies continued during the 1950s and 1960s. Protest movements began in the 1960s, with activists drawing links between racial discrimination in Australia and the United States. By 1970, all states and territories had repealed child removal legislation, although removals still occurred under child welfare legislation (see Haebich, 2000, for a definitive history). An estimated 20,000 to 25,000 children were affected by removal policies and practices between 1910 and 1970 (Manne, 2000, p. 27).

The immediate catalyst for the Commonwealth Government's response was a finding by the Royal Commission into Aboriginal Deaths in Custody (1991) that 43 of 99 Aboriginal people who had died in custody had been separated from their families as children (cited in HREOC, 1997, p. 274) and the 1994 *Going Home* conference in Darwin, the Northern Territory. In May 1995, the Commonwealth Attorney General commissioned the HREOC to conduct a national inquiry on the past and present practices and policies of separation and removal of Indigenous children; and in August, the terms of reference were revised to include advice on 'compensation' for those affected by policies of child removal (p. 15). The inquiry was co-chaired by HREOC President, Sir Ronald Wilson, and Aboriginal and Torres Strait Islander Social Justice Commissioner, Mick Dodson. Their report, *Bringing Them Home,* was tabled in Parliament in May 1997. It concluded that policies of forcible child removal and placement in residential and out-of-home care deprived children of their liberty and their 'parents of parental rights' (pp. 219–20), and that carers and government officials abused their powers and breached their duties as legal guardians (pp. 222–6). One recommendation was establishing a National Compensation Fund to avoid the 'pitfalls of costly, time-consuming litigation' (p. 267). An apology and commemorations were also among the recommendations.

The Commonwealth rejected financial payments in its 1997 response; and to date, its position is that if payments are to be made, relevant state or territory jurisdictions should carry out the role. Since 1997, the Commonwealth has funded a range of services, an oral history project, and memorialization. A sincere Commonwealth apology was made in 2008. Before then, all state and territory governments and church organizations had apologized.

Child Migrants (AU3)

This case includes all institutions, both government and non-government, that participated in the British-Australian child migrant policy. The Senate Report (2001) estimates a total of 52 institutions in all the states (but not the territories). The policy began in 1912, and the last Child Migrants were flown to Tasmania in 1970.

Between the 1600s and the mid-1960s, an estimated 100,000 to 180,000 British children were sent to Australia, Canada, the Caribbean, New Zealand, Rhodesia, South Africa, and the United States (Senate Report, 2001, p.13). For Australia, the start of British child migration was 1912, when Kingsley Fairbridge, the founder of the Fairbridge Society, established a Farm School in Pinjarra, Western Australia. Before World War II, the government's rationale to receive children was rural development; after the war, it was to increase Australia's population (p. 19). In 1946, legislation was passed that made the Australian Government the children's guardian. However, the federal minister delegated guardianship powers to state welfare authorities, who in turn, transferred responsibility to the receiving agencies and institutions. The care and protection of children suffered as a result.

Some parents sought to have their children placed in a migration scheme or consented to their placement, but most children were sent without parental consent. This occurred when parents expressed wishes against their child being sent, a sending agency was unable to locate or contact a child's parents, or a sending agency did not advise parents that their child was being sent. 'Consent' was sometimes gained through deception or duress (Senate Report, 2001, p. 60). In Australia, on-going communication between children and family members was discouraged or prevented, and siblings were intentionally separated. Children were told they were not wanted by their parents or country (pp. 74–5). An estimated 7,000 children were affected. About half were sent to Western Australia. In 1950, the Maltese Government and the Australian Catholic Church entered into an agreement, with the approval of the Australian Government, to permit Maltese children to migrate to Australia. Between 1950 and 1965, about 310 Maltese children were sent.

Several investigations were undertaken by the British Government in the 1950s. One, the Ross Report (1956), criticized institutional care in Australia, citing the lack of trained staff, the separation of siblings, lack of education and employment opportunities for residents, isolation of the institutions, and the exploitation of residents' labour (Senate Report, 2001, p. 37). It called for radical change, if child migration were to continue. In 1987, Margaret Humphreys, a British social worker, established the Child Migrants Trust (CMT), which campaigned to bring the policy and practices to public attention, to represent the interests of Child Migrants, and to expose the operations of churches and other receiving organizations, who gained financially from the policy. Significant newspaper exposure began in 1987 and continued thereafter with a range of media (books, television, and film).

In 2000, an Australian Senate inquiry on the policy of child migration to Australia was announced. Senator Andrew Murray, a former Child Migrant, was a significant figure in moving the idea forward. The Senate Report (2001) found evidence of the 'brutality of life in some institutions, where...indifferent care was the norm'. Child Migrants suffered a 'loss of identity [and] sense of belonging' (p. 7). The Report did not recommend financial recompense in 2001, but another Senate Report did in 2009, when a follow-up inquiry was carried out. The Australian, British, and Maltese Prime Ministers apologized; several state governments apologized; and public church apologies were given in Australia and Malta.

Forgotten Australians (AU4)

This case includes all institutional care facilities in Australia: orphanages, residential homes, industrial and training schools, and juvenile detention centres. The institutions were administered by state governments, religious orders, and charitable organizations. *Forgotten Australians* is the third in the Commonwealth's inquiries into policies and practices concerning children in institutional care, which began with the *Stolen Generations* (HREOC, 1997) and *Child Migrants* (Senate Report, 2001). While estimates vary, conservatively, there were over 500,000 Australians in residential and out-of-home care (foster care) during the 20th century (Senate Report, 2004, pp. xv, 29).[32]

The Senate Inquiry into Children in Institutional Care was announced on 4 March 2003 (Senate Report, 2004, p. 1). Having gathered considerable evidence of institutional care and foster care, the Senate Committee produced two reports. The first, Senate Report (2004), was on children in institutional care between the 1920s and the 1970s, and the second, Senate Report (2005), was on children in foster care, children with disabilities in state care (both foster and institutions), and children in detention centres. My analysis of the case focuses on the first report.

Among the recommendations in the Senate Report (2004) were that the Commonwealth establish a national reparations fund for eligible care leavers, to be funded by governments and relevant church and other organizations. The government rejected the idea, saying it was a matter for state and territory jurisdictions. A follow-up Senate inquiry was announced in September 2008 to review the implementation of the recommendations made in the Senate Reports (2001, 2004) on *Child Migrants* and *Forgotten Australians*. The resulting Senate Report (2009) said that those giving evidence were disappointed by the lack of implementing the recommendations in *Forgotten Australians*, and they 'consistently described' the Commonwealth's response 'as a failure of national leadership' (p. 9) because it devolved responsibility to the states and territories. The report's recommendations encouraged jurisdictions to establish redress schemes (for those that had not yet done so), to commit funding to the Child Migrants Trust, and to provide recurrent funding to survivor advocacy and support groups.

In 2009, funding increased significantly for support services to care leavers. In addition, the Commonwealth funded memorials, an oral history project, and museum exhibit. The Prime Minister's apology to Child Migrants and Forgotten Australians was made at the same time in 2009. All the states and the ACT apologized, and there were many church apologies.

Australian redress schemes only

Two Australian cases are redress schemes only. The Tasmanian scheme flowed from recommendations in HREOC (1997), and *Redress WA* responded to recommendations in HREOC (1997) and the Senate Reports (2001, 2004).

Tasmanian Stolen Generations (AU7)

In October 2006, the Premier of Tasmania, Paul Lennon, announced legislation to provide financial payments (*ex gratia*) to Aboriginal people who had been affected by policies of forcible removal in Tasmania (Tasmania Department of Premier and Cabinet, 2008, p. 6). In November 2006, the *Stolen Generations of Aboriginal Children Act 2006* was passed unanimously. It created a $5 million fund to provide *ex gratia* payments to eligible members of Tasmanian Stolen Generations and their children.

Tasmania was the first Australian jurisdiction to enact such legislation, and it is the only jurisdiction to offer *ex gratia* payments in recognition of the policy wrong and practice of removing Aboriginal children from their families. The *Act* came into operation in January 2007. In addition to the *ex gratia* payment, there were limited services. A total of 84 people were validated as members of *Tasmanian Stolen Generations*, and 22 as biological children of deceased Stolen Generations members.

In 1997, the government had apologized, in response to the HREOC (1997) report.

Redress WA (AU8)

This case includes all children who were abused or neglected while in state care in Western Australia, including all those in institutions as a result of policies or practices of child migration or Aboriginal child removal from families. About 156 residential facilities were identified, which were run by the government or jointly managed by it and private agencies, church organizations, and non-denominational groups. Since 1920, an estimated 56,000 children had been placed in state care in Western Australia (Western Australia Communities, 2009).

On 17 December 2007, the Western Australian Government announced a redress scheme, with a maximum payment of $80,000. In July 2009, after a change in government, it was announced that because there was an unexpectedly high number of claimants, the maximum would be reduced to $45,000 for all those applying to the scheme. Advocacy groups held protest rallies in September to November 2009.

In addition to the *ex gratia* payment, limited counselling services were provided. Of the 10,000 people who had registered with Redress WA by November 2009, 'children from Aboriginal communities [were] 50 per cent of applicants; former child migrants ... 13 per cent; and other children ... placed in state care, 37 per cent' (Western Australia Communities, 2009, p. 2). Of the 10,000 registrants, of 5,917 completed applications, 5,345 were validated. (My analysis of *ex gratia* payments in Chapter 6 is of a somewhat smaller group of 5,210 validated claimants, who were not in the special categories of interim payment only, deceased person, or unclaimed monies.) Government apologies had been made previously to Stolen Generations members, former Child Migrants, and Forgotten Australians.

Observations

Two Canadian cases, *St John's and St Joseph's* and *Grandview*, became models or were considered in the initial design of redress schemes in other Canadian jurisdictions. These were *George Epoch*,[33] *Nova Scotia Institutions*, *Ontario Schools for the Deaf*, *Jericho Hill*, and *Indian Residential Schools*. More Canadian than Australian cases moved into the public arena with prosecutions and criminal convictions of institutional staff, whereas more Australian cases were prompted by nation-wide or state public inquiries.

The significant differences in the federal government's response to *Indian Residential Schools* in Canada and *Stolen Generations* in Australia can be explained, in part, by the substantial number of civil litigation cases against the Canadian Government and religious organizations, which in turn was prompted by criminal convictions for sex offences. In addition, in Canada, the statute of limitations was relaxed in the Indian Residential School civil cases, but not in the Australian Stolen Generations civil cases (Kune, 2011; Marchetti and Ransley, 2005). Although I have called *Indian Residential Schools* and *Stolen Generations* core-plus-two cases, with policy wrongs against children and against a group of people, the key legal decisions in both countries did not recognize the 'policy wrong'. Instead, in successful litigation in Canada, what was proved was that government (or church) officials owed those children who had been removed a duty of care *and* that their abuse by staff meant that this duty was not fulfilled (Cassidy, 2006; Jacobs, 2007). The only successful civil litigation case for *Stolen Generations* in Australia, *Trevorrow v South Australia (No 5)* (2007), was won on the grounds that Trevorrow's removal was made knowingly, outside the scope of relevant legislation (McRae et al., 2009, pp. 615–17).[34] Although 'loss of language and culture' with a policy of forced assimilation by the residential school system was not won in the Canadian courts, it was incorporated as an element in the IRSSA. Thus, redress schemes may offer a more satisfactory result than court, when wrongs flow from government policy.

This chapter has sketched the history and legal developments in each case, but it is essential to know what happened when children were placed in institutions. The next chapter presents their memories of institutional life.

3
Institutions for Children and Memories of Institutional Life

In this chapter, I review the historical emergence of institutions for children and the factors that enabled physical and sexual abuse of children in residential care. I consider whether abuse is more prevalent in institutions than outside them, and the role of social construction in framing accounts of abuse. I then present care leavers', former residents', and victim/survivors' memories of institutional life and its impact.[1]

Institutions for children

Institutions for poor, abandoned, or neglected children emerged in western affluent nations in the 1750s. Others have written in detail on this history; here I sketch developments in the briefest of terms, having in mind Australia, North America, and England and Wales (Anderberg, 2009; Corby et al. 2001, chapter 1; Dozier et al., 2012; Liddell, 1993; Tomison, 2001). In reviewing research from the late 14th century to the mid-18th century in England, Corby et al. (2001, p. 19) identify three themes: 'a reluctance to use residential care for children [until the mid-18th century], the importance [of making] deprived children work..., and a preoccupation with costs'. Although the first changed, the second and third continued into the latter half of the 18th century and throughout the 19th and 20th centuries.

The modern beginnings of institutions for children can be traced to Elizabethan poor laws in the 17th century, which created alms houses for children and adults. These were sources of cheap child labour: British children were sold to businesses in the American colonies in the 17th century as indentured servants; and children in the American colonies were apprenticed or indentured on work contracts. Parents indentured their children, as did receiving homes for British Child Migrants to

Canada, a practice that continued through the 19th century. Specialized institutions for children such as orphanages and homes emerged at the start of 19th century in Australia, Canada, and other countries. During the 19th century, placing children in institutions was a common practice when parents or family members could not care for them, but by the end of the 19th century, 'boarding out' to family-based care became more prevalent (Tomison, 2001, p. 49). Throughout the 20th century, family-based care (fostering and group homes) was used alongside institutional care. However, during this period, the 'care pendulum' oscillated between institutional and family-based care (p. 49).

In the latter part of the 19th century and throughout the 20th century, the names given to the institutions varied: orphanages, homes, residential schools, training schools, farm schools, and youth centres. In addition, institutions were created for children (and adults) with special needs (Deaf, hard of hearing, blind; or having mental disabilities). In all cases, as the Law Commission of Canada (LCC) (2000, p. 3) notes, residential facilities 'were conceived because... [it was] concluded that they were an appropriate response to what [was viewed] *as problems*' (emphasis added). In some cases, parents willingly sent their children to homes or facilities or were unable to care for them; but in other cases, children 'were found to be neglected or abused, or judged to be "unmanageable" or truant', and thus were sent to facilities as state wards. Some children in youth detention or training schools had committed criminal offences, but many, especially girls, were adjudicated delinquent for breaches of status offences.

The LCC's review and the five Australian Commonwealth and state inquiries all say that the picture of institutional life cannot be depicted as uniformly bad, depending on the place and time. For example, the LCC (2000, p. 3) points out that 'many children acquired an education and life skills'. Nor can the staff working in the institutions be cast in entirely negative terms. The LCC (2000, p. 3) suggests that 'most people... did their very best to fulfil their roles as educators, caregivers, and guardians, often with inadequate resources and support'; and Forde (1999, forward) acknowledges 'the many hardworking, good, dedicated people who have selflessly devoted their lives to the care of children over many years', saying that 'such innocent people may feel hurt by the findings of the inquiry'. Despite this and depending on the place and time, institutions more often resembled prison-like conditions. They had highly regimented schedules, feeding times, and rows of beds in one room; children were not permitted to have a sense of individuality; and children were viewed by staff as contaminated, tainted, and unworthy.

Although a 'dehumanizing environment' itself could be considered a form of abuse, as Penglase (2005, p. 48) suggests, the LCC (2000, p. 4) identifies a set of 'circumstances and attitudes' that facilitated physical and sexual abuse of children.

Enablers of abuse

The enablers of abuse were the status of the children, the status of the staff and organizations running the facilities, and the invisibility of institutional life to outsiders. Children came from poorer families, had parents who were unable to care for them, were members of racial or ethnic minority groups, or had mental and physical disabilities. They were treated by staff and viewed by the general public as 'undeserving' and requiring 'moral reclamation' (Ferguson, 2007, p. 136). They had no voice; and even when they did report offences to authorities, their stories were not believed or acted upon. When their mothers, fathers, or other family and community members complained to authorities about too severe beatings and 'indecent practices' (the term for sexual abuse), these were typically not followed up or investigated.

By contrast, staff workers, both members of religious orders and lay, were trusted members of society. During the abuse time frame (as recalled by adult survivors, the 1930s to the 1990s, depending on the institution), the organizations running the institutions 'wielded significant social power and [were] potent symbols of authority' (LCC, 2000, p. 5). In some cases, the significant economic gain from state-church funding arrangements inhibited any type of independent government oversight (as in *Duplessis Orphans* in Canada and *Child Migrants* in Australia) or the practices were carried out by medical authorities without oversight (as in *Duplessis Orphans* and *Alberta Sterilization* in Canada). The more that the financial interests of government and church entities were aligned, the less likely there was effective external oversight, and the more likely that abusive regimes could flourish. Most members of society would have found it 'incredible' that government officials would not have children's welfare in mind, and 'unthinkable' that church authorities, 'priests, nuns, or members of lay orders would commit acts of physical and sexual child abuse'. The 'deference accorded to governments and churches' (to which I would add medical authorities and charitable organizations) meant that policies and practices went unnoticed and unchallenged (LCC, 2000, p. 4). Moving offending staff to other institutions, whether they were members of religious orders or lay staff, was the typical response up to the 1990s.

In this way the reputation of governments and church and charitable organizations was maintained.

Finally, there was little effective oversight of day-to-day institutional practices. Officials might visit to inspect, but because visits were scheduled or anticipated, the institution could appear to be operating effectively and humanely. Forde (1999, p. 100) suggests there was 'extensive cleaning and improving of external appearances... Quilts were placed on beds, the unappealing refectory tables were covered, and boxes of toys were brought out in the infants' section'. Even when government authorities issued specific directives to change institutional practices, as occurred in Ontario in the 1940s and 1950s, the institutions did not comply. Not until 1990 to 2010, depending on the country, were there concerted efforts to address the failures and legacy of institutional care.

Is abuse more likely in institutions for children?

Save the Children UK shows unequivocally that institutional care has negative physical, psychological, and emotional effects on children's development, particularly from infancy to 3 years of age (Browne, 2009, pp. 11–15). However, is physical and sexual abuse more likely for children who live in institutions than outside them? Intuitively, we may say yes, this must be true, for all the reasons the LCC (2000) gives. With the exception of recent research by Euser et al. (2013) on the prevalence of sexual abuse in residential and foster care (reviewed below), no research has substantiated this claim. Until recently, the prevalence of physical or sexual abuse of children was not measured, whether inside or outside institutions. To make accurate comparisons of abuse in different care contexts, the same questions must be asked, the same definitions of 'abuse' must be used, and random samples are required. Meta-reviews have attempted to compare prevalence by type of care context, but they run into problems of sample comparability in definitions and questions asked. Barth (2002, pp. 8–10) reviewed studies from the United States and England on abuse in foster and group care, but the findings were conflicting and inconclusive. Browne (2009) presented survey results of physical and sexual abuse of children in Romanian residential facilities, but like other studies, the sample of respondents, although large, was non-random.

There is now more definitive research from the Netherlands, with data gathered in 2010 (Euser et al., 2013), although the focus is on sexual abuse. Using four items from the NPM-2010 self-report survey,[2] the annual prevalence of sexual abuse for youth (12 to 17 years old) in residential care is greater (over 2.5 times greater) than those in foster care or in an average Dutch home. Specifically, the annual prevalence was 19.4 per cent in residential care compare to 5.5 per cent in foster care and 7.4 per cent in a Dutch home (p. 227). Rates of reported sexual abuse were higher for girls than boys (p. 228).[3] Of those who reported sexual abuse, nearly half (46 per cent) said they did not want to report their relationship to the perpetrator. For youth in residential care who reported the relationship, 44 per cent of identified perpetrators were the victims' peers in the same residential facility (p. 228). Confirming the residential and foster care figures reported in Euser et al. (2013), a parallel Dutch study by the Samson Commission (2012), which analyzed 'hands-on' sexual abuse, found that the prevalence of sexual abuse was 2.5 times higher in residential care (22.9 per cent) than foster care (8.8 per cent).[4]

Recall that these estimates of annual prevalence are for 2010, not many decades earlier, when residential care facilities were less well regulated and less subject to oversight and when carers had little or no professional training. In saying this, I am not implying that abuse prevalence may have been higher in previous decades. Although we may intuitively believe that this is so, it cannot be known and is compromised by retrospective understandings of 'abuse'. Moreover, the population of children in residential care today in countries like the Netherlands, Australia, and Canada contains more 'deep end' behavioural cases, that is, of children who are harder to place in foster care, than the population in previous decades. In addition to the enablers of abuse identified by the LCC (2000) for historical institutional abuse, the Samson Commission (2012) identified enablers of sexual abuse in residential care today. They argue that the 'risk of sexual abuse is inherent in juvenile care' and the 'risk of detection and reprisals for perpetrators is low' (p. 146). The interrelated factors facilitating abuse are the organization of care, children's needs for affection and its expression in sexual activity, the 'deeply troubled background' of children who are living together in care, and the power of professionals and foster parents (p. 146).

The Dutch research is of one country, and until research in other countries is carried out, we need to be cautious in generalizing. A significant contribution is estimating sexual abuse prevalence across three care settings (Euser at al., 2013) and explaining why sexual abuse is expectable in residential care (Samson Commission, 2012), even if it is experienced by a minority of residents in any one year. A potential drawback is a focus on sexual abuse alone, when as we shall see, what is remembered by historical abuse survivors as much or more is harsh physical discipline and the cruelty of carers.

Social construction and 'accounts'

Smith (2010, p. 306) suggests that 'inquiry into historical abuse might, most charitably, be described as naïve realist, where...accounts given by former residents of children's homes [are] assumed to accurately mirror the way things were'. He believes that the correction of past responses has swung too far: moving from one extreme of not believing victims' stories, to another, of accepting them without further investigation. He argues that claims of abuse should be subject to a greater degree of critical analysis. I agree, but wish to clarify the point.

By taking a critical analysis, I do not mean that survivors' or care leavers' stories should be criticized. Rather, all stories or 'accounts' – whether of the present or past, of sexual abuse or any other victimization, by perpetrators or victims, by government, church, and other officials – are socially constructed. They are constructed and presented to another person or an audience for a purpose, they may justify and neutralize a person's actions, they may include professional language used and absorbed in therapy sessions, and they may incorporate positions of both victim and offender. All of this has been part of the sociological toolkit for more than half a century (see Sykes and Matza, 1957; Scott and Lyman, 1968 for early works). When accounts are of events that occurred many years ago, we can expect imprecision, even distortion. Thus, researchers should read accounts that *pronounce* or *mobilize* a social problem of institutional abuse as critically as those that *deny* it (or have denied it in the past). Such accounts are put forward not only by survivors, but also by government, church, and other officials; therapists, counsellors, and social workers; and lawyers, journalists, and researchers, among others. In the current political context, few can easily deny the problem; thus, it takes courage to ask critical questions about the sources and intensity of mobilization when it occurs. Smith (2010, p. 316) argues for a 'more rounded approach' by drawing on the memories of a range of participants, not solely victims and survivors. Such an approach features in five cases in my sample: *Alberta Sterilization, Indian Residential Schools, Stolen Generations, Child Migrants,* and *Forgotten Australians*.

Memories of institutional life

Much has been written and recorded on the experiences of former residents, care leavers, and survivors. Books and articles have also been published by care leavers themselves. One, by Penglase (2005), is remarkable in tracing her story of being in care, within a broader analysis of children's experiences in Australian residential care. Other contributions come from journalists, researchers, and public inquiry submissions. In addition, television documentary dramas, DVDs, museum installations, and oral history projects have been produced (see Appendix 6).

For those familiar with institutional life from adult survivors' perspectives, my encapsulation will not reveal anything that has not been said or written before. However, it is essential to show the range of wrongs and harms that did occur, which are now subject to redress by government, church, and other entities. The selection of stories was not easy. I did not want to pick the most sensational or worst cases, and nor am I attempting to present an analysis of institutional life within and across all the cases. I decided to focus on a set of common themes in the literature, which are indicative of the regimes of care in total institutions. All the cited work draws from the materials and people who were part of the 19 cases; when names are given, they are in the public domain, having been quoted by name in books, research studies, government reports or inquiry submissions, and in one case, a DVD. All are of remembered experiences in institutions from the 1930s to the 1990s.

Although memories of institutional life often show similar experiences, there were, as Penglase (2005, pp. 178–85) suggests, 'better' and 'worse' places. The worse places were training schools or detention centres; and among the residential homes, those run by 'some Catholic religious orders, the Protestant sect homes, many of the Salvation Army homes, the Christian Brothers homes, and those run by the Sisters of Mercy' (p. 183). Practices in these places are often termed 'sadistic'. Penglase's observation for Australia holds for Canada, where schools run by the Christian Brothers or other Catholic religious orders, and training schools or detention centres comprise over half of the 11 cases. I have not sought to differentiate care leavers' memories by type of institution (for example, training schools and homes); in any event, state wards and voluntary placements were often in the same institution. Another potential source of variation is the size of a home or institution, but Penglase (2005, pp. 176–8) suggests that the 'philosophy of care' mattered more than the size of the facility. When staff attitudes were 'unsympathetic' and regimes were rigid and punitive, abuse was more likely.

In this chapter, I depict memories of institutional life with themes of isolation and separation, control and fear, and degradation and neglect. Acts we now call physical and sexual abuse are readily apparent, but it is a total institution's regime – its environment of control and regulation, and of carers' attitudes toward children – which comes through strongly in the accounts. I begin, however, with the positive, not the negative, memories.

Positive memories

In his submission to the Senate inquiry on Forgotten Australians, a former resident of Tally Ho Boys' Home in Burwood, Victoria, recalled:

> I was transferred to Tally Ho Boys' Home in May 1939, aged 9 years and 5 months. I remember that when I went to Tally Ho, I started wetting the bed for about 18 months until I settled down. I was never punished for this. At Tally Ho they taught you to make your bed, wash your clothes, and we shared laundry duties, farm duties, cooking, separating milk, harvesting. I found the homes to be a good environment...The only fights I saw were between the boys. (Senate Report, 2004, p. 46)

Some institutional carers were kind. For example, Grant Hartley, a former resident of St Joseph's said about one the Christian Brothers:

> He was a very nice man. He always had a cookie or candy for you. He was a great big Brother. He worked in the kitchen. He also worked around the garden, and I never saw him mistreat anybody. He always had something for somebody – always. (Hoffman, 1996, p. 221)

The Truth and Reconciliation Commission [TRC]'s (2012) analysis of the Indian residential school system points out that former students completed post-secondary education, and some took on leadership positions in Aboriginal and church organizations and in politics. The TRC study is unusual in having a separate section devoted to positive experiences of children in institutional care (TRC, 2012, pp. 45–9). Some former students expressed 'their gratitude to former teachers', the enjoyment they received from sporting and creative activities, their education, and religious education. One said:

> My experience at the residential school was good. That's one thing I'll tell you, it was really good to be able to go to school and to learn how to read and write. And the other thing, the best of all, I was happy to learn about God. (p. 47)

For some, being in a residential school was better than an abusive home. A former student, who was orphaned, lived with relatives who had abused and neglected her. At 12, afraid for her safety, she telephoned an Indian agent and asked to be placed in Shubenacadie, a residential school in Nova Scotia. Although she 'acknowledged that many negative things happened at the school,...she never regretted going there' (TRC, 2012, p. 46). In Queensland, Forde (1999, p. ii) 'heard from a small number of [care leavers], who came forward to express strong support for the institutions where they were resident'.

Ryszard Szablicki, a former resident of several Catholic institutions in Victoria, has no positive memories. However, he recalled a conversation he had with a man at a CLAN (Care Leavers of Australia) rally in 2008. The man said to Szablicki that he had read his book, *The Orphanage Boy* (2007), but 'he didn't experience the trauma I wrote about. He said he was one of the lucky ones in the orphanage...and had come along to support the children of yesteryear's institutions' (Szablicki, 2010, p. 67). What struck Szablicki 'was the poignant reality that the care each individual child received...was at the whim of luck. As a child behind the walls, that was how I lived it' (p. 67). The 'whim of luck' and being (or not being) 'one of the lucky ones' are phrases often mentioned by survivors.

Isolation and separation

Within this theme, I consider separation from family and culture, the community surrounding the institution, other residents in the institution, and one's self.

Family and culture

Many Indigenous children were not permitted to speak their native language or practice their culture. If they did, they would be punished. The following examples are of Australian and Canadian Indigenous people, respectively:

> Y'know, I can remember we used to just talk lingo. [In the home] they used to tell us not to talk that language, that it's devil's language. And they'd wash our mouths with soap. We sorta had to sit down with Bible language all the time. So it sorta wiped out all our language that we knew. (Human Rights and Equal Opportunity Commission [HREOC], 1997, p. 133)

> After a lifetime of beatings, going hungry, standing in a corridor on one leg, and walking in the snow with no shoes for speaking Inuvialuktun, and having a heavy, stinging paste rubbed on my face,

> which did not stop us expressing our Eskimo custom of raising our eyebrows for 'yes' and wrinkling our noses for 'no', I soon lost the ability to speak my mother tongue. When a language dies, the world it was generated from is broken down too. (Royal Commission on Aboriginal Peoples [RCAP], 1996, p. 372)

Children were isolated and separated from their families by control of communication between children and family members. In some cases, mail from family members was not given to residents, and their letters to family members were not posted. For example, a former Child Migrant, who had been placed in St John's in Canterbury, Victoria, said:

> When I was 14 and started to work, which meant moving from the home to the hostel, I was given a bundle of letters from my mother. Those had been written over the 8 years I had been [at the home]. In the meantime, I had thought that my mother did not love me and did not want me back. (Senate Report, 2001, p. 74)

For some children, visits by family members were not allowed. A parent of a former resident of residential school on Kuper Island, British Columbia, said that when he arrived, 'I could not see my boy, and the priest who was the principal would have nothing to do with me' (TRC, 2012, p. 24). A care leaver told the Forgotten Australians inquiry:

> I was very angry to read [in] my earlier files how my mother and maternal and paternal grandmothers all tried for access visits. They were denied each time [because] my mother was deemed to have fallen from grace. My father...was also denied access. If only I could have met them, I would at least have had a mental picture to remember of them. (Senate Report, 2004, p. 106)

For other children, there was limited access to family members. For example, in a Queensland institution, children were allowed monthly visits only if their behaviour had been 'satisfactory', and the visits could be only for one hour (Forde, 1999, p. 79). Visits by family members were difficult when the institution was at a considerable distance from the family's home. A former resident of a youth detention facility in Shelburne in Nova Scotia, whose family lived some distance in Cape Breton, said it was 'inconvenient because my parents [had] to drive 9 hours to visit for 4 hours, and the telephone bill [wasn't] pleasant either' (Samuels-Stewart, 1995, p. 56).

Community surrounding the institution

Children were isolated and separated from those in the community surrounding the institution, although some attended schools away from the care facilities. Former residents of several institutions in Queensland (Silky Oaks, Nazareth House, Enoggera Boys' Home, and Blackheath) told the Forde inquiry of feeling stigmatized when attending school. Staff and students looked down on them as 'Home kids', nuns told them they were 'receiving their education free of charge', and their clothing marked them as different because they did not have the school uniform (Forde, 1999, p. 85). In a Salvation Army facility in Queensland, the boys attending an external school were not allowed to talk to any girls during their lunch breaks; otherwise, they would be punished.

Alice Quinton, a former Duplessis Orphan,[5] was transferred to the St Julien Hospital for psychiatric patients when she was 7. (The hospital is located 200 kilometres [125 miles] east of Montréal.) She lived there for 16 years; and during that time, she remembered having one trip outside, when she 'saw ordinary children who walked about freely and did not appear frightened [to] laugh out loud or talk with their friends'. She had 'never imagined such a life was possible' (Nickerson, 2000, p. 2). A former residential school student said, 'We were so totally isolated in this boarding school. All around the schoolyard, there were fences, beyond which we didn't set foot' (TRC, 2012, p. 24).

Other residents and siblings

Interactions between siblings were watched and regulated, and siblings were sometimes banned from speaking to each other. A former residential school student said she remembered this exchange with her brother in the classroom:

> I went over to talk to him, and he was really nervous. He said, 'don't come over and talk to me'. I asked, 'Why...' And he was saying, 'You're not supposed to'. I told him, 'Why, you are my brother'. And right away I was taken to the front of the class, and I was given the ruler on the palm of my hands. (TRC 2012, p. 23)

A former resident of the Ballarat Orphanage in Victoria said:

> The staff saw no reason to treat brothers and sisters as part of a family. Instead, children were separated into age groups, and some siblings were even sent to different orphanages depending on what room was available here, there, and elsewhere. (Senate Report, 2004, p. 107)

One child recalled seeing her brother every week at church but only waving to him because she was not allowed to speak to him. In a Queensland institution, siblings were not permitted to see each other at all because it 'wasn't permitted' (Forde, 1999, p. 78).

Children were not allowed to talk to each other, depending on the time of day or sex of student. One former residential school student said, 'during certain periods of the day we were not allowed to talk, which only led to hand motions and sneaking around in secrecy' (TRC, 2012, p. 23). Care leavers told the Forde inquiry that they were forced to sit together without moving or speaking; otherwise, they would be punished (Forde, 1999, p. 71). They were also punished for '...talking during meal or study time,...talking to girls or playing with them in the school grounds,...[and] talking on the way to school....' (p. 72). Children were often separated by sex, and boys and girls were not allowed to speak to each other. A former resident of the Salvation Army Home for Boys in Indooroopilly (Brisbane) said:

> [Staff]...discouraged boys having anything to do with the opposite sex, boys were brainwashed that talking to girls was filthy and were punished if they were heard by an officer...I now believe this is why I seem to have trouble starting a relationship with the opposite sex. (Senate Report, 2004, p. 95)

In an Indian residential school, the children '...used to have to use this sign language to communicate [with each other]' (TRC, 2012, p. 23).

Self

Institutional care often meant regimented treatment as a group, not as individuals. Children were called by their last name, or if more than one child had the same last name, by their last name and a number, or simply by a number. A former resident of a Queensland institution said:

> You were just a number on the book, or somebody's name on their books. But as far as a person goes, I could have been some dog that wandered in off the street. (Forde, 1999, p. 78)

A former Child Migrant, who lived in Clontarf Boys Town (located in Waterford, a suburb of Perth), said that 'our clothes were numbered and we were not a name just a number. Any names we were given were terrible racist taunts' (Senate Report, 2001, p. 74). In an Indian Residential School, a former student said that they were '...given a number and were called by that number. Our heads were shaved bald, and we were all dressed the same.…' (LCC, 2000, p. 31). Another former student said: 'I was number one hundred and sixteen. I was trying to find myself; I was lost.…I wondered if I was the only one to feel that way' (TRC, 2012, p. 23).

Children were not permitted to have their own possessions. A former student at Lynwood Hall in Guildford, New South Wales, said that '…everything that my foster parents had given me, clothes, jewellery, shoes, my treasures and my bank account were taken from me. I never saw any of them again' (Senate Report, 2004, p. 87). A former resident of Bidura Children's Home, New South Wales, reported that when she arrived,

> I was taken to a room where my bag containing everything I owned in my life was taken away and nothing was ever returned. Even the clothes I had on were taken from me…I was told to put on the stock clothing. (p. 87)

Former residential school students spoke of culturally meaningful clothes that family members had given them being removed and replaced with standard clothing. One said that she later wondered whether 'maybe…they wanted us to dress like them' (TRC, 2012, p. 22). Another said that after his head was shaved, he was told 'Now you are no longer an Indian' (p. 22). A *Grandview* survivor reflected on the impact of these institutional practices: 'at Grandview I had to be who they wanted me to be…I couldn't draw attention to myself' (Patricia Griffiths, *Until Someone Listens*, 1999).

A significant example of separation of self was the lack of recognizing children's birthdays. Three care leavers said in their submissions to the Forgotten Australians inquiry:

- I never had a birthday party or cake (Georgina Fraser, St Catherine's Orphanage, New South Wales).
- There were so many children, the orphanage did not celebrate birthdays (Frank Golding, Ballarat Orphanage, Victoria).
- No birthday parties, no presents, no kindness; just fear and regimentation to keep us in line (Les Johnson, Murray Dwyer Orphanage, New South Wales). (Senate Report, 2004, p. 94)

Control and fear

Social groups and the socialization of children require order and control. Furthermore, adults do have greater power than children such that 'powerlessness, some might say, is a natural condition of childhood' (LCC, 2000, p. 26). The following examples are of a different type of social control and use of power: when carers impose rigid, arbitrary, or disproportionate rules and punishments, including power to control the most intimate aspects of an individual's body. As Penglase (2005, p. 105) suggests, 'it is no exaggeration to say that most children living in Children's Homes felt fear on a daily basis' (p. 105). This fear could be used to further dominate and control the children and to re-enforce the authority of carers.

Punishment

Punishments were physical (direct violence to the body) and mental and physical (solitary confinement, for example). Care leavers' experiences with, witnessing of, and participating in physical punishment, including severe punishment that resulted in bleeding and bruising, are evident throughout all the materials. Thus, it would be pointless to offer one or two general examples; therefore, I consider different contexts and meanings of punishment.

In addition to an abuser's hands, fists, and feet, all types of instruments were used: 'straps, belts, whips, canes, planks of wood, and keys' (Tasmanian Ombudsman, 2004, p. 17); sawed-off goalie's hockey sticks, extension cords, and strappings while tied up (Hoffman, 1996, pp. 139–40); and a hot iron, scissors, rulers, and a garden hose (Forde, 1999, pp. 71–2). A former student of St John's School (Ontario) summed it up this way: 'they liked to punish us; you could tell they liked it' (Hoffman, 1996, p. 139). Punishments could be arbitrary and without explanation, for example, being punished for left-handedness ('to get the Devil out of them') or punishing a group for offending by one or a few children (Forde, 1999, p. 71). Punishments could be groundless:

> [A] former resident described how a staff member beat him with a cane for failing to complete a chore, after which he was thrown into the Brisbane River. He described having to pull himself from the water against the current only to receive another beating with the cane by the same staff member because 'he had been swimming'. (Forde, 1999, p. 73)

Punishments could come out of the blue, with a ferocity that survivors could not comprehend, as occurred when a Mount Cashel brother, whom Shane Earle had understood to be 'his friend and protector [and whom he] adored because of his gentle nature, began beating him mercilessly' with a belt (Harris, 1990, p. 58). The apparent reason was that Earle told the brother that a library card was missing from a book they were about to return to the library.

A common punishment for boys was forcing them to hit and hurt other boys. The Tasmanian Ombudsman (2004, p. 19) describes a 'makeshift boxing ring in the gymnasium' in the 1960s and early 1970s, in which

> the participants were often deliberately unevenly matched, which… resulted in the smaller boy being 'punched out'. Boys who refused to box or did not demonstrate that they were trying hard enough, were punished. This often took the form of beatings by staff, or sometimes by other boys at the instigation of staff.

The following account is from a former student of St Joseph's in 1956, who said that the 'fear [the] brother would instil by his actions was just as bad as the fear when he hit you'. He continues:

> I watched an incident where one kid had a broken arm, and a brother sent his favourite to fight the kid with the broken arm. And the kid with the broken arm was winning, so the brother beat up the kid with the broken arm. The violence boggles you. (Hoffman, 1996, p. 59)

Children were witnesses to physical abuse and were shown the effects of punishment: 'the worse beating I ever saw was when [the] brother beat H. unconscious' (a St Joseph's student, 1965); and 'I will never forget the beating that [the brother] gave to __. He showed us his body, and it was black and blue with welts from the strap' (a St Joseph's student, 1958) (Hoffman, 1996, pp. 139–40). In the St Vincent's Orphanage in Queensland, older children, both boys and girls, were used to 'enforce discipline':

> Older boys were permitted to patrol with straps, ready to administer a flogging to any smaller boy who stepped out of line…Older girls exercised their power with beatings, punching, 'Chinese burns', and the locking of younger children in cupboards. (Forde, 1999, p. 72)

Penglase (2005, p. 137) gives examples of 'sexualised punishment' in Australian institutions. Boys would be made to wait naked for a shower, and staff would hit them on their penis if they had an erection. A former resident of Mittagong Homes in New South Wales recalled that

> a common practice was polishing the floorboards of the building. Five or six boys, 5 or 6 years old, maybe more, would polish…We would

> wear pyjama tops but no bottoms...Matron...would walk through the hall and smack bottoms with a wooden hair brush at random, sometimes absentmindedly.

Children were punished for disclosing physical or sexual abuse. A survivor from St Joseph's Orphanage in South Australia described what happened after he was told by a nun that 'some people' [potential foster parents] were taking him out for the weekend:

> ...Friday, I [slept] in the lounge room, they would talk to me. On the Saturday the man and the woman performed sexual acts on me for their own pleasure. I was told if I said anything, I would be punished. When I got back to the Home, I complained to the head sister and told her what happened...and I was taken down to the dungeon under the home...and was told by the sister the Devil is going to come and punish me. She then closed the door. It was pitch black...I was frightened as I was waiting for the Devil to come...I was down there a long time. (Penglase, 2005, p. 276)

Numerous accounts are given of solitary confinement. This type of punishment instilled fear not only in the children who were sent to solitary, but also other children.

Threats and fear

Survivors spoke of 'living in constant fear, the fear of being the next one to be beaten', but then 'feeling relieved when it was someone else being beaten, then feeling guilty for feeling that way' (*Grandview* survivor Patricia Griffiths, *Until Someone Listens*, 1999). Threats and fear were used by carers to encourage compliance and non-disclosure of abuse, particularly sexual abuse, and to intentionally scare children and enforce authority.

In some Queensland institutions, staff would 'always [wear] thick leather straps over their shoulders that they used to discipline children' (Forde, 1999, p. 71). The straps frightened children into compliance and were used to punish those perceived as having committed infractions. In one Queensland institution, the 'threat of transfer to [another institution] was used to enforce compliance and to frighten, since [it] was...a much harsher and more punitive environment' (Forde, 1999, p. 72). In HREOC (1997, p. 138), a former resident reported:

> They were very cruel to us...I remember once, I must have been 8 or 9, and I was locked in the old morgue. The adults who worked there

> would tell us of the things that happened in there...I screamed all night, but no one came to get me.

A Queensland care leaver illustrated the diffusion of fear, which created an 'atmosphere of tension and fear':

> [The institution]...was a place of extreme violence, institutionalized cruelty, both physical and emotional. Severe public floggings and bashings and verbal abuse and poor diet created an atmosphere of tension and fear, which adversely affected all of the boys, not only those directly assaulted, but those who witnessed those assaults. (Forde, 1999, p. 129)

The relationship between fear, guilt, self-hatred, and witnessing violence is illustrated in the following haunting passage from Penglase (2005, p. 149), who says that the 'worst experience of my childhood was seeing my sister punished day in and day out [by Betty, the home's matron], and doing nothing to prevent it'. She continues:

> I witnessed [my sister] being beaten and kicked by the woman I felt my survival depended upon...I was afraid it was going to happen to me next, and if it did, I would be annihilated....So I would watch, in a form of dissociation from the horror, torn between my terror of being abandoned by Betty if I spoke up, and shame and self-hatred for not doing so.

Sexual use and abuse

Penglase (2005) coined the term 'sexual use' to capture the ways that 'children...were used by adults for their own sexual gratification'. It is an apt expression. A former resident of a Western Australian institution said, '...we meant no more to them than the moment's pleasure' (p. 144). Sexual use and abuse ranged from carers' watching children showering, touching their genitals, to rape. Sexual offences were committed by employees, carers, visitors, adults outside of the institution, and other residents.

Sexual abuse was mentioned by male and female residents as a routine part of 'pat searches' in two youth detention facilities in Nova Scotia (Samuels-Stewart, 1995, pp. 34–6). One boy recalled that he

> was sort of touched too much in certain places by staff. On another occasion my pants came unbuttoned, I turned around and hit the

> counsellor's hand away from me. I was scared. I got five days in [the] cell. (p. 36)

A care leaver told the Mullighan inquiry in South Australia that he awoke one night in his dormitory to a man penetrating him. He tried to resist him, but the man threatened to kill him if he did not 'shut up'. Staff came to his dormitory and removed the man. The next day the police came to talk to the boy. He recalled one officer saying:

> The bloke that did it, the man that did it, was a policeman, and the police have the right to come on to [the grounds] and have a boy any fuckin' time they want one, so you all better keep your bums clean in case, for when they come back.

For a few days 'he and the other boys did not wash or wipe their anuses in the hope of avoiding assault' (Mullighan, 2008a, p. 51).

Sexual use and abuse evolved from what appeared to be a 'protected' relationship. A *Grandview* survivor said:

> [It] started off slowly as a father/daughter type relationship. He gave me privileges, and I was able to get away with things that the other residents didn't. In time he expected sexual favours in return for these privileges: manipulation, total manipulation. I thought this person was on my side, I thought they were there to protect me. (Bev Mann, *Until Someone Listens*, 1999)

Another example of an initially protected relationship that progressed to sexual offending is described in Henton and McCann (1995, p. 66). A former resident of St John's School in Ontario said a Christian Brother 'would sit on the edge of the bed', and the two would talk. At the time, the boy believed that the brother 'seemed genuinely concerned' about his welfare. Thus, he 'was not overly concerned' when the brother 'gave him an affectionate kiss on his forehead before leaving one night'. However, in the time 'the kissing became more sexual' and the brother's actions more sexually coercive and controlling. A third example comes from the Nova Scotia School for Girls. Counsellor George Moss (who was later convicted for sexual assault) would initially present himself as a '...a warm and understanding person,...as a father figure to the girls' (Stratton, 1995, p. 39), but then he would escalate to sexually coercive behaviour. This 'alarmed [one resident] because she had a fear of sex at that early age and believed sex could cause pain'. She decided to run away from the school, but was returned to the school, and placed in confinement (p. 40). Exemplifying the complexity of abuse in institutions, several girls believed that Moss loved them and were jealous when they learned that Moss was 'doing the same things to other girls' (p. 43).

George Epoch, a Jesuit priest and prolific offender, decorated his rectory in Cape Croker, an Aboriginal reserve, to entice children. He gave the boys money for sex, but in an indirect way. A survivor recalled:

> We could do what we wanted, and Father couldn't do anything. We could take money from his wallet, or his wallet would disappear. He never really gave us hell.... He would say things like: 'When I come back in this room I want my wallet on the table', and it would be put back with no money, and he couldn't do anything because of what he was doing to us. (Mussell, 1995, p. 5)

Epoch fondled the boys' genitals, kissed, and masturbated them, and had oral, anal, and group sex with them (p. 6), but it was 'extremely confusing to them'. The following passage demonstrates why such sexual activity was confusing: it was experienced as 'not right' and as a source of comfort:

> For some, they knew it wasn't right because their bodies told them it wasn't right. For others, the abuse was acceptable because his way of abusing was less severe than what they had grown accustomed to in their family of origin. For still others, it was the gruesome price paid for a warm bed, a hot meal, [and] safety from a severe beating. (p. 8)

Another example of receiving rewards for sexual use is recalled by Shane Earle, former resident of Mount Cashel. A favourite of one of the brothers, Earle said that the brother '... used to touch me sexually quite often... Almost always after these incidents, he would give me money. I always had money and everyone used to wonder where I got it' (Harris, 1990, p. 43).

Fear was part of sexual abuse because care leavers did not know when it would occur. This account comes from a former resident of Goodwood Orphanage in South Australia:

> You're laying in bed and you're listening for the beads and you're listening for the Angelus... to be sung and I used to think, 'Will she come tonight? I hope she doesn't,' and then I'd say, 'Our Father, and

> Hail Mary' and you know, and then you hear the click of the beads and she would come, yes, and she would take me and come up to the attic.

In the attic, the nun would sexually abuse the girl and tell her not to tell anyone (Mullighan, 2008a, pp. 81–2).

Sexual abuse by residents was learned and encouraged by staff. When Jericho Hill School was first investigated in 1982, a psychologist and social worker called attention to abuse not only by staff of residents, but also by the older boys of the younger girls and boys (Berger, 1995, pp. 18–19). A lawyer close to the case said that the residents were told by staff that coercive sexual activity was 'normal behaviour' and 'how to show someone you loved them'; this then evolved to the older boys abusing the younger boys and girls (Anne Sheane, personal communication, 9 January 2014). Peer physical and sexual abuse in children's institutions is often hidden in case materials or given oblique reference, with more attention paid to abuse by staff (Barter et al., 2004). It took courage by Phil Fontaine, an Aboriginal leader and former residential school student, to say in television and radio interviews in 1990 that 'what often happens is the abused becomes the abuser' and with respect to sexual abuse, 'you do what is done to you' (Fontaine, 1990a, 1990b).[6]

Degradation and neglect

All the preceding examples of physical and sexual abuse are one form of degradation. Here I consider other forms that reminded children that they were 'no good' and would 'never amount to anything', of 'being emotionally beaten down and having one's self-confidence and pride continually undermined' (LCC, 2000, p. 25). Examples are humiliating punishment, inadequate food, food used to humiliate, coarse living and learning, and lack of privacy. These were daily reminders to children that they were worthless and had little chance of making something of themselves.

Humiliating punishment

Stories of humiliating and public punishment for bed wetting are common in the materials. A former residential school student said: 'I have seen Indian children having their faces rubbed in human excrement...the normal punishment for bed wetters...was to have his face rubbed in his own urine' (RCAP, 1996, p. 373). Survivors of a Tasmanian institution recalled that boys who bed wet had to sleep in 'special' dormitories. They also remembered that bed wetters were

> 'belted' and then lined up in front of all the other boys in the dining room and called names in front of everyone. The other boys were not allowed to start eating until the bed wetters had been beaten and ridiculed. (Tasmanian Ombudsman, 2004, p. 19)

Those punished for bed wetting recalled that the public humiliation was worse than the actual physical hurt. Being naked while being punished was also remembered for the humiliation it caused:

> The nun in charge pounded into the dormitory brandishing a very thick strap. She stripped me naked and proceeded to savagely flog me, showing no mercy. She was like a woman gone mad, cruelly beating me until she had crushed and shamed me. The pain was unbearable and I had been humiliated beyond imagination. To be stripped for all to see, at 15 years of age, was horrendous. (Senate Report, 2001, p. 80)

Punishment in segregation was degrading. A *Grandview* survivor describes the notorious 'hole' at Churchill House, the secure facility at the school:

> Physical altercations against staff or other residents resulted in solitary confinement, known as a 'trip to the hole', where residents sometimes spent days screaming, singing, or cursing. The hole at Churchill was a small cement room containing a dirty mattress on the floor and a toilet. The walls were covered in graffiti and blood. To eliminate the possibility of suicide, girls were forced to remove their clothing and sit naked on the mattress. Refusal to do so would result in intervention by male staff members, whereby a resident's clothing was forcibly removed. (Dubinsky, 2007, p. 10)

Food, hunger, and humiliation

Residents knew that their food was inferior to what the staff ate. William McLeary, a former resident of Burnside in New South Wales, said in his submission to the Forgotten Australians inquiry:

> Staff took their meals at the same time and sat at tables covered with crisp white starched tablecloths and napkins, silver cutlery and

> serviette rings. We would sit and drool at their food. They had chicken, meat, bacon and eggs, toast with real butter, scones with fresh cream. (Penglase, 2005, p. 117)

Likewise, a former student at a residential school in Saskatchewan remembered 'walking past the staff dining room and noticing that they were having steak and chicken. It looked like a king's feast. We had baloney sandwiches' (TRC, 2012, p. 34). Although the children's food was inadequate, in both quality and quantity, it improved when inspectors and other visitors came. A Métis former residential school student in Alberta recalled: '...the welfare was coming this one time, [and] they used to put tablecloths on the table and give us bacon and eggs to make it look like it was really good food, you know'. The students told 'the inspectors that this was not their regular fare [but] were not believed' (TRC, 2012, p. 34).

Douglas Mann, who was in a home in Western Australia in the 1950s, relayed his memories of hunger to the Forgotten Australians inquiry: 'Hunger pains were always with us. There was never enough food. I used to always offer to do the dishes so that I could scrape the pots and eat the scraps' (Penglase, 2005, p. 120). George Manuel, who became a prominent Canadian Aboriginal leader, recalled that when he was at the Kamloops residential school in British Columbia, 'hunger is both the first and the last thing I can remember about that school...Every Indian student smelled of hunger' (TRC, 2012, p. 31). In some schools, boys would '...trap gophers and roast them over open fires to supplement their diets, occasionally sharing these treats with the girls....These were acts of desperation, not a return to traditional diets' (TRC, 2012, p. 33).

Food was bland and inadequate, and at times rotting and covered in weevils. There are many accounts of being served rotten food or of children being so hungry they had to 'scrounge in the town dump' or eat the scraps in the kitchen (HREOC, 1997, p. 137). During her stays in several homes in Victoria, a former resident recalled 'protein-moving Weeties, sometimes with warm milk, other times, cold':

> [The Weeties] moved because of the weevils that inhabited them. No matter how much protein they thought we required, weevils just could not cut it. Yet we were made to sit, and sit, and sit until we ate it, little worms and all. (Penglase, 2005, pp. 117–18)

Children were force-fed and made to eat their own vomit if they became sick from what they ate. A former resident of Sir James Whitney School recalled that he vomited after eating stewed tomatoes, but then was forced by a staff member to eat them, and who threatened to 'strap all the other students' if he didn't do so. He said that he ate the tomatoes, but '...to this day I can't eat stewed tomatoes, or cabbage or lettuce' (Girard, 1998). A similar account was given to the Forgotten Australians inquiry:

> At one meal time I was served lambs fry, which made me gag and dry retch. I vomited on the plate. I was then served the same lambs fry for the next three meals until I ate it. I did not eat it and was severely punished. (Senate Report, 2004, p. 57)

Penglase (2005) says she has 'never forgotten' Tracy, a child in her home.[7] She 'would never eat the morning porridge, and as a result she had to stand in the corner in her nightie with a lump of porridge in her mouth'. Penglase continues:

> There she stayed all morning, or perhaps all day, and refused to swallow. I can still see her skinny little legs, blue with cold, her white nightie and fine pale hair..., and the dogged look on her face, as she stood there unmoved by slaps and harsh words, determined to remain true to herself. (pp. 119–20)

Tracy, how brave and determined you were.

'Coarse' living and learning

Goffman (1961, p. 20) says that when people enter total institutions, their possessions are removed and the replacement is typically of a '"coarse" variety, ill-suited, often old, and the same for large categories of inmates'. In general, when one shifts between the 'home world and the institutional world', the 'self is systematically...mortified' (pp. 12–14). For some children, the shift is not apt because the institution and 'home world' were the same, as occurred to Penglase who was placed in a home at 8 months. The children's home was her world, the only world she knew: 'I would never have dared set foot outside the Home without permission, and – what I now see was worse – I did not want to' (Penglase, 2005, p. 123). For others, who had come from abusive families or foster families, coming into an institution was an improvement, as Dereck O'Brien (1991, p. 117) recalled about Mount Cashel School: 'I wasn't stuck in a basement anymore, I could watch television and play in the gym...' However, for many children, the shift is apt. I use the phrase 'coarse living and learning' to apply not only to clothing and bedding in institutions, but also to work, education, and play.

When Maree Giles arrived at Paramatta Girls' Home, she encountered the standard features of a stripped identity and coarse replacements, in moving between the 'home world and institutional world':

> She confiscated all my clothes, all my belongings, then used a pair of large black shears to cut off my shoulder length hair. There was no care taken to style the hair, it was HACKED. I was issued with regulation clothing, a number (43), horrible long dresses made of rough material, clumpy shoes and disgusting bloomers and singlets. I was not given a bra. (Senate Report, 2004, p. 87, emphasis in original)

Reinforcing Goffman, Forde (1999, p. 67) found that the removal of personal clothing was a 'particularly sore point' because it removed 'a link with the outside world'. Their clothes were replaced with generic, ill-fitting items. When children attended school away from the residential facility, their clothing singled them out as a 'homies', which was stigmatizing and humiliating. Not being given appropriate clothing reminded children that they did 'not deserve to be treated with care' (Penglase, 2005, p. 290). As a boy in Parkerville in Western Australia, Douglas Mann remembers 'crying all the way to school in winter' because 'we weren't allowed to wear shoes...' The trip was 2 to 3 kilometres (1 to 2 miles) each way on a gravel road, and Mann said 'my feet really hurt, chilblains were common, and in summer, we would get blisters because the road was so hot' (p. 290).

In Barambah, Queensland, a reserve for Indigenous people was created in 1901 as part of the state's protection–segregation policies of removing Indigenous families from their homes. Renamed Cherbourg in 1931, the settlement had a reformatory school, training farm, and dormitories for women and children. Drawing from inspection reports in the early 1930s, Forde (1999, p. 52) describes the dormitory conditions as 'appalling':

> Each night, women and children scrambled for blankets, and some slept on the floor with a mattress over them for warmth. Others pushed two or three beds together and slept seven or eight together for warmth, covered with only a couple of blankets, most without pillows...[The girls' dormitory] was literally alive with bugs. The beds, bed clothing, pillows and mattresses [were] all infested...All

> pillows were filthy because the previous matron withheld pillow slips in order to save washing.

Forde (1999, p. 51) devotes a separate chapter to institutions for Indigenous children in Queensland, noting that conditions 'fell well short of the standards prevalent at other institutions accommodating state wards'.

Children worked long hours to keep the institutions running. In some institutions, work is all they did, according to Penglase (2005, pp. 124–8). The girls did the 'inside' chores, and the boys, the 'outside' ones. In Ken Carter's submission to the Forgotten Australians inquiry, he wrote of his memories in a state home and a Salvation Army boys' home in Victoria: 'WORK, FLOGGINGS... FLOGGINGS, WORK was my whole life at the homes, which now seem to me nothing but concentration camps' (Penglase, 2005, p. 102, emphasis in original). By 'keeping children busy' with work under adult 'surveillance and control', children were not able to 'explore their own childhood domain through unsupervised play' (p. 126). In one Queensland institution there was a 'play room' filled with toys and books, but children were not allowed to touch them. In a submission to the Forde inquiry, a former resident recalled:

> It was just a pretend room. When they brought visitors in, and I don't know who the visitors were... They'd bring them in, and they'd open up the doors to this pretend playroom to show the visitors; and when the visitors went, you know, they'd close the doors again. (Forde, 1999, p. 81)

The provision and quality of education varied. In institutions dedicated to providing labour for commercial purposes, it did not exist. For Australia, Penglase (2005, p. 129) believes that perhaps in a majority of facilities, children 'did receive schooling'; and for the Canadian cases, I would estimate a slim majority. In a residential school, a former student recalled that 'school... was mostly memorizing, not much teaching and talking. Lots of copying and memorizing. The sisters were not really teachers, but they did their best' (TRC, 2012, p. 26). Another said that the focus of education was on religious education: 'All we ever got was religion, religion, religion. I can still fall on my knees at 72 years of age and not hurt myself because of the training and condition I got... ' (TRC, 2012, p. 26).

In Québec, Bruno Roy, a former *Duplessis Orphan*, who became a well-known poet and university professor,[8] recalled the transformation of Mount Providence in 1954, from an orphanage to a psychiatric institution:

> It happened almost overnight... Bars were put on the windows, a fence was raised around the orphanage, and four busloads of crazies – adults, some drooling, some catatonic, some dangerous – were brought to live among us. Our education was suspended; no more classes. Instead, we were set to work washing the backs and bed linen of insane old men. (Nickerson, 2000, p. 2)

In his review of Québec's practice of reclassifying children and institutions as 'psychiatric' or 'mentally retarded', the Ombudsman listened to and received statements from many survivors (Québec Ombudsman, 1997, p. 1), including this one:

> The first injury I suffered was not being taught, not getting an education to cope with adult life. Another was being treated as if I didn't exist, and not receiving even the slightest amount of human affection.... But the greatest injustice was being called mentally retarded and of generally mediocre appearance. That is *unforgivable*. (emphasis in original)

Also unforgivable is that government, church, and other officials used children as a means to an end, to raise money. Similar 'uses' of children were made in other ways: to test new drugs or eugenics theories (Penglase, 2005, pp. 99–101, 319–20).

Lack of autonomy and privacy

Former residents describe being under 'constant surveillance' and having to ask permission to step outside, to talk to other residents, or to use the toilet. At times, requests to use the toilet would be denied, and children would urinate and defecate on themselves or in front of others (Corina Hayward, *Until Someone Listens*, 1999). A concern for girls was access to sanitary items, which were 'heavily controlled'. Stories range from being given sanitary pads in front of other children, being given one pad at a time (which was recorded in a book), having to 'show a soiled pad before receiving another', and being made to use rags which the girls then had to scrub 'spotless' (Senate Report, 2004, p. 91). In some facilities, toilet paper was rationed. Penglase (2005, p. 115) recalls that in her home, 'each child was allowed two pieces per visit for a "number 2"'.

Children bathed together or had to share bath water. In her submission to the Forgotten Australians inquiry, Helena Dam said her bath time was 'horrendous' in the Catholic Nazereth House in Brisbane:

> We used to bath only once a week. The water wasn't changed at all. If you went in first, the water was very hot, hot enough to scald you. If you were one of the last ones in the bath, the water was usually cold and muddy, as it was never changed. (Penglase, 2005, p. 115)

A similar account was given to the Tasmanian Ombudsman (2004, p. 22) of being 'bathed only once a week, two girls in the bath at the same time, with the water usually changed after seven pairs of girls had used it'. There was no privacy in bathing: children would be lined up naked to wait their turn, to shower, and to share a towel with many others (Senate Report, 2004, p. 91).

Impact and legacy

What does this add up to? The stories are similar, no matter where the child is living. The problem is broad and diffuse: not acts of physical and sexual abuse alone, but a 'dehumanizing institutional environment' of fear, non-care, and bleakness (Penglase, 2005, p. 48). The message to children is you are worthless, not wanted, and do not matter to anyone: you are 'bad, delinquent, no good, bad blood, poor stock,...' (Penglase, 2005, p. 151). Szablicki (2010, p. 66), who was placed in a Catholic Home when he was 4 years old, says he still struggles 'with the ingrained belief that I am undeserving to ask for anything. I was raised and abused to accept worthlessness as my core...' Penglase (2005, p. 36) uses nearly identical language:

> People who have grown up in 'care' are often afraid to speak up, and indeed unable to do so, because in the very roots of our being we feel...that we don't matter to anybody and so have no right to speak.

She describes the problems she faced in writing her PhD on children's experiences in care:

> It was a great struggle...I feared that a thesis...based on my own experience was not valid because *I* was not valid. I was sabotaged daily by the question, 'Who do you think you are?'...The answer for us as children was: nobody, nothing. (p. 36, emphasis in original)

The Senate Report (2004, pp. 145–6) identifies 'a range of legacies' of childhood spent in institutional care in the 20th century:

> low self-esteem, lack of confidence, depression, fear and distrust, anger, shame, guilt, obsessiveness, social anxieties, phobias, recurring nightmares, tension migraines, speech difficulties ... difficulties forming and maintaining trust in relationships ...

To these, Wolfe et al. (2002) add 'loss of trust, and fear or disrespect of authority'.

Of course, not everyone growing up in institutional care has experienced these problems. Nor does everyone have higher-than-average levels of alcohol and drug abuse, unemployment, difficulties forming and maintaining relationships, getting into trouble, and being imprisoned, which are often associated with those growing up in care (Penglase, 2005, p. 312). Nor can problems that manifest in adulthood all be traceable to experiences in care (Smith, 2010). Three elements may explain variation in the degree to which care leavers face problems in their adult years: individual strengths as a child; degree and type of trauma experienced as a child; and supports after leaving care, especially marriage or having a child (Perry et al., 2006).

In the early years of negotiating the agreement in *St John's and St Joseph's*, the survivors' advocacy group, Helpline, commissioned a survey to identify the number of men abused, the severity of abuse, and its impact. The survey was carried out early in 1992; at the time Hoffman (1996) estimated that Helpline's total membership was 250 men. A total of 152 men participated in the survey. Circumstances did not permit a random sample, but it is the only case in my sample that estimates the prevalence of abuse at the time, along with the men's current circumstances. Excerpting from Hoffman (1996, pp. 68–73), here are some findings.

- Almost all (97 per cent) the men said they had been physically assaulted; 66 per cent said they were sexually assaulted; and 49 per cent, severely sexually assaulted when they were at St John's or St Joseph's Schools. The time period of abuse was 1930 to 1974. Abuse was frequent, with 'all describing themselves as living in a state of fear of assault'. (p. 69)
- Nearly 80 per cent said the problems encountered after they left the school were 'related to the abuse they suffered in the school ... The men as a group are bitter, poor, marginalized, and lack self-esteem ... Some

> 70 per cent are unemployed, ... 83 per cent have been convicted of a criminal offence, ... they have poor life skills, ... many cope or have coped with drug and alcohol use, participate in criminal activity, and some have become perpetrators themselves'. (p. 70)

The estimates of abuse prevalence need to be interpreted with care because they reflect a person's entire time in the institution; furthermore, the estimates of problems in adulthood may not be generalizable to residents of other institutions. However, the findings reinforce the message from researchers, advocacy groups, and professionals that a substantial share of those born in affluent nations from the 1920s to the 1970s, who were placed in residential care, now live with a range of needs for acknowledgement, support, and care (Alliance for Forgotten Australians, 2011).

As we shall see in the next chapter, there were many early indications of poor management and poor care of children. Institutions were chronically underfunded, and staff numbers and training were inadequate. Children were invisible and out of sight, both physically and socially. Institutional personnel were able to hide abuse and neglect. All of this began to change in the 1980s when institutional abuse became visible.

Part II

The Response

4
Time and Knowledge

Why did institutional abuse of children begin to emerge as a social problem in the 1980s in affluent nations of the developed world? What were the immediate events that led to a response? This chapter addresses these questions, along with three gaps in the research literature.

Three gaps

An interpretive gap exists in understanding time, knowledge, and reports of abuse. Reports from public inquiries and investigations note that care leavers and survivors, who were alive to make submissions or give evidence, described abuse that occurred many decades ago, as early as the 1930s, but more typically, in the 1940s to the 1990s. This is characterized as a 'delay' between when abuse occurred and when it was reported to authorities. In this chapter, I turn the tables on 'delay'. I ask, how many years were officials aware of the problem of abuse, but did nothing about it; and for those who tried to change institutional practices, why did they not succeed? There is ample evidence that children (or family and community members) reported physical and sexual abuse to the police, child welfare, or other authorities at the time it occurred. In some cases, authorities took action, but in many others, they did not.

Second, a theoretical gap exists between detailed analyses of individual cases (such as Corby et al., 2001, for North Wales; Harris, 1990, for *Mount Cashel*; Henton and McCann, 1995, for *St John's and St Joseph's*) and sociological analyses of broader societal contexts of 'threats to children' (such as Best 1990 on the rise of the 'child-victim'), especially the threats of sexual victimization, sexual predators, and paedophilia that emerged in the 1980s (Angelides, 2005; Jenkins, 1998; Pratt, 2009; Scott

1995). An analysis of individual cases is important for understanding the evolution of each case, including the actors and events that moved it to public attention and the factors that motivated official responses. A sociological analysis is important for understanding the structural basis and discursive character of social action and social problem construction. With the exception of Corby et al. (2001), few have attempted to work across the individual case and societal levels in understanding the emergence of institutional abuse of children as a social problem. In addition, with the exception of Davis (2005), few have grasped the significance of survivors' 'public stories' for social problem construction.[1]

Third is an apparent memory gap. When reading the reports and recommendations in the 19 cases, I am struck, as others have been before me, by how much knowledge had already been accumulated; how much human endeavour had already gone into understanding, preventing, and responding to institutional abuse; and how similar the findings and recommendations were. I wondered, how much time has been taken, for the 19 cases alone, to understand and respond to institutional abuse of children? How many pages have been written, and how many recommendations made? If, as some argue, public inquiries are expensive and time consuming, and their findings and recommendations are often repetitive, why do so many continue to be established? I cannot readily answer that question. However, I can show a significant investment of time and thought has been spent on understanding and responding to institutional abuse of children.

Inquiries and investigations, 1850 to 1970

Inquiries and investigations of child maltreatment or the negative effects of institutions on children began in the 19th century. Over the next century, these focused on physical abuse ('harsh discipline') of children in reformatory or training schools or inadequate care of children in orphanages or homes. I highlight a selected set of inquiries in Canada, Australia, and England and Wales up to 1970.[2]

For Canada, the Brown Royal Commission was established in Ontario in 1848 to 'investigate complaints that the warden and staff of Kingston Penitentiary had watched over a cruel, indiscriminate, and ineffective disciplinary regime' (the Honourable David Cole, forward to Henton and McCann, 1995, p. ix). Over the next century, according to Cole, there were '15 other royal commissions in Ontario' that investigated the maltreatment of children not only in training schools and detention centres, but also in orphanages (p. ix). The Canadian Department of

Indian Affairs (as it was then called) carried out investigations as early as 1886 on the mistreatment of children in residential schools (Le Beuf, 2011, p. 28).

Dr. Peter Bryce, who was appointed chief medical officer for the Departments of Interior and Indian Affairs in 1904, documented mortality rates of Aboriginal children who had entered residential schools. Bryce (1907) showed an average mortality rate of 30 per cent for schools located in the western provinces; and in an addendum to his 1907 report, Bryce (1909) showed an especially high rate (50 per cent) in Alberta. The cause of death was almost always tuberculosis. Bryce was critical not only of the health problems and poor conditions of the schools, but also church–state partnerships in managing them. Although his report led to some change in sanitary and health conditions, he was removed from his post in 1913 and retired from the civil service in 1921.[3] From 1868 and into the first several decades of the 20th century, there were numerous complaints by government officials and parents about severe punishments, meagre diets, and building conditions, and of sexual assaults by teachers and principals of residential school students (Royal Commission on Aboriginal Peoples [RCAP], 2006, pp. 365–73; TRC, 2012, chapter 2; see definitive histories by Miller, 1996; Milloy, 1999).

For Australia, in 1855, the Governor General of New South Wales criticized the 'utter inefficiency' of large institutions 'to produce any good effect upon the children maintained in them' (cited in van Krieken, 1991, p. 72). The New South Wales Public Charities Commission was established in 1873 to investigate conditions in institutions for the care of 'destitute children, the aged, and needy'. Its 1874 report concluded in part that 'large charitable institutions for maintenance of pauper children are unsound in principle and pernicious in results' (1874, p. 86). The Commission wanted to see children 'raised within respectable families, or at least family-like settings, and ... removed from previous associations' (van Krieken, 1991, p. 73). In addition, the Commission noted with concern the 'violence meted out to the girls at the Biloela Asylum, many of whom had black eyes, bruises, and bloody noses' (Senate Report, 2004, p. 20).

In a significant 1934 New South Wales commission of inquiry into government-run institutions for children (including correctional institutions, hostels, and homes for those with mental disabilities), chair J. E. McCulloch 'expressed surprise at the persistence of complaints about ... problems which appeared never to be resolved and ... resurfaced time and again at regular intervals' (van Krieken, 1991, p. 118). McCulloch had reviewed 'all the inquiries that had taken place since 1874', and found that 'many of the current problems...were old ones, and many of his recommendations had already been anticipated and...not acted upon'. The recurring problems were 'inadequate training and staff levels, cruel and excessive punishment, and poor organization' (p. 118).

In England and Wales in 1944, Lady Allen of Hurtwood 'led a publicity campaign' to establish a committee of inquiry on children's residential care. She received a 'large number of letters' from former residents of children's home, all but one of which was negative, giving examples of 'monotony, strict discipline, stigma, poor material and dietary standards, poor quality of staff, inappropriate placements, and lack of contact with birth families' (Corby et al., 2001, pp. 26–7). This launched the Curtis inquiry in England and Wales, and the Clyde inquiry in Scotland, which reported in 1946; they were the first in the two jurisdictions to investigate residential and out-of-home care of children. Both inquiries reached the same conclusion: large residential institutions for children should be reduced and foster care increased. Their reports led to legislation in 1948 that significantly re-organized care for children in both jurisdictions.

Two major investigations were undertaken in the 1950s by the British Government on institutions housing Child Migrants sent to Australia. These resulted in the Moss Report (1953), which criticized the isolation of the institutions and poorly trained staff, and the Ross Report (1956), which was critical of the policy of child migration and far more critical than the Moss Report of the conditions of institutional care. The Ross Report cited a lack of trained staff, the separation of siblings, a lack of a 'homely atmosphere, too little privacy, lack of educational and employment opportunities', and isolation of the institutions from local communities (Senate Report, 2001, p. 40). The Australian Government decided not to publish the Ross Report until Australian officials visited the institutions themselves. A delegation visited several institutions, but concluded there was no reason to change the policy of child migration. The British Government responded by saying, 'as we feared, the Australian authorities focus only on material things like bathrooms and carpets and ignore what has been said about atmosphere and management'. The Australian response 'confirms...that the Australian and UK thinking on child care matters is poles part' (p. 41).

Whispers of 'sexual acts', 1950 to 1970

As early as 1868 in Canada, charges had been laid against the principal of an orphanage for 'sexually violating' two students,[4] which led to closing the orphanage. And as early as 1920 in Australia, after many boys complained of 'systematic sexual abuse' at Clontarf Orphanage (Western Australia), Christian Brother Philip Carmody was charged; he pleaded guilty to three counts of 'indecent dealing beyond the course of nature' (Coldrey, 1993, pp. 385–6). Here I focus on developments in the 1950s, when there are glimmerings of awareness by government and department officials of coercive sexual activity by adult males of boys in residential care and training schools. It would take several more decades for the general public and officials to see such activity as 'widespread', not isolated.

Depicting the British context, Rollinson (2006, p. 23) says that 'it is somewhat perplexing that…people had such difficulties in seeing, naming, and acting upon harmful practices and regimes'. He describes a circular distributed by the Home Office to heads of residential care units in 1952, which outlined 'in precise detail…what should be done when "indecent practices" were committed on boys either by other boys or by staff':

> It reads very much like best advice today when it instructs that if there is knowledge or suspicion of serious indecent acts, which if proven, would constitute a crime, then the police are to be called in to investigate. (pp. 23–4)

This 1952 circular appears to be the earliest evidence of a government's interest to address *sexual acts* against children in care, which would be considered a crime. Rollinson (2006) says that the circular 'seems to have sunk without a trace', until it was '"discovered" over 40 years later by David Berridge during his…research into abuse in residential care' (p. 24). Rollinson (2006) suggests that officials 'could well have been struggling at the extremities of their capacities to regard such acts…as anything other than unthinkable and unspeakable'. He says that no other document in England and Wales from 1950 to 1989 dealt with such acts directly and as 'something other than an isolated incident carried out by a very rare, sick individual' (p. 24).[5] If government officials had difficulties comprehending the problem and were silenced by 'discomfort, embarrassment, shame, and guilt', then we might expect that children or staff in residential facilities would feel the same.

As early as 1940, authorities in Ontario were writing to the head of St Joseph's School that using the lash on the boys was illegal, although a 'regulation school strap may be used for more serious offences' (Hoffman, 1996, p. 80). The first investigation by Ontario authorities of sex offences against children was in 1958, when several boys said that a brother at St Joseph's School was coercing the boys 'into committing homosexual acts' (p. 88). A department official spoke to the boys and the brother, but found 'there was not sufficient evidence to warrant further investigation, and it appeared indiscreet to continue' (p. 80). An internal investigation was undertaken in 1960 after a probation officer had heard 'rumours and stories about the treatment of boys' in 1959 at St Joseph's School. Department officials visited the school in January 1960, and the boys relayed accounts of physical maltreatment and said that a 'staff member was trying to persuade [them] into homosexual activity' (p. 93). The officials thought that much of what was said was 'exaggeration', but they were later informed by Cornwall detention centre staff worker that several St Joseph's boys were there, having run away from the school. The staff worker said that 'the boys were frightened to the point of being terrified and implored her "to do something about conditions at the school"'. At the time, department officials were 'reluctant to believe all they had heard'.

In March 1960, another investigation was undertaken of St Joseph's School. This time it was by Donald Sinclair, Executive Director of the Advisory Board for Ontario's training schools. He concluded there was 'no evidence ... to support the charge of homosexual practices ... by [the] staff member', who had also been the subject of an investigation in 1953. However, inappropriate punishment practices were clearly evident (pp. 92–5). Many years later, Darcy Henton interviewed Sinclair; and he asked him why the boys' allegations were not reported to the police. Sinclair said that 'things were done differently in those days ... it was not the practice to *charge* people [but to] *discharge* them ...' (emphasis added). Sinclair said he 'knew damn well from what the kids said that there was a great deal of brutality at St Joseph's', but 'I couldn't stand up in court and say I knew and had hard evidence of abuse' (Henton and McCann, 1995, p. 102).

Department officials were not able to enforce regulations because they had to rely upon church authorities to remove offending brothers. This was not easy, as the Chief Inspector of the Department of Reform Schools said to the Deputy Minister in August 1960 about corporal punishment at St Joseph's School:

> The Brothers are a closely knit organization, and the boys are reluctant to 'squeal'. It is and always has been very difficult to obtain information on this institution. It is equally difficult to offer a solution ... unless the Diocesan authorities are willing to take disciplinary action

with any Brother disobeying the Superintendent or the Department. (Hoffman, 1996, p. 98)

In 1992, it was revealed that a brother at St Joseph's, Sylvio Valade, had admitted in 1960 to a Ministry of Corrections investigator that he had sexually assaulted a boy. The boy reported what had happened to his mother, who reported it to provincial authorities.[6] Although Valade had admitted the offending at the time, no criminal charges were laid, although he was 'voted out of the Brothers of Christian Schools' (Hoffman, 1996, p. 103). In 1992, he pleaded guilty to indecent assault. Although many *St John's and St Joseph's* boys had reported sexual assaults by the Christian Brothers to family and community members, department officials, and mental health workers in the late 1950s and early 1960s, they were not believed. It was not until the convictions of offenders in the 1990s that the boys (now adults) were vindicated. Likewise, for *Mount Cashel*, the boys had reported sexual offences to the police in 1975, but it was not until the Hughes inquiry that these became known to the general public and in the 1990s, subject to prosecution and conviction.

Complaints of abuse by residents and families

Children and youth protested institutional conditions in the 19th and 20th centuries.[7] Riots occurred at the Newcastle Girls School, New South Wales, from the year it first opened in 1867: the girls 'protested their confinement with wild rioting, obscene language, lewd behaviour, and frequent escapes' (Ison, 2012). A major riot occurred in 1871, causing the school to close. Riots were frequent at the Parramatta Girls' Industrial School in New South Wales (later called Parramatta Girls' Home). The first took place the year the school was opened (1887), and there were 12 others from then to 1961, although the Parramatta Female Factory Precinct website, Parragirls (2013), suggests that 'for every riot at least another dozen were quelled before they got out of hand'. In 1957, four girls escaped from Lynwood Hall in New South Wales; they went to a newspaper, *The Sun*, describing harsh conditions at the school. Of all the 19 cases, this 1957 newspaper story is the earliest I have sourced of a media-generated exposé that draws from accounts of residents.

A constant theme is children and youth running away. Penglase (2005, p. 297) quotes a former Neerkol (Queensland) resident who said, 'Kids ran away and no official every asked why'. There was a cyclical pattern of too harsh punishment, running away, being caught, and then 'returned back to the orphanage to another belting', a New South Wales survivor recalls, who said she ran away 50 times from a nun she was 'absolutely terrified of' (p. 297). For Canada, Miller (1996, chapter 12) suggests that running away meant 'a plea, either a cry of loneliness or a howl of protest. It clearly was a form of student resistance to the oppressive atmosphere that prevailed too often and too long...' (p. 368). Some children froze or died when trying to run away. In 1902, when nine boys ran away from the Williams Lake School (British Columbia), all were caught except one, who froze to death. In 1937, four boys died when running away from 'too harsh discipline' at the Lejac Indian Residential School in British Columbia (TRC, 2012, p. 39).

Methods of capturing runaways and subsequent punishment were extremely harsh and often exemplary, that is, carried out to instil fear in other students and to degrade the runners. Despite knowing the punishment that awaited them, the children's desires for freedom were stronger. Runaways were caught by the authorities and returned to the institution; or alternatively, they made it to family members' homes, but then, were subsequently brought back to the institution. Some were able to disclose abuse to family or community members, who in turn reported what happened to the police, as these examples from *St John's and St Joseph's* show.

In the earliest documented report to the police in *St John's and St Joseph's*, in 1957, a St John's student had been punished severely for running away. His mother took him to the doctor, and then to the police station. According to Henton and McCann (1995, p. 29), 'Chief Fred Oliver expressed astonishment when he saw the extent of the boy's injuries. "Jesus!" he exclaimed. "What bastard did this?"' However, because St John's School was outside Oliver's jurisdiction, he did not investigate it. During 1958–59, a St Joseph's student had attempted to escape several times, but unsuccessfully. In his fourth attempt, he and other boys were caught and placed overnight in a home, to await collection by the brothers the next day. In the morning, the boys told the woman running the home about abuse they had experienced. When the brothers arrived, one assaulted a boy and then kicked him. The woman witnessed the assault and alerted authorities (Henton and McCann, 1995, pp. 33–7). These and other incidents during 1958–62 were the focus of internal investigations and sharp letters by department officials to the heads of the schools. Such efforts had little effect: cases kept coming until St Joseph's closed in 1973, and St John's, in 1977.

Reports to authorities were conveyed in different ways. In a 1992 news story, when the *St John's and St Joseph's* trials were underway, a retired police officer spoke to a newspaper reporter about an incident at St Joseph's in the early 1960s. The officer, John Williams, said that the boys tried to tell the police about physical abuse at the school, but in an unusual way. At a 'sports day' held at the school, the boys slipped a one-page typewritten page into the day's program, which described the punishments the brothers used. Williams was angered by what he had read; the next day he discussed it with his supervisor, who said that the boys 'deserved everything they got'. Williams wanted to 'apologize to the men now [in 1992] for not doing something about it then' (Hoffman, 1996, p. 109).

For *Mount Cashel*, one boy ran away in November 1975, but within 2 hours, was observed by a police officer who ordered him to stop. The boy ran instead. 'They chased after me and caught up with me...I fought...they handcuffed my wrists...and legs and...threw me in the back of the car', he recalled in his testimony nearly 15 years later at the Hughes inquiry. Once in the police car, the boy begged not to be returned to the school. The police took him to a social worker, where he described in 'great detail...what was happening'. He named the brother who was abusing him, the 'man...that scared me the most'. But then, the social worker took him back to the school, and 'they handed me to the same man I told them about...It was like taking me and throwing me into a fire' (Harris, 1990, pp. 93–4). Interviewed in July 2012, former Detective Robert Hillier, who conducted the 1975 investigation, said that 'there were so many boys escaping from Mount Cashel...We were out all night long looking for them'. He continued,

> You did everything...to get them back into the home. They screamed until they got to the door. When they got to the door, they were just scared. And we just threw them into the lions' den. (Sweet, 2012)

Note the similar expressions used by the boy and police officer, respectively: of the police 'throwing me into a fire' and 'into the lions' den'. Could the police have handled it differently? At the time, there appeared to be no other place for the children to live. They were captives to the abuse they tried to run from, and the police were not necessarily their allies. These circumstances were especially acute for Aboriginal children in Australia and Canada, for whom the police were also the enforcers of protective segregation and forced assimilation policies toward their communities (Human Rights and Equal Opportunity Commission, [HREOC] 1997; Le Beuf, 2011).

By today's standards, the contexts in which children's complaints were investigated were inappropriate. For example, as part of his investigations of *Mount Cashel*, Detective Hillier asked that the boys be transported to the police station. How did they get there? The brother in charge, Douglas Kenny, who was feared by the boys as 'the worst, the enforcer' (O'Brien, 1991, p. 108) drove them. According to a former resident, Dereck O'Brien, during the car ride to the police station, Kenny told the boys 'don't say anything about me or [another brother] ... Don't mention our names' (p. 143). When the interviews were finished, the boys went downstairs, where Brother Kenny was waiting to take them home. Hughes (1991, p. 197) believed that the boys' fear of retaliation 'must have had a stultifying effect on many of their statements', but despite this, 'many deadly allegations were made'.

Reporting abuse to authorities was not a simple equation for children, balanced against other aspects of institutional life. For example, in *Jericho Hill*, the students saw the school as a place where they could participate in Deaf culture. Thus, if they reported sexual abuse, they were concerned that the school would be closed, and they would be sent 'home', away from Deaf culture and 'into a hearing culture that they could not communicate with and had no real affinity with' (Anne Sheane, personal communication, 9 January 2014).

From the 1850s through the 1970s, there were numerous reports to the police and other authorities of maltreatment, many official investigations, and clear signs of children's distress by their running away from institutions. Individual offending was, in some cases, prosecuted and resulted in convictions, or an offending individual was dismissed or moved to another institution. However, institutional practices did not change. The reasons were funding arrangements, whereby government authorities relied on the low-cost labour of those in religious orders and charitable organizations; deference paid by government authorities to religious and medical personnel and an inability to enforce regulations; a general inability by authorities to 'see' abuse; and the success of institutional carers to conceal 'children's bruises and other injuries' and to give 'an impression of adequate care' when inspections were carried out (Ferguson, 2007, p. 128). All of this began to change in the 1980s.

Emergence of a social problem

What made institutional abuse of children a 'social problem' that demanded a response? Several elements coalesced to define it as a social problem: changing concepts of childhood, new concepts that facilitated 'seeing' abuse, significant cases of clergy sexual abuse, and a 'sexual turn' in the institutional abuse story.

Changes in concepts of childhood

Corby et al. (2001) argue that a societal shift occurred in the early 1960s in affluent nations of the developed world toward a more child-centred world, a 'prizing of childhood' (p. 43) that came with increasing affluence, higher standards of living, lower birth rates, and better treatment of child illnesses. 'The expectation that childhood will be *a protected time* is key...*expected to be protected* from illness, from accidents, from harm from outsiders and...from harm in the home' (p. 48, emphasis added). This shift prompted new ways of 'seeing' corporal punishment and what had been termed 'homosexual abuse' between adults and boys.

New concepts

The discovery of 'baby battering' in the early 1960s centred on intra-familial *physical* abuse; and in the 1970s, there was the (re)discovery of intra-familial *sexual* abuse. In the mid-1970s, Gil's concept of *institutional abuse* helped people to begin to 'see' it. Much is made of parents or family members, residential staff, and doctors not 'seeing' the signs of children who may have been physically or sexually abused. David Berridge's experiences as a social worker suggest that even he (and his colleagues) were unable to 'see' it. Berridge (2005, p. 113) recalls hearing, for the first time, the concept of 'institutional abuse' at a conference he attended in Paris in 1981 or 1982 (he is not sure). He says 'it did not resonate with my experiences and observations in residential care...', and he was 'unaware of any instances of physical or sexual abuse...reported...in 20 children's homes' where he and a colleague 'lived for a week in the early 1980s'. He raises an 'unpalatable question for researchers' (including himself): 'how [did we] miss the physical and sexual abuse that was occurring'? He goes on to suggest that the same skills that sexual abusers 'used to befriend children and mislead management' may also 'have been used to discourage researchers' (p. 113).

Clergy abuse and 'homosexual abuse'

Major cases of clergy abuse first came to notoriety in the United States in 1984 with media stories about Gilbert Gauthe's sexual abuse of boys. Gauthe's offending, like that of other priests, took place 'in the rectory, on [boating and fishing] trips, and in the church after Mass' (Lytton, 2008, p. 1), that is, in community-based settings. However, Gauthe's and other priests' admissions of sexual offending made more 'thinkable' and 'credible' children's reports of sexual abuse committed by members of religious orders in residential care institutions for children.[8]

Several years before the revelations in the United States, there was alleged sexual abuse by lay staff in boys' homes in Northern Ireland. In 1980, a newspaper story in *The Irish Independent* suggested there had been a cover-up by the Royal Ulster Constabulary in its investigations of criminal activity and 'homosexual abuse' in the Kincora Boys' Home in East Belfast (McKenna, 1980). His Honour Judge William H. Hughes was appointed in 1984 to head a Committee to investigate 'a series of cases of homosexual abuse' in nine homes; the inquiry spanned 24 years, from 1960 to 1984. The Committee found that allegations of sexual abuse had been reported by the boys to authorities as early as 1967 and throughout the 1970s. At the end of the report, Hughes (1986) concluded that what occurred at Kincora and other schools 'can no longer be regarded as exceptional':

> [It] must perhaps now be recognized as earlier symptoms of a general malaise permeating the United Kingdom. The physical and sexual abuse of children has even been described as having reached epidemic proportions. (p. 342)

How Hughes had come to think there was a 'general malaise' or that physical and sexual abuse[9] of children had 'reached epidemic proportions' is uncertain because he gives no basis for these claims. However, as I show next, sexual abuse in institutions became 'observable' in the 1980s.

The 'sexual turn'

A strong belief that 'something must be done' about institutional abuse of children can be traced to three factors. First, the alleged abuse was sexual; it was not harsh physical regimes or corporal punishment, for which 'there was a fair degree of acceptance' of its use in care settings. By contrast, sexual abuse was 'a more disturbing form of abuse' (Corby et al., 2001, p. 83), particularly sexual abuse by adult men of boys, which could not be easily brushed aside as 'discipline'. Second, when cases began to emerge in Northern Ireland, Canada, and England and Wales from 1980 to the early 1990s, there seemed to be a 'constant stream of revelations', which raised questions about 'why it was apparently so prevalent' (p. 87). Third, and related, it became 'observable'. As Pratt (2009, p. 70) suggests, citing Hacking (1998, p. 82), it must be 'strange, disturbing *and* noticed'. It must have a 'quantifiable element' and be 'newsworthy as well'.

In Canada, observability was facilitated by early estimates of prevalence in Toronto in 1982, which were re-estimated in the Badgley Report (1984). These estimates were not solely of sexual abuse of children in institutions, but sexual abuse of children and youth more generally in Canada. However, 'as the problem became more observable, so there was an escalation in reported cases' (Pratt, 2009, p. 72) in both non-institutional and institutional settings.

In Australia, Scott (1995, p. 119) marks 1986, the year the International Society for the Prevention of Child Abuse and Neglect held its conference in Sydney, as the 'turning point from the re(discovery) of child sexual abuse to... its diffusion', that is, as being seen as a widespread social problem. There was an escalation of interest in the research literature. Scott and Swain (2002, p. 161) analyzed the academic journal, *Child Abuse and Neglect*; they found that the share of articles on child sexual abuse went from '10 per cent in 1980 to 51 per cent in 1994. The share of articles on physical abuse was 5 to 15 per cent over the period.

A crucial feature of observability was adult survivors' first-hand accounts of abuse. Davis (2005, p. 27) argues that up to 1970, 'standing up in public and telling a personal story of childhood molestation was a revolutionary thing to do'. There had been survey research on sexual experiences as early as the 1920s, as well as clinical assessments, but 'first person public accounts... outside a legal context were non-existent'. Davis marks the shift as occurring in 1971 at a feminist conference in New York when Florence Rush spoke publicly of being sexually victimized as a child. Up to that point, Davis argues, 'there were no public victim stories because there was no collective victimization story' (p. 28). In the early 1970s, Rush's public victim story was of intra-familial sexual abuse of girls by men; but in the late 1980s, the public victim story began to include institutional sexual abuse of boys by men.

The speed of change from 'not seeing' to 'seeing' sexual abuse of children (Wolmar, 2000), and some would say to 'over-seeing' it (Webster, 2005) is remarkable. Writing in the early 1990s, the British Columbia Ombudsman (1993, p. 40) said that 'in 1982, society did not have the same level of understanding of the dynamics of child abuse as we have today, and adults did not believe the statements of children who disclosed abuse' (the reference is to sexual abuse, the subject of *Jericho Hill*). In just 10 years, there was rapid change, not only in the recognition of, but also concerns with child sexual abuse. But how, more precisely, did such concerns spark government, church, or other relevant authorities to respond?

What sparked responses?

During the 1980s, there were heightened concerns about child sexual abuse in the media and by politicians in affluent nations, including Canada, Australia, Northern Ireland, England and Wales, and the United States. Drawing from Cohen (1972), Jenkins (1998) terms the 1980s as the decade when a 'moral panic' over child sexual abuse took hold. A 'moral panic' occurs when fear over a social problem is 'wildly exaggerated and wrongly directed' (p. 7). Jenkins' analysis focuses on changing periods of quiescence and panic over perceived dangers of those who sexually offend. Such fears in the 1980s (which ranged from sexual abuse in child day care, to paedophilia and satanic ritual abuse) may have 'jumped' to residential care facilities for children. However, in the Canadian and Australian cases, the claims were not exaggerated.[10] My analysis of the evolution of responses suggests that in addition to alleged sexual offences against children, other political and legal factors motivated responses by authorities.

As foreshadowed in Chapter 2, the cases differ, and in ways that affect responses to institutional abuse. By a *response*, I mean a government or church initiation of sustained actions to address a perceived social problem. In all the cases, the response sought to address the failure of authorities to protect and care for children. However, in the policy cases, there was, in addition, recognition of policy or practice wrongs by authorities against certain groups of children (*Alberta Sterilization* and *Duplessis Orphans* in Canada; *Child Migrants* in Australia) and of such wrongs against children being part of a more general discrimination against a political minority group (*Indian Residential Schools* in Canada; *Stolen Generations* in Australia).

Core cases

Of the 19 cases, 12 are 'core' cases.[11] They contain allegations of adult sex offending against children, perceptions of widespread prevalence, media stories, and at times, victim group advocacy. Almost all the core cases have histories of reports to the police or other authorities that were not investigated or for which no charges were laid. Failed or closed investigations were emphasized in media coverage about the case and formed part of the negative press about its handling by authorities. *Mount Cashel* and *St John's and St Joseph's* were unusual in having a relatively large number of criminal cases underway when the response began. Other core cases had a smaller number of prosecuted and convicted offenders, but their histories of offending against children were longstanding

(*Nova Scotia, New Brunswick,* and *Queensland Institutions*). In *George Epoch,* sexual offending by the priest was prodigious, which gave rise to significant civil litigation; however, Epoch's offending was reported to the police only after he died.

As depicted in Chapter 1, *Mount Cashel* was the 'perfect storm'. There were allegations of a cover-up between government and church authorities in 1975; and the sexual offending was not just by men against boys, but religious men. Newspaper publisher Michael Harris encouraged Shane Earle to write his public account of sexual abuse at the school. Hughes (1991, p. 190) opines that the newspaper editorials and articles by Harris and Earle galvanized the government to establish a Royal Commission. Other Canadian cases were affected by *Mount Cashel*. Most directly, it affected the mobilization of *St John's and St Joseph's* survivors because David McCann recognized his experiences as similar to *Mount Cashel* survivors'. Because of *St John's and St Joseph's,* I suspect that the two *Grandview* survivors were confident in coming forward to the media in 1991. *The Boys of St Vincent,* which was based on the events in *Mount Cashel,* influenced the Canadian and Australian public and brought many survivors forward.[12]

St John's and St Joseph's first came to public attention with Darcy Henton's news story in March 1990, with more stories by him and other journalists in 1990 and 1991. Likewise, *Grandview* first came to public attention with survivors telling their 'public stories' on television, and asking others to contact the police or provincial authorities. Media stories, especially public stories by survivors, played a significant role in sparking official responses to abuse in four of eight Canadian core cases (*Mount Cashel, St John's and St Joseph's, Grandview, Jericho Hill*). Print and television media, especially public stories by survivors, played a more significant role in these cases than in *George Epoch, Nova Scotia Institutions, New Brunswick Institutions,* and *Ontario Schools for the Deaf.* In the latter cases, the main factor motivating official responses were victims' (or staff members') reports to police or other authorities, which subsequently led to investigations and prosecutions.[13] In Canada, the initial response was investigation (six cases) or a public inquiry (two cases). The response start years were 1989 to 1992.

Three Australian core cases – *Queensland, South Australian,* and *Tasmanian Institutions* – were sparked principally by media stories. Two (*Queensland* and *South Australia*) were also associated with failed police investigations and alleged cover-ups, and one (*Queensland*), with victim group advocacy. *Tasmania* was unusual in that one survivor, Walter Tusyn, told his 'public story' on television in July 2003.[14] It was *after* the government response (that is, the announcement of the Ombudsman's review) that victim group advocacy began. Another Australian core case, *Forgotten Australians*, was sparked by previous inquiries and victim group advocacy. The response start years were 1998 to 2004.

I sketch *Queensland Institutions* to show that the evolution of the case was not one perfect storm, as it was in *Mount Cashel*, but a set of linked, separate 'storms' that swirled for over 10 years before the Forde inquiry was announced in 1998. The first, in 1988, was an alleged rape of a 14-year-old girl by several boys while under youth correctional authority. An inquiry into the management of the youth centre, conducted by Magistrate Noel Heiner, began in 1989, but ended abruptly after 4 months. A new government had been elected; and the cabinet approved the destruction of documents gathered in the Heiner inquiry because it was concerned that the government could face civil litigation for defamation. The matter, variously termed 'Shreddergate' and the 'Heiner Affair', has only recently been settled after many investigations and inquiries.[15]

The second storm was 'organized paedophilia', which had received attention by the Wood Royal Commission into the New South Wales Police Service (1995–97); among other outcomes, the Commission exposed sexual and physical abuse of children by teachers, state-employed caregivers, police officers, and members of churches. In May 1996, Queensland signed on to a national strategy by creating a Children's Commission, which a member of the Legislative Assembly argued would have the 'authority to get rid of this national scandal – this disgrace' (Queensland Legislative Assembly, 1996, pp. 865–6). In 1997, soon after publication of the Children's Commission's report, there were media stories of alleged 'cover-ups and other impropriety by police officers and others regarding the investigation of paedophilia ..., both historical and contemporary' (Criminal Justice Commission [CJC], 1998, p. 1), which led to a CJC special investigation.

The third storm was allegations of sexual abuse at St Joseph's in Neerkol, which had been known for some time. When Broken Rites, a support organization for Catholic clergy abuse victims, established a national Australian telephone hotline in 1993, its first callers were former Neerkol residents (Broken Rites, 2013), who alleged sexual abuse by a priest, Reginald Durham, which had occurred as early as the mid-1960s. When, in 1996, a child abuse hotline was established by the Queensland Government, there were over 400 callers, 'nearly 70 per cent ... were adults reporting abuse experienced during their childhood ... while residents at ... Neerkol' (Children's Commission of Queensland 1997, pp. 68–9).

The Neerkol Action Support Group pressed for a public inquiry, which was announced in August 1998.

In *Queensland Institutions*, the main factor sparking the response was media stories; but in addition, other political and legal elements included failed police investigations, allegations and investigations of police and government cover-ups, and victim group advocacy.

Core-plus cases

Common to core-plus cases is a moral claim of a policy wrong or practice committed by the government or both government and church (or charitable) organizations. For the core-plus-two cases, the historical beginnings of the (now recognized) wrong were in 1883 for *Indian Residential Schools* and 1900 for *Stolen Generations*, which was somewhat earlier than the start year for the core-plus-one cases (1910 for *Child Migrants*, 1928 for *Alberta Sterilization*, and 1930 for *Duplessis Orphans*). What the moral claim brings to each case, and especially the core-plus-two cases, is a significant group of people who challenge relevant authorities on political grounds. Such advocacy has a broader political base than that associated with core cases.

Compared to the core cases, the core-plus cases moved into the public arena and sparked a response for different reasons: political advocacy group campaigning (*Duplessis Orphans*, *Stolen Generations*, and *Child Migrants*) and the pressure of significant civil litigation (*Alberta Sterilization* and *Indian Residential Schools*), not allegations of sexual or physical abuse. Although allegations of (and convictions for) abuse were relevant, they were secondary to the moral claim of a policy wrong, which was the basis for political advocacy. Of the five policy cases, just one (*Duplessis Orphans*) was associated with previous failed investigations by the police and allegations of cover-ups by government and church officials. Media coverage of advocacy group campaigns gave these cases visibility, but the cases had developed a large cultural platform of print and visual media before the response start year.

Child Migrants is a good illustration of advocacy group campaigns: the Child Migrant Trust, formed by Margaret Humphreys in 1987, began to bring the policy wrong to public attention, which led to a response first by the British Government in 1998, and then by the Australian Government in 2000 (the response start year) with the announcement of a Senate inquiry. Also in 1987 a Western Australian newspaper published a feature article on the experiences of Child Migrants in the state, which was the first significant media exposure in Australia. Books began to appear: Melville and Bean's (1989) *Lost Children of the Empire*,

Humphreys' (1994) *Empty Cradles*, and Gill's (1997) *Orphans of the Empire*. A documentary drama mini-series, *The Leaving of Liverpool*, was aired in 1992 (see Appendix 6). A crucial element was a determined politician, Andrew Murray, a former Child Migrant, Australian Senator, and member of the Democratic Party. In Murray and Rock (2003, p. 149), he recounts the 'forces of luck and timing' that led to a Senate inquiry. This included a chance meeting with Margaret Humphreys in 1999 when she was visiting Perth, and with Kim Beazley, Leader of the Labor Party (in opposition), who 'delivered the numbers to get the Senate…inquiry up' (p. 150).

Compared to *Child Migrants*, the evolution of *Duplessis Orphans* is more tortuous, and advocacy groups are still campaigning to bring to light what they identify as additional harms against children such as medical experimentation. As noted in Chapter 2, public awareness of *Duplessis Orphans* first emerged in 1961 with *Les fous crient au secours* (Pagé, 1961). Many other works, including biographies and autobiographies, have been published (Appendix 6). A television program, hosted by Jeanette Bertrand in 1989, gave significant exposure to the case. An advocacy group, Comité des Orphelins et Orphelines institutionnalisés de Duplessis (COOID), was formed in the early 1990s; and despite trying to bring criminal cases and a class action suit forward, this did not occur. After all routes of potential redress had been pursued, COOID sought review by the Québec Ombudsman, whose 1997 report concluded that the government should address COOID's claims in a non-adversarial manner.

Alberta Sterilization is unusual as a core-plus case because the policy wrong was identified in arguments put forward by Leilani Muir's legal team.[16] Muir first contacted lawyers in the fall of 1989. Her civil trial began in June 1995 and lasted 4 weeks; Madame Justice Veit's judgment was issued on 25 January 1996 (the response start year). Lawyers for Muir drew, in part, from expert testimony on the eugenics movement. After the judgment, Muir's lawyers sought independent university research to assemble the files and decisions of the Eugenics Board in anticipation of future litigation. The research was not used at trial because some 900 civil cases were settled; however, it was later published (Grekul et al., 2004). The cultural platform in this case was built *after* the response in 1996, not before it. A documentary was produced by the National Film Board of Canada (1996); a university-based project, *Living Archives on Eugenics in Western Canada*, was funded (2010–15); and a play on Muir's life, *Invisible Child*, was performed in 2012.

For *Indian Residential Schools* and *Stolen Generations*, the histories and rationales for the policy wrongs were similar: white colonial governments sought to forcibly assimilate Indigenous people into mainstream society. Social movement activism against residential schools in Canada and against removal of 'half-caste' children from families in Australia began at about the same time in both countries (1920) and strengthened in the 1930s and 1940s. By 1970 in Australia, legislation had been repealed; and by 1986 in Canada, the government 'came to the end of the residential school road' (Milloy, 1999, p. 238). In Canada, criminal convictions of residential school staff for sexual assaults of students began in 1988, after which successful civil litigation followed. In 1996, the Canadian Government created a special unit to address mounting litigation. In Australia, growing Indigenous activism from the 1960s was building momentum for significant social change, and the *Going Home* conference in 1994 was the start of mobilizing for redress of child removal policies. In Australia, there were no criminal convictions, and all but one civil case has been unsuccessful. Both cases have huge cultural platforms, built during the century before official responses in the 1990s, which continue to the present.

Quantifying responses to abuse

I sought to quantify the 19 case histories of abuse, official knowledge of it, and when a sustained response began by creating several variables. Each is a simple calculation, but considerable research time was taken to decide what year should be used. The variables are:

- ***Potential window of abuse***: the difference between *establishment year* (year an institution or policy was established) and *end year of abuse* (year an institution closed, policy ended, or response year began). The establishment year is important for understanding the age of institutions. The potential window of abuse is important for appreciating how long the institution(s) had housed children before an official response began. I would not argue that abuse occurred from the year the school opened (or policy began); this cannot be known in most cases because detailed histories are lacking.
- ***Time to respond***: the difference between *year of first complaint* and official *response year*. This variable defines the length of time for which there was official knowledge of a problem of abuse to the year that a sustained response began.

A third variable, time to tangible result, is reported in Chapter 6. This variable taps the 'wait time' from a survivor's perspective from the start of a response to receiving a financial payment.

Potential window of abuse

Although this measure may seem straightforward, sources varied on when precisely an institution 'opened' or 'closed'. When a case had many institutions, as the Australian state cases did, the year that legislation was passed, establishing institutions for children in the relevant state was used. For *Forgotten Australians*, the year by which most states had enacted legislation to 'protect' children from maltreatment was used (1895; see Tomison, 2001, p. 49). For the five policy cases, three (*Alberta Sterilization, Duplessis Orphans, Child Migrants*) were straightforward: policies or legislations began and ended in well-defined years. For *Indian Residential Schools*, I drew authority from Miller (1996, p. 103) and the TRC (2012, pp. 5–6), in identifying 1883 as the start year. For *Stolen Generations*, I computed the average (mean) of the start years of state and territory legislation (excluding that in Tasmania) that enabled the removal of children from families; that year is 1900.

Time to respond

To estimate how long it took officials to respond to knowledge of sexual and physical abuse, two time points had to be identified: Time1, the year of officials' awareness of abuse; and Time2, the year of official response. Each measure required careful definition and consistent application across the cases. For Time1, identifying and deciding upon the right year took considerable effort and reflection. In some cases, I considered several potential start years; and in others, serendipitous new information came along that changed what had been a settled start year. I give examples of how some cases were coded.[17]

Time1, year of awareness, is defined as the year when a complaint of sexual or physical abuse was lodged by a victim, family or community member, or staff member to the police or other authority.[18] This variable, 'year of first complaint', was sourced from the primary documents, coupled with academic research and newspaper articles. To clarify, Time1 is the year when *a complaint was made to an authority*, not the year when officials were aware of physical or sexual abuse or became aware of it in retrospect. For example, in *St John's and St Joseph's*, departmental authorities were aware of and concerned with too severe physical punishment in 1940, and Hoffman (1996, pp. 50, 58, 80, 140) gives examples of survivors' memories of abuse as early as the 1930s and 1940s. However, I chose 1957 as the 'year of first complaint' because in that year a mother reported her son's injuries to a police chief (discussed above). Thus, the 'year of first complaint' is a conservative estimate of when complaints to authorities began. For the core-plus cases, the 'year of first complaint' is the year a victim or family member of a victim, or a political advocacy group lodged a complaint about *the policy*, not of physical or sexual abuse (examples are given below).

Time2, year of response, is defined as the first year of a sustained response by authorities to a perceived social problem of institutional abuse or policy wrong. In 15 of 19 cases, the 'response start year' was when an inquiry was announced or official investigations (by the police or other authorities) began in a sustained way. For two cases (*Tasmanian Stolen Generations* and *Redress WA*), the start year was the year the government announced a redress program; and for two (*Duplessis Orphans* and *Indian Residential Schools*), consideration was given to several possible years (discussed below) before coming to a final decision.

Core case examples

In *Mount Cashel*, Hughes (1991, p. 221) reports that a complaint to a police constable was made in 1954 of an indecent assault on a boy at the school; and the start year of response was 1989, with the announcement of the Royal Commission. Thus, for this case, the time from first complaint to response is 35 years. For *Queensland Institutions*, Forde (1999, p. 68) reports that a letter was sent in 1931 to the Catholic Archbishop of Brisbane alleging physical abuse and neglect against a nun at St Vincent's Orphanage (north of Brisbane); the start year of response was 1998, with the announcement of the Forde inquiry. Thus, the time from first complaint to response is 67 years.

Core-plus case examples

These cases posed more challenges in determining the year of first complaint and, in some cases, the response year. For *Child Migrants*, although a Christian Brother pleaded guilty in 1920 of sexual offences against boys at Clontarf (Coldrey, 1993, p. 386), that year was not used because the 'complaint' did not concern the policy. Instead, I chose 1987 because it was the year of the founding of the Child Migrant Trust and the year of a significant news story that was critical of the child migration scheme (Gill, 1997, p. 497). Another challenging case was *Duplessis Orphans*. I chose 1961 as the year of first complaint, with the publishing of *Les fous crient au secours* by a former orphan. Other sources (such as Bédard Commission, 1962; Institute for Human Resource

Development, 1998) credit the book as being the first public knowledge of the problem. The year of response was more difficult. There were a large number of police investigations of complaints in 1992–93, but the Attorney General decided not to prosecute. I chose 1997, the year the Québec Ombudsman's report was released, which called for a redress scheme (Québec Ombudsman, 1997, p. 36). The Ombudsman's decision to review the case was a turning point in what had been, up to then, Québec Government's resistance to recognize its policy wrong against children.

For the 'year of first complaint' in the core-plus-two cases, I chose the year when there was a *national* level of complaint from Canadian and Australian political groups about the policies and practices of forcible assimilation.[19] Thus, for *Indian Residential Schools,* the year of first complaint is 1946, when hearings began in the federal parliament with 'strong representations from Indian groups for "an end to the policy and practice of segregated education"' (RCAP, 1996, p. 346). For *Stolen Generations,* the year of first complaint is 1938, when the Australian Aborigines Progressive Association and the Australian Aborigines League staged a one-day protest 'on the 150th anniversary of the British occupation of Australia' (26 January 1938), in which activists called for citizen rights and castigated white Australian policies of 'protection' as 'killing us off' (HREOC, 1997, pp. 38–9).

The response year for *Stolen Generations* is clear (1995, when the HREOC inquiry was announced), but that for *Indian Residential Schools* is not. After considering several options,[20] I chose 1996 as the response year for two reasons. RCAP (1996) had a chapter on Indian Residential Schools and one recommendation called for a public inquiry on the residential school system; and in 1996, the Canadian Government created a Residential Schools unit to address significant increases in litigation associated with residential schools (Russell affidavit, 2006, paragraph 12, p. 6). For these cases, the time from first complaint to response was 50 years for the *Indian Residential Schools* and 57 years for *Stolen Generations*.

Findings for time

On average (using the mean), the year that institutions opened or policies began was 1900, and the year that the institution closed or policy ended was 1987; thus, the potential window of time that children were exposed to abuse was 87 years (Table 4.1). The year of first complaint was 1959, and the response start year was 1996. Overall, it took government and church authorities, on average (using the mean), 37 years to respond. The time to respond ranged widely: from less than a year to 73 years.

The averages mask differences for Canada and Australia. The institutions (or policies/practices) began about 15 years later in Canada (1905) than in Australia (1892), which may explain in part, why the year of first complaint is 18 years later in Canada (1967) than in Australia (1949). However, the response year for Canada is 10 years earlier (1992) than in Australia (2002). Thus, the time from first complaint to response is shorter for Canada (25 years to respond) than in Australia (53 years to respond). Although the differences in response time initially seemed large, on closer inspection, they can be explained by the earlier year of first complaint for Australia and the 10-year lag in Australia's response compared to Canada. That, in turn, may be explained by the different character of Canada's cases: eight of 11 cases (all 'core' cases) were clumped in the response years 1989 to 1992. All were of one to five institutions; none was province wide. In addition, for three, the time from the year of first complaint to response was unusually short (less than a year to 10 years).

I shall use the average for the two countries as a pooled indicator of time. The findings suggest that *hypothetically*, had authorities been able to respond more decisively, say in 1960, to address physical and sexual abuse, victims' 'delay' in reporting victimization would have been substantially less. However, as we know, physical abuse of children was not known as a concept until the 1960s, and sexual abuse, a decade later. It took another decade, the 1980s, for institutional abuse to become known as a concept. Imagine, however, the question of 'delay' from a care leaver's perspective. If you tried to report victimization in 1960, but no one believed you or you were punished for saying things institutional staff did not want to hear, you would not pursue it further. Instead, you would bury the memory and keep quiet, as so many survivors today have said they did.

Turning the tables on 'delay'

It is essential, then, to shift the onus of responsibility for 'delay': it should not be placed on care leavers and survivors, as people do unwittingly by saying that 'the abuse happened long ago' or there is a 'time lag' between when abuse occurred and when adult survivors came forward with complaints. Rather, the onus should be placed on societal beliefs and attitudes about children and their credibility, especially children growing up in adverse circumstances or having a parent unable to provide or care for them. For the policy cases, societal beliefs about the appropriate 'uses' of children for government (or church) purposes are responsible. These were for labour, population growth, and income generation (*Child Migrants*); implementing eugenics theories (*Alberta Sterilization*); income generation (*Duplessis Orphans*); and the forced assimilation of colonized people (*Indian Residential Schools* and *Stolen Generations*). From a survivor's perspective it took, on average, nearly four decades for authorities to begin to respond to complaints of sexual and physical abuse or to policy wrongs against children or groups. This puts 'delay' in a different, but more accurate, light.

Knowledge and human endeavour

As the project evolved, I identified the primary documents in the 19 cases. By *primary documents*, I mean those that would be required for a minimum understanding of each case. It took considerable time to decide which materials were primary. After many revisions, I identified 83 documents.[21] They fell into these categories: inquiry reports (11); investigation and review reports (10); government reports responding to inquiries or reviews, including responses to recommendations (29); independent evaluations or recorders' reports (16); academic research (10); and court judgments, settlements, or legislation (7). Most were produced by government (31 per cent) or at arm's length or critical of government or church authorities (27 per cent). The arm's length activities included all the inquiries, independent investigations, and reviews that were authorized and paid for by a government or church authority, but were carried out with a degree of independence from that authority. The remainder were generated by independent evaluators (16 per cent), academic researchers or journalists (12 per cent), courts or legislature (8 per cent), or victim or community-based advocacy groups (6 per cent). I created several measures of knowledge and human endeavour: document length, time taken to carry out the activity, and the number of recommendations.

Document length is a count of the total pages in a document, including the relevant appendices. Time to carry out the activity is the time from the start of the activity to the end. It is not a measure of person years, which could not be estimated. For example, the Hughes inquiry in *Mount Cashel* began in April 1989, and the report was delivered to the government on 31 May 1991, a time span of 26 months. However, I do not know how many staff members contributed to the inquiry's work or final report. Thus, the time measure is a gross underestimate of the

Table 4.1 Institution (or policy) time, first complaint, and response

CANADA AND AUSTRALIA (N = 19)

	year institution opened or policy began	year abuse or policy ended	potential window of abuse (yrs)	year of first complaint	response start year	time from first complaint to response (yrs)
mean	1900	1987	87	1959	1996	37
median	1895	1991	97	1961	1996	35

CANADA (N = 11)

	year institution opened or policy began	year abuse or policy ended	potential window of abuse (yrs)	year of first complaint	response start year	time from first complaint to response (yrs)
range	1865 to 1946	1965 to 1996	35 to 126	1946 to 1991	1989 to 1997	<1 to 50
mean	1905	1984	79	1967	1992	25
median	1895	1989	82	1961	1991	31

AUSTRALIA (N = 8)

	year institution opened or policy began	year abuse or policy ended	potential window of abuse (yrs)	year of first complaint	response start year	time from first complaint to response (yrs)
range	1865 to 1912	1969 to 2006	58 to 133	1931 to 1987	1995 to 2007	13 to 73
mean	1892	1991	99	1949	2002	53
median	1895	2000	108	1943	2003	56

actual time taken by many people to gather and assess information and produce final documents, which could have a multiplier of 5 to 50 or more, depending on the case. It is better viewed as a 'window of time' that was spent to carry out an activity. In creating this measure, I took care to estimate human endeavour as precisely as possible. Thus, for example, a primary document for *Indian Residential Schools* is chapter 10 of the RCAP (1996) on residential schools. Only that chapter (not the set of five RCAP volumes) was used to count that document's page length. Likewise, I estimated a fraction of time that the RCAP spent on residential schools (not the entire length of the inquiry), and my count of recommendations was only those directly related to residential schools (one of 16 RCAP recommendations was). The measure for the number of recommendations is a simple count of them for each relevant document.

Findings for knowledge and human endeavour

The 83 primary documents had a total of 13,505 pages. That is just over 27 reams of paper, which if stacked would be 1.4 metres (4.6 feet) high. Assuming 250 to 300 words per page, the estimated number of words is 3.4 to 4.1 million. For time spent to carry out an activity, I excluded the 17 documents produced by academics or journalists, courts or lawyers, or a legislature; there was too little information to identify precise start and end dates. For 66 documents, the window of time spent to produce them was 888 months (74 years). The breakdown of time by type of document or activity shows that the 21 inquiries and investigations took 370 months (31 years); the 29 government responses to recommendations or reports on schemes, 305 months (25 years); and the 16 independent evaluations or recorders' reports, 213 months (18 years). By country, Canada spent 496 months (41 years), and Australia, 392 months (33 years). However, when taking into account the larger number of Canadian cases, the average spent per case is similar (Canada, 45 months; Australia, 49 months), or about 4 years per case.

Of the 19 cases, most (15 or 79 per cent) had recommendations in one or more documents; and the relevant 28 documents contained 805 recommendations. More intriguing, of course, is an analysis of the recommendations themselves, which I carried out in a limited way for the public inquiries (see Chapter 6). If previous analyses of public inquiries are a guide, recommendations are repeatedly made for better trained staff and more robust procedures in detecting abuse and responding to reports of it. Public inquiries are but one activity producing recommendations. Other reports and recommendations focus on the failures of government to implement recommendations made in previous reports, optimal justice mechanisms to address institutional abuse, and community-based responses. An analysis of recommendations from inquiries alone does not give a complete view of proposed ideas for change.

Several other points should be emphasized. First, my analysis of primary documents scratches the surface of the number of relevant documents and human endeavour spent in the 19 cases, not only in describing and responding to institutional abuse of children, but also in investigating previous investigations and practices, and in creating and implementing justice responses. There were many other related documents and activities, whose girth and scope are substantial. For example, in *Nova Scotia Institutions*, the Internal Investigations Unit (IIU) conducted an investigation into 'veracity and verifiability of the many claims of abuse levelled against past and present employees [of three institutions]' (Kaufman, 2002, p. 326). The IIU's final report was 529 pages, with an additional 23 volumes of appendices. It was based on 'interviews of numerous individuals and a review of between 1.5 to 2 million documents' (p. 327). Second, the human endeavour to create and implement redress schemes is not included in my estimates. Some redress schemes have been open for 10 years (*Duplessis Orphans* and *Tasmanian Institutions*). Third, it is not just government or church officials who are spending time on responding to institutional abuse. Many citizens, advocacy groups, and survivors are too. In the Forgotten Australians inquiry, the number of submissions (440) was the largest ever received up to then by a Senate inquiry. (These were not included in the page count for the primary documents.) Other people have produced or participated in films, documentaries, plays, museum installations, oral history projects, memorials, and many types of commemorative projects and activities (see Appendices 5 and 6). All of this activity is not included in the estimates of human endeavour in responding to institutional abuse.

Making sense of time and knowledge

This chapter has considered the role of time and knowledge in constructing institutional abuse as a social problem and responses to it. Many inquiries and investigations were carried out from the mid-19th century onward, which identified failures and problems in providing adequate and appropriate care for children in institutions. Inquiries were coupled with protests and complaints by residents, family and community members, and officials. Early evidence and concerns with 'indecent practices' and 'homosexual acts' by men against boys in children's institutions emerged in the 1950s, although criminal convictions had occurred in the 19th century and early decades of the 20th century. My research finds that the average (mean) year of first complaint is 1959, pooling the Canadian and Australian cases. This year marks the start of victims, family and community members, or staff coming forward with allegations of institutional abuse, or the year that a policy wrong began to be challenged. Although abuse was 'known' and acted upon by those who had reported it, authorities could not 'see' it or they denied it, and institutions hid it. To say that authorities could not 'believe' the accounts of children (or family members and others) overlooks an essential point: they chose *not to believe* the accounts in most, although not all, cases. This began to change in the 1980s, with the coalescing of several factors that built upon the discovery of physical abuse (1960s) and sexual abuse (1970s) in families.

The new concept of 'institutional abuse' began to achieve lift-off in the 1980s, aided by major cases of clergy sexual abuse; it was adult male sexual abuse of boys, in particular, that was 'disturbing'. The 1980s is also associated with a 'moral panic' about child sexual abuse as a social problem. However, a moral panic analysis is not sufficient for understanding why *institutional* abuse of children emerged as a social problem and what motivated responses to it. Public concern with and official responses to institutional abuse began in the 1980s, but have continued through the 1990s and first decades of the 21st century, as evinced by the many inquiries that have been recently completed or are underway. There are, as yet, few signs of decline. This is due, in part, to strong survivor advocacy groups, who have pressed (and continued to press) for the 'truth' to be known and for redress, and in part, to survivors who continue to come forward with public victim stories.

Governments and church authorities were motivated to respond for varied reasons. It would be inaccurate to say that the 'core' cases were simply 'scandal-driven', although the media played an important role. In addition to allegations of sex offending by adults against children, common themes in the core cases were failed police investigations and cover-ups in the past. This lent weight to suspicions that officials 'had knowledge', but in failing to act on what they knew, many children may have suffered needlessly. In the core-plus cases, advocacy groups named policy wrongs against children, or wrongs against children and discrimination against a group of people as the social problem. It was not sexual or physical abuse alone that brought core-plus cases forward; rather, it was the moral claim of government and church wrongs against children and groups.

My estimates of response time, knowledge, and human endeavour are conservative. It took nearly four decades, on average, for Canadian and Australian Governments (and church organizations) to begin to respond to institutional abuse, or in the core-plus cases, the policies or practices that led to institutional abuse. The knowledge produced from 83 primary documents associated with the cases is prodigious: about 13,500 pages, 3.4 to 4.1 million words, and 805 recommendations. The question must be asked: is anyone reading? My estimate of 74 years to produce 66 primary documents is not person years, for which multipliers by the number of staff would need to be considered. Nor does it include numerous post-response activities and secondary documents, or the wider circles of human endeavour in advocacy, commemoration, creative works, and research. As we shall see in the next chapter, the initial 'response' is only the first step in a chain of activities that will take more time and human endeavour.

5
Redress Structure and Process

Once a government or church authority begins to respond to institutional abuse, what happens next? Published sources do not provide ready answers. In my sample of 19 cases, just two (*Jericho Hill* and *Tasmanian Stolen Generations*) produced a publicly available report of both processes and outcomes of redress schemes. For all the others, I had to seek information from government departments or others close to the case to determine what the outcomes were. This chapter presents new information on what happened after inquiries were concluded, agreements and redress schemes were decided, and major civil litigation cases were settled. My focus is on the structure and process of redress schemes, but I give attention to other justice mechanisms.

For the 19 cases, the trajectory of activities *after* the response start year varied. Of the seven cases that began with a public inquiry, four subsequently moved to major civil litigation and settlements (*Mount Cashel*) or some type of redress scheme (*New Brunswick Institutions, Queensland Institutions, South Australian Institutions*); three provided services or benefits but no redress scheme (*Stolen Generations, Child Migrants, Forgotten Australians*). Of the eight cases that began with police or other official investigations, all moved to a redress scheme (*George Epoch, St John's and St Joseph's, Grandview, Nova Scotia Institutions, Ontario Schools for the Deaf, Jericho Hill, Duplessis Orphans*, and *Tasmanian Institutions*). In addition to the Jericho Individual Compensation Program (JICP), a government-stipulated redress scheme for *Jericho Hill*, the case had a class action settlement (*Jericho Hill Class Action*). For the four remaining cases, one began with a civil judgment that led to substantial civil litigation and settlements (*Alberta Sterilization*); another began with the press of substantial civil litigation, which subsequently resulted in a class action settlement agreement (*Indian Residential Schools*). Two Australian cases began with legislation or a government announcement of a redress scheme, which was then implemented (*Tasmanian Stolen Generations* and *Redress WA*). Of the 19 cases, 14 had financial payments to survivors from redress schemes, and two others from larger civil settlements after the response year. In addition to redress schemes, three other justice mechanisms were used: criminal prosecution, civil litigation, and public inquiries.

Criminal prosecution and civil litigation

Of the 19 cases, 14 had criminal prosecutions that resulted in convictions. Three had a large number of convictions: *Mount Cashel* (15), *St John's and St Joseph's* (16), and *Indian Residential Schools* (20). The five without criminal convictions were redress scheme only cases (*Tasmanian Stolen Generations* and *Redress WA*) or no charges were laid (*George Epoch, Alberta Sterilization*, and *Stolen Generations*).

Of the 19 cases, 16 had civil litigation that resulted in out-of-court settlements.[1] Of this group, seven have had settlements with 70 to 900 litigants.[2] An eighth case, *Indian Residential Schools*, had a very high number of litigants: over 4,000 claims had been settled by July 1996 (see Appendix 1, column 8).[3] Of the eight cases, two had major civil settlements only (*Mount Cashel* and *Alberta Sterilization*), and two had class action settlements with a significant redress package (*Jericho Hill Class Action* and *Indian Residential Schools*).

Public inquiries

Survivors of institutional abuse often push strongly for an inquiry to 'bring out the truth' of their abuse claims or to recognize them as a group in ways that criminal prosecution and civil litigation often cannot. As the Law Commission of Canada (LCC) (2000, p. 249) suggests, there are two broad types of public inquiries: one is established 'to investigate specific events, to make findings about them, and ... to make recommendations' about preventing 'future occurrences' (type 1) and another 'to investigate and make recommendations concerning a broad area of public policy' (type 2). Often the two roles are combined (LaPrairie and Stenning, 2004). The Canadian inquiries were closer to type 1: their terms of reference focused on questions of police cover-ups and whether or not physical and sexual abuse (*Mount Cashel*) or sexual abuse (*New Brunswick Institutions*) was committed by adult staff against child residents. The Australian inquiries were a mix: the Commonwealth inquiries (*Stolen Generations, Child Migrants*, and *Forgotten Australians*) were type 2; and the two state inquiries (*Queensland* and *South Australian Institutions*) were a blend of types 1 and 2, although both gave greater weight to policy. The South Australian inquiry had two reports, as did the Commonwealth inquiry on institutional and out-of-home care. For the 19 cases, then, there were seven public inquiries, which produced nine reports.

I analyzed public inquiries with attention to their duration (when they began and when the final report was submitted), the number of submissions or witnesses, whether the non-confidential submissions are accessible (for example, on a website or in a library), the character of the oral hearings, the number of recommendations, and whether recommendations were given for 'compensation' (see Chapter 6 for discussion of this term).

For the two inquiries in Canada, the time from the start of the inquiry to report completion was 2 to 2.5 years; the inquiries had 280 (*Mount Cashel*) and 157 (*New Brunswick Institutions*) witnesses or submissions. The Mount Cashel inquiry was televised (except for two private hearings), but the New Brunswick inquiry was not. For both inquiries, written submissions are not easily accessible. However, the proceedings from the televised Mount Cashel hearings were excerpted in a two-part television documentary on the Christian Brothers by Raidió Teilifís Éireann (2001); this suggests that tapes may be accessible in an archive. Hughes's (1991) report excerpts testimony from former residents, whereas Miller's (1995) for schools in New Brunswick gives synopses of incidents, but contains no direct victim 'voice'. The two reports generated 55 recommendations, and both recommended a compensation scheme.

For the five inquiries in Australia, the time frame from the start of inquiry to report completion ranged from 10 months (Forde inquiry in Queensland) to 3.5 years (the two-part Mullighan inquiry in South Australia); the three other inquiries took about 1 to 2 years. All had extensive witness evidence and submissions. *Stolen Generations* contained oral and written submissions from 535 Indigenous people; *Child Migrants* had 80 witnesses and 253 written submissions; and *Forgotten Australians* had oral hearings with 171 individuals and received 614 submissions, the largest volume of 'personal evidence ... of any Senate inquiry'.[4] *Queensland Institutions* held 105 private hearings and conducted 166 interviews (both mainly of former residents) and received about 200 written submissions. *South Australian Institutions* (city/town component) held 762 hearings (496 were with individuals alleging abuse in care, of which Mullighan concluded that 242 came within the inquiry's terms of reference); and the inquiry received 448 written submissions. The APY Lands component heard from about 100 people (as individuals or in a group), held 147 meetings, and received ten written submissions. The Australian final reports contain a wealth of victim 'voice' material gathered in hearings or submissions. However, it is easily accessible in only two cases (*Child Migrants* and *Forgotten Australians*). Non-confidential submissions to the *Stolen Generations* inquiry are available upon request. The Queensland submissions are housed in the Queensland State Archives. The catalogue has a 60-year restriction on access (to year 2059), although one may lodge a request for documents to the Queensland Department of Justice and Attorney General. For South Australia, all victims' submissions are treated as confidential and cannot be accessed. All but one Australian inquiry (*Child Migrants*) recommended that a compensation scheme be established or considered. However, some years later, in a review of the Senate's (2001, 2004) reports on *Child Migrants* and *Forgotten Australians*, a Senate (2009) inquiry recommended that a compensation scheme be established for both groups.

What is redress?

Victim redress can be defined broadly as all the activities, processes, and outcomes that recognize and provide a compensatory mechanism for harms or wrongs against an individual or group.[5] The term refers generally to varied types of corrective justice, which aim to rectify private wrongs, as compared to criminal justice, which responds to public wrongs by criminal prosecution, trial, and punishment. Applied to institutional abuse, redress is more than a financial payment. Broadly conceived, it includes all the processes that occur when claimants seek financial payments, benefits, and services: how well informed they are and whether they understand the redress process; how they are treated; and whether they have a role in shaping the process and desired outcomes. In addition to financial payments, benefits, and services, redress outcomes may also include public apologies, memorialization, commemoration, and other types of memory projects. The latter activities have a wider audience and larger purpose: they seek to remember and reinterpret past wrongs, and they attempt to imagine new futures and identities of wronged individuals or groups.

Redress, as I define it here, takes two forms in responding to institutional abuse or related policy wrongs. One is civil litigation, when, if successful for the plaintiff, a money amount (damages) is awarded to recompense 'injury'. Two of the 19 cases had major out-of-court settlements only (*Mount Cashel* and *Alberta Sterilization*); in these cases, lawyers for the government (or church) and the plaintiffs, together with other actors (such as insurers and judicial actors) determined the scope and individual amounts in the financial settlements. Information on outcomes for these cases is limited to the total number of litigants, how long the process took, total amount paid, and other outcomes such as apologies or memorialization. The second form of redress is a 'redress scheme'. Such schemes can range from a negotiated redress *package* or structured civil settlement with financial payments, benefits, services, and other outcomes, to a more pared back, government-stipulated[6] redress *scheme* with payments, but perhaps few or no benefits, services, or other outcomes.[7] Some schemes are devised with a greater degree of survivor group participation than others. They also vary in the processes used to determine eligibility and outcomes, with some more 'victim-centred' than others. The meaning of 'redress' for survivors may be entirely different from what is contained in a redress scheme (see Case example 5.1).

Case example 5.1 Redress schemes and survivor scepticism

In light of the abuses suffered as children, redress schemes can be meaningless to some survivors. For example, the scheme in *Queensland Institutions* had two levels of payment: level 1 ($7,000) for declaring that abuse had occurred and level 2 ($33,000 maximum) for documenting serious incidents and impact in greater detail. Reflecting on the scheme, Bob Toreaux, a former resident of the Riverview Training Home for Boys, run by the Salvation Army south of Brisbane, said '"$7,000? $33,000?"' He laughs, poking his skull with his forefinger, '"Is that going to get this out of my bloody brain?"' (Dalton, 2009). Another survivor, John Munt, has been collecting Freedom of Information documents on Riverview. Munt said to a journalist, 'I've gotten so angry about all of this. The redress scheme means nothing'. He then handed his bag of documents to the journalist and said, 'Please bring this to light' (Dalton, 2009).

In Canada, some schemes had names such as the 'ADR project' (for alternative dispute resolution) or 'reconciliation agreement'. In both Canada and Australia, some schemes are termed a 'healing process'. I shall not be concerned with whether or not a scheme describes itself as 'alternative' or whether it strives to achieves reconciliation, healing, reparation, or restoration. Although often used, these terms are variably defined and too imprecise for my purposes (Daly and Proietti-Scifoni, 2011). Nor will I use restorative justice or therapeutic jurisprudence to analyze the schemes, except to make several points. First, elements of restorative justice practices may be part of redress scheme processes and outcomes; for example, schemes may include respectful listening to survivors' stories, sincere apologies, or outcomes that are related to past abuse, or in some cases, that have broader political and educational objectives. Likewise, practices thought to yield 'therapeutic effects', such as attention to how decisions are made and the participation of claimants, may have relevance. Instead of these concepts, I use the construct of *victims' justice interests.*

Introducing victims' justice interests

I developed the construct of *victims' justice interests* to describe and compare different types of justice mechanisms (for example, criminal trials, civil litigation, public inquiries, restorative justice conferences, victim impact statements, specialist family or sexual violence courts, redress schemes, among many others) in different contexts of victimization. I devised the construct because criminologists and victimologists, among others, place too much reliance on asking victims whether they are 'satisfied' with processes or outcomes of justice mechanisms, when most of us would say that the satisfaction variable is overly simplified and largely uninterpretable (Pemberton and Reynaers, 2011, pp. 238–9). It is crucial that we find additional ways to assess justice mechanisms and victims' experiences or judgments of them than asking whether they are satisfied.

Victims' justice interests[8] contains some elements of procedural justice (that is, aspects of participation and voice; see Tyler 1990; Wemmers 2010), but the construct encompasses more than respectful and fair treatment. It also includes validation, vindication, and offender accountability. These five elements – participation, voice, validation, vindication, and offender accountability – have been identified by others as important to victims' sense of justice (Auckland University of Technology Centre of Restorative Justice, 2010; Backer, 2012, personal communication; Herman, 2005; Koss, 2006; van der Merwe, 2009), although relevant elements will (and should be expected to) vary by the context of victimization. For example, in post-conflict societies affected by inter-ethnic or state violence, transformation and state-building are justice interests. Likewise, the construct will require modification to be relevant to contexts of institutional victimization.

Based on its consultations with institutional abuse survivors, the LCC identified ten justice elements: these included two values that should structure a justice response and eight needs of adult survivors of institutional abuse (LCC, 2000, pp. 71–100). My set of five elements is a neat and more parsimonious overlay of the LCC's elements. However, the LCC lists two elements I would consider 'coping' or 'rehabilitation needs' (access to counselling and education or training). While these are important, they are not *justice* needs. In this chapter, I analyze participation as it affects the design of redress schemes; and in Chapter 7, I apply all five elements to claimants' and survivors' experiences with redress schemes and public inquiries.

Participation

I designed victims' justice interests to be adaptable to diverse contexts of victimization (individual, organizational-occupational, institutional, and collective) (see Daly, 2014). Each of the five elements of victims' justice interests is generically defined; therefore, each requires modification to the context studied. In what follows, I first give a generic definition of participation and then modify it to be relevant to victims' interests in redressing institutional abuse.

Although my focus is on redress schemes, ideally, one would want to compare participation in redress schemes with that in civil litigation or criminal prosecution. The Institute for Human Resource Development (IHRD) provides some insight into survivors' experiences with litigation in *Mount Cashel* and *Alberta Sterilization*, which I incorporate in Chapter 6. For criminal prosecution, there is no information on victims' participation in sentencing for the relevant cases.

Defining participation

The *generic definition* of participation is as follows: being informed of options and developments in a case, including the different types of justice mechanisms available; discussing ways to address offending and victimization in meetings with (admitted) offenders and others; and asking questions and receiving information about crime (for example, the location of bodies or the motivations for an offender's actions). This definition pays attention to victims' interests in a criminal justice process, but requires modification to include other justice mechanisms. I *modify* the generic definition to be inclusive of participation in redress schemes, civil litigation, and public inquiries.

The *modified definition* of participation is as follows: being informed of options and developments in a case, including different types of justice mechanisms available; active participation in shaping the elements of redress, including optimal modes of implementation;

being informed of negotiations and having a say (or vote) in ratifying a redress scheme (or settlement agreement); and understanding how the process works.

To operationalize the definition for analyzing participation in redress schemes, I created several variables. One is whether or not the scheme resulted from negotiations between the parties (typically by lawyers representing clients, including victim advocacy groups). When redress schemes are negotiated, lawyers representing victims and survivors can strengthen their bargaining position, as compared to a scheme that is stipulated entirely by a government or other organizational entity. The second is whether or not victims (including advocacy groups) *participated* in shaping elements in the redress scheme, and the third, whether or not they had been *consulted*. Fourteen of the 19 cases had redress schemes, but *Jericho Hill* had two: a government-stipulated redress scheme, JICP, with some survivor consultation, and a structured class action settlement (*Jericho Hill Class Action*), which was negotiated between lawyers and had a greater degree of survivor participation. Thus, my analysis is of 15 redress schemes.

Participation in designing redress schemes

Negotiated schemes and victim participation in shaping them featured in the Canadian, but not Australian cases. Of the ten Canadian schemes, seven were negotiated; in six, victims (including advocacy groups) participated in shaping the design of the scheme; in a seventh case, survivors were consulted. By comparison, none of the five Australian redress schemes was negotiated, that is, all were government-stipulated. Nor could I find evidence of victim participation in these cases. Consultation occurred in one case (*Tasmanian Stolen Generations*), but it appears, not in the others.

Case studies of participation

Participation by victims and advocacy groups can take different forms, which depend on the bargaining power of the advocacy group and the size and strength of the legal team. In three of the six Canadian cases in which victims participated in designing the scheme (*St John's and St Joseph's*, *Grandview*, and to a lesser degree, *George Epoch*), victims or an advocacy group, represented by a lawyer, negotiated the terms of a redress scheme with government and/or church organizations. In a fourth case (*Duplessis Orphans*), a major advocacy group and legal team, although large, had less bargaining power. The advocacy group, the Comité des Orphelins et Orphelines institutionnalisés de Duplessis

(COOID), had struggled for some years to achieve recognition, but was pushed back by the government, prosecutors, and the court's denial of class certification. *Duplessis Orphans* is one of three Canadian cases that did not have a negotiated agreement, although it had strong victim advocacy in shaping the outcome, if only by voting to accept (or not) the government's offer. In the two remaining cases (*Jericho Hill Class Action* and *Indian Residential Schools*), the legal team had substantial bargaining power after the class was certified. For *Jericho Hill Class Action*, the case was initiated by several survivors working with lawyers, who sought class action certification; once that was achieved, the lawyers encouraged participation of survivors in shaping the outcomes of the scheme. For *Indian Residential Schools*, the elements in the class action settlement arose from many years of collaborative activity by lawyers and Aboriginal advocacy groups, the latter specifically concerned with recognition for loss of language and culture. With the exception of *St John's and St Joseph's, Nova Scotia Institutions*, and to a lesser degree, *Indian Residential Schools*, we lack evidence on the sequence of activities that brought a redress scheme to fruition.

What happened in *St John's and St Joseph's* may be atypical. At the time, it was claimed to be 'unprecedented in North America' (Henton and McCann, 1995, p. 172) by Douglas Roche, the lawyer who negotiated the package with Helpline (the advocacy group), the Ontario Government, the Archdioceses of Toronto and Ottawa, and the Ottawa Christian Brothers.[9] Negotiations began in 1990 and were finalized 2 years later in December 1992. All the key players – for the government, church, and advocacy groups – were new to redress schemes that promised reconciliation instead of adversarial litigation; they were new to thinking about what the processes of validation might be, and new to imagining appropriate levels of financial payments, benefits, and services. Except for civil litigation and criminal injuries compensation schemes, there was little to go on. This, coupled with the many government and church actors involved, made for a difficult negotiation process (Case example 5.2).

Case example 5.2 Victim advocacy group negotiating an agreement

Helpline, the survivor advocacy group for *St John's and St Joseph's*, was established in 1990, and over the next 2 years, it grew in size to about 250 to 280 members. David McCann, Helpline's president, visited Newfoundland in 1990 to learn about *Mount Cashel*; he spoke with victims, counsel for the Hughes inquiry, and others in St John's. Toward the end of 1990, he and the

Helpline executive committee came to the conclusion that an inquiry was 'a distant prospect' and may not be 'worth the time, money, and terrible personal anguish' for Helpline members (Henton and McCann, 1995, p. 145). A decision was made to pursue an agreement. Roche brokered a negotiated agreement, but he relied on Helpline members to put their desired elements forward. The process was difficult: although McCann knew what he wanted ('a simple, non-confrontational, easily understood ... process, over which the victim feels somewhat in control') (p. 156), getting all the parties to agree and make financial commitments was arduous (Henton and McCann, 1995, chapters 11 and 12). The Toronto Christian Brothers were the 'largest single impediment to progress' because they refused to 'acknowledge responsibility' (p. 146); and when they backed out the agreement, Helpline members felt betrayed.

The process took a toll on McCann and other Helpline members; they attended many meetings, but had little idea of how long the negotiations would take and became increasingly angry and impatient. A deal was reached in August 1993, but not finalized until December of that year. Then, it was estimated that the cash payment to each man would average $23,000, and counselling and other benefits, an additional $10,000 (p. 177). Money was not the main demand, however. McCann was convinced that Helpline members would not ratify the agreement unless there was a commitment of apologies from church leaders, archbishops, and the Christian Brothers. Helpline also wanted to see 'new policies and procedures to deal with child abuse in the church' (p. 156).

Helpline's experience shows that victim group participation in fashioning elements of an agreement may, in the abstract, seem like a positive thing; but it can come at a cost to members' spirits and mental health. Ultimately, Helpline members voted overwhelmingly in favour of the agreement, in accord with David McCann, who was 'not interested in spending the next 10 years of my life fighting in court' (p. 175). Compared to *St John's and St Joseph's*, negotiated agreements in *Grandview* and *George Epoch* took less time to achieve and exacted less of a toll on victims and advocacy groups.

For *Duplessis Orphans*, victim advocates had struggled since 1992 to have their concerns recognized by the Québec Government. It took nearly 10 years for a redress scheme to materialize; and as of 2014, the case remains contested as advocacy groups and individuals continue to press their case against the government, Roman Catholic orders, and medical groups (Comité des Orphelin(e)s de Duplessis Victimes d'Abus [COVA], 2012). Claims have been made of cover-ups and genocide (Vienneau, 2008/2012) (see Case example 5.3). Although this case had significant victim group advocacy, which had vetoed an earlier government proposal, the outcome was not fully satisfactory.

Case example 5.3 Victim advocacy group participation by veto power

In 1992, Hervé Bertrand met with a lawyer, Robert Fauteux, to launch a class action suit against the Québec Government. Fauteux assembled a team of four other lawyers and they contacted nearly 1,800 people who had been in seven institutions. The Comité des Orphelins et Orphelines institutionnalisés de Duplessis (COOID) was formed. The legal team grew to include two more lawyers, a sociologist, a psychologist, and a historian. COOID sought financial assistance to pursue a class action, but was unsuccessful; and its efforts to be recognized as a class were not accepted by the courts. After several years, with at times 20 people working full time, COOID's attempts to be recognized as a class ended in the mid-1990s. During 1992–93, there were significant police investigations, but no charges were laid.

In response to the Ombudsman's (1997, p. 36) recommendation that the victims be offered 'no fault compensation', the government announced an offer in 1999, which included an apology and $3 million, which would go into a trust fund to be distributed among claimants (an estimated $1,000 per person). COOID rejected it. It took 2 more years for the government to make an offer that COOID could accept. Although COOID had proposed that validated survivors receive, on average, $50,000, it accepted the government's offer of a formula that would pay claimants $25,000, on average, because 'they [were] reaching the end of their lives' (CBC Digital Archives, 2001, citing Bruno Roy). In 2007, a second program of financial payments was announced by the government and accepted by COOID, which recognized a larger group of those who had been placed in other institutions; each validated claimant would receive a flat payment of $15,000.

The class action settlement agreements in *Jericho Hill Class Action* and *Indian Residential Schools* were forged in strong bargaining contexts for the plaintiffs, and advocacy groups were better able to advance their goals. These cases had structured agreements with many elements. *Jericho Hill Class Action* had a two-level payment, in which eligible class members could elect to receive a flat payment of $10,000 (level 1) or apply for higher amounts (levels 2 and 3), the latter based on sexual abuse while at the school and consequent impact. In addition, the agreement included funds to establish a trust fund for education and employment assistance and to continue counselling, among other elements. *Indian Residential Schools* also had a two-level payment outcome: level 1, the Common Experience Payment (CEP), which recognized the policy wrong (time spent in a residential school and consequent loss of language and culture); and level 2, the Independent Assessment Process (IAP), a payment based on abuse and consequent impact while in a residential school. In addition, the agreement included funds to establish (or continue) healing projects and centres, commemorative activities, mental health and emotional support, a truth and reconciliation commission, and a national research centre.

Indirect or no participation in designing redress schemes

Four Canadian agreements were decided between government lawyers or officials and plaintiffs' lawyers, with little or no victim group participation. Although government officials in *Nova Scotia Institutions* had hoped in 1995 to enter into an agreement with a small number of lawyers representing a survivor group, this did not occur. Rather, by 1998, 62 private lawyers, representing over 800 claimants, billed the province's compensation program for their services (Nova Scotia Auditor General, 1998, section 13.34), which exacted a toll on program costs. In *New Brunswick Institutions*, the largely government-stipulated agreement was finalized in 1995; and by 2001, over 400 claimants had applied, with some 20 lawyers representing them (Kaufman, 2002, pp. 354–5).

Evidence on the role of victims is scant for *Ontario Schools for the Deaf* and *Jericho Hill*-JICP in Vancouver. In Ontario, former students from Sir James Whitney School initiated meetings with two government departments some time in 1993. It took 4 years for a negotiated agreement to be finalized, and sources suggest that one lawyer negotiated the agreement for former residents. In Vancouver, Thomas Berger was appointed Special Counsel in 1993 to consider 'the extent and severity of abuse, the province's responsibility... and remedies' (Berger, 1995, p. 1). He recommended that the province establish a compensation scheme. An interministry working group, the Jericho Coordinating Committee, consulted with 12 community representatives (ten Deaf, one DeafBlind, and one blind. However, the outcome was not negotiated, but government-stipulated (Morley, 2001, p. 5).

All the Australian redress schemes were government-stipulated, not negotiated, with little apparent victim participation in shaping the elements. I must err on the side of caution in characterizing the Australian cases: there is too little information to know precisely what happened in the early phases of redress scheme creation. There may well have been consultation with advocacy groups, but except for Queensland, there is no published information. For *Queensland Institutions*, Walsh (2010, p. 188) says that the redress scheme was 'a significant outcome after years of advocacy by the Historical Abuse Network (HAN)'. However, although HAN 'advocated for a redress scheme, it did not at any point have the negotiating power to influence eventual outcomes'. For *Tasmanian Institutions*, the Ombudsman's review of abuse in state care was announced on the night that survivor Walter Tusyn told a television audience of his experiences of sexual abuse in state care. Six weeks later, the government announced a redress scheme, but there is no indication of survivors' participation in shaping it. Tusyn refused to participate because he believed 'restrictions [were] placed on claimants' access to information' held by the government (Macgregor, 2011). For *South Australian Institutions*, in 2010, an interpretation of a rule about the Attorney General's discretion to disburse payments from the Victims of Crime Fund facilitated the ability of victims to seek a financial payment for historical abuse in state care. However, there was no negotiation with advocacy groups or victim participation in coming to this decision. For *Redress WA*, although a survivor advocacy group, CBERS (for Christian Brothers Ex-Residents and Students Services) assisted claimants in completing redress scheme applications, I found no evidence of their participation (or that of other advocacy groups) in designing the scheme. In a letter published in *The West Australian* (4 August 2009, p. 18), two members of the CBERS Redress Service expressed strong criticism of the government's having lowered the maximum cap from $80,000 to $45,000. In outlining the state's redress scheme, they suggest it came 'out of the blue' to survivors. One Australian case, *Tasmanian Stolen Generations*, consulted with community groups: the Legislative Assembly Hansard for the second reading of the bill says there was 'wide consultation' with Tasmanian Indigenous groups (Tasmanian Legislative Assembly, 2006, p. 17).

Redress scheme structure

Redress schemes are structured by content and constraints. Content has three dimensions: (1) the logic used in deciding financial payments ('money logic'); (2) the types of processes used to validate and assess applications; and (3) the inclusion of benefits, services, and other outcomes. The content of a scheme may change over time, and it may use a combination of logics in deciding financial payments. Redress schemes are constrained by (1) the amount of money the government (and/or other contributing participant) is willing to spend and (2) the number of claimants who may apply. Circumscribing both are decisions on what is to be redressed: any type of abuse or neglect? sexual abuse only? time spent in care? what types of care? which institutions? If scheme designers expect a high number of claimants, decisions need to be made on the trade-offs between spending money on *processes* used to assess applications and *outcomes* for claimants. All of this assumes that decision-makers have complete information in advance and that decisions are guided by economic rationality. Both may be lacking. From the available information, for example, we know that the number of redress scheme applicants often exceeds officials' forecasts.

In describing money amounts in this chapter, I use each country's currency without continually referencing Canadian or Australian dollars. In Chapter 6, in my analysis of financial payments, I give attention to adjustments for inflation and currency exchange.

Redress scheme design may be based on what is familiar to actors. For example, the money logic used in *St John's and St Joseph's* was tied to amounts paid by the Criminal Injuries Compensation Board in Ontario (which in both 1990 and 2014 has a cap of $25,000). By comparison, the processes and money logics used in other Canadian schemes had grids or tiers that were more closely aligned with damage awards in civil cases (although at the low end of the scale, typically capped at $60,000). In Australia, the bands used in *Redress WA* were similar to those in the Canadian cases (from less to more serious abuse, with few to serious ongoing effects). However, South Australia's scheme was (and is) placed within the Victims of Crime Fund; thus, decisions on financial payments for 'abuse in state care' use a similar logic as those for victims of crime.[10]

Except for one case, *Nova Scotia Institutions,* we lack evidence on what was in the minds of authorities in designing redress schemes. A July 1995 memorandum to the Cabinet by Paula Simon and Alison Scott, Nova Scotia Department of Justice (Kaufman, 2002, Vol. 2, appendix E, pp. 537–47) compared the different political, economic, and moral costs associated with litigation and two types of redress responses (*Grandview,* negotiated between the government, one lawyer, and a victim advocacy group; and *New Brunswick Institutions,* government-stipulated, many plaintiff lawyers, and no victim advocacy group). Projected economic costs to the government for litigation and a redress scheme were about the same; but as importantly to Simon and Scott, the *Grandview* model was preferable to that used in *New Brunswick Institutions* and to litigation on moral grounds: they believed it had more 'buy-in' for victims, relied on fewer lawyers, and there would be 'fewer legal bills' for victims. Simon and Scott wanted to 'engage victims in the process by allowing them to participate in the negotiation of an agreement that attempts to meet their needs' (p. 540). Their aspirations were not realized, however, because as negotiations evolved in 1996, plaintiffs' lawyers expressed no interest in having one or two represent a victim group; and their numbers swelled. Simon and Scott had initially estimated 170 eligible claimants, but when the program closed in 2000, over 1,220 had applied, and 1,101 were deemed eligible for a financial payment. The projected costs in 1995 for payments to claimants were \$10 to \$20 million, but the final cost of payments was \$31.5 million. The total cost was \$73.5 million, which included payments to claimants, administrative costs, counselling, claimants' legal costs, other legal fees, Internal Investigations Unit (IIU) salaries, and payouts to union employees.[11]

Redress scheme content

Money logics

The logic of financial payments has two dimensions: *how* to decide and *how much* to pay. *How to decide* can either be individualized or equal (same) treatment of eligible claimants. Individualized assessments use bands, grids, or scoring systems to assess abuse severity, and where relevant, both severity and impact of offences. For equal treatment, claimants receive the same amount as a flat payment, or another equality-based formula is used, such as the number of years spent in an institution. *How much to pay* can be open-ended, with a high maxima; or it can be capped, with a lower maxima; or it can be a flat payment. Of the 15 redress schemes, some used a combination of money logics; thus, there are 20 financial payment outcomes. Of these, 12 were based on individualized assessments, with capped and lower maxima; one was individualized with higher maxima; four had flat payments, and three used another type of equality-based formula. Money logics affect the types of processes used to validate and assess applications. Flat payment or other equality-based approaches do not require probing of the claimants' experiences of abuse, and depending on the scheme, can be based on government records of placement histories or time spent in institutions. It is of interest that of the five money logics in the core-plus cases, four used a flat payment or other equality-based formula (*Duplessis Orphans* [in phases 1 and 2], *Indian Residential Schools* [level 1, CEP], and *Tasmanian Stolen Generations*).

What is the source of money amounts?

Where, then, did the flat payments or capped (lower maxima) amounts come from? In a report for the LCC, IHRD (1998, p. 38) states:

> We were unable to determine from any source how the amounts involved in the compensation grids were chosen.... If there is some derived formula, which attempts to incorporate the body of existing knowledge about child abuse impacts with tort law principles, we did

> not uncover it. Our belief is that no such formula exists, and that the grids or matrices or level systems are *the creation primarily of lawyers acting for governments*. (IHRD, 1998, p. 38, emphasis added)

The authors are right: there is no clear justification in any of the Canadian or Australian schemes for why certain amounts were chosen as caps or flat amounts, and how these related to the type, frequency, and impact of abuse.[12] One report sheds some light on the matter. In proposing a compensatory mechanism for *Jericho Hill* (what would later be the JICP), Berger (1995, section VII) gave consideration to amounts awarded in Canadian courts for sexual abuse, as well as a civil settlement amount for sexual abuse at Jericho Hill School. He also considered different categories of damages (pecuniary, non-pecuniary, punitive), but concluded that 'pain and suffering' (non-pecuniary) was most appropriate. Berger proposed that *Jericho Hill* use a tiered approach, like that in *Grandview* ($3,000 to $60,000 maximum).[13] He acknowledged that the amounts were probably 'not as generous as awards made by courts', but were 'reasonable in light of the difficulties of proof of liability and damage that a plaintiff would face' (Berger, 1995, p. 29).

For the individualized Canadian and Australian schemes, with decisions based on severity (or on severity and impact), the maximum amount, which range from $33,000 to $120,000, might have been sourced from outcomes in previous civil cases; however, no case or authority is cited. (By comparison, for the Irish Residential Redress Board, the Compensation Advisory Committee's [2002] report is exemplary in identifying five redress bands, their points range, and monetary ranges in calculating *ex gratia* payments, after reviewing relevant case law.) For flat payments, which range from $7,000 in *Queensland Institutions* to $25,000 in *George Epoch*, no justification is given in any public document. Comparisons might have been drawn to other flat payment or *ex gratia* schemes, but except for Berger (1995), no such consideration is given.[14] In part, the size of flat payments may be explained by constraints. The Queensland redress scheme allocated $100 million for financial payments; although I cannot be certain, it is possible that the state's scheme designers calculated the level of the flat payment based on the estimated number of claimants.

Tasmanian Stolen Generations used an equality-based formula to distribute a fixed pool of $5 million. After $100,000 was paid to eligible family members (children of deceased members of the Stolen Generations), the remaining $4.9 million was distributed equally to eligible members of the Stolen Generations. Another type of equality-based formula is based on the number of years spent in an institution. For *Duplessis Orphans* in time 1, the formula was $10,000, plus $1,000 for each year spent in an eligible institution. For *Indian Residential Schools*, the CEP was $10,000 for the first year, plus $3,000 for each additional year spent in an eligible residential school. An institutional time formula has much to commend: by linking money to time spent in an institution, the amount may better symbolize claimants' realities of institutional life than a tort logic of 'pain and suffering', which is tied to incidents of abuse. A problem with any time-based formula is determining which institutions are eligible and why.[15]

Scheme process: oral hearings and other outcomes

Table 5.1 shows differences in scheme elements and the degree to which redress can be more of a larger 'package' than a smaller 'scheme'. The table does not itemize all the outcomes; for now, I sketch broad patterns across schemes.

Applications can be assessed in oral hearings (or interviews) with claimants, or by reading documents without a hearing. All but one (*Duplessis Orphans*) provided counselling as a service or a benefit; three also provided an Opportunity Fund, to which claimants had to apply for additional vocational, educational, or other benefits; and the two class action settlements had a significant package of benefits and services. I captured this variability with 'invest', a measure that tapped a scheme's investment in claimants by listening to them in interviews or oral hearings and by providing benefits and services. (For the moment, I shall set financial payments to the side.) Invest is not a measure of the total amount an organizational entity may have spent on a scheme because the costs to administer a scheme and pay legal costs can be substantial. Rather, it is the amount of time, benefits, and services offered to claimants.

Using this measure, the scheme with the least investment in claimants was *Duplessis Orphans*: although hearings were held by request in phase 1, no counselling was offered. Next, with low investment, were almost all the Australian schemes (*Queensland Institutions, South Australia Institutions, Tasmanian Stolen Generations*, and *Redress WA*) and two in Canada (*Nova Scotia* and *New Brunswick Institutions*) with no hearings, but the provision of counselling. With greater investment were two Canadian schemes (*Ontario Schools for the Deaf* and *Jericho Hill*-JICP) and one in Australia (*Tasmanian Institutions*), with hearings and counselling (in Tasmania, processes were streamlined in phases 3 and 4 and counselling reduced in phase 4). The five remaining cases are redress *packages* more than *schemes* because they offered a larger set of benefits and

Table 5.1 Schematic of redress schemes

Case	Invest[16]	Money logic (in local CAD or AUD currency)	Process used to validate and assess	Other outcomes (excludes legal costs)
George Epoch	3-high	flat ($25,000)	oral hearing	counselling, Opportunity Fund, and Recorder
St John's and St Joseph's	3-high	individualized, lower maxima ($25,000 government share)	oral hearing (groups 1 and 2, optional over time); optional for post-group 2	counselling, Opportunity Fund, and Recorder; benefits reduce (post-group 2)
Grandview	3-high	individualized, capped ($60,000)	oral hearing (group 1); lawyer for province (not adjudicator) assesses in group 2	counselling, Opportunity Fund, and general and individual benefits; services and benefits reduce (group 2)
Nova Scotia Institutions	1-low	individualized, capped ($120,000)	no hearing and more stringent criteria over time	counselling
Ontario Schools for the Deaf	2-high	individualized, capped ($60,000)	oral hearing (ASL assisted)[17]	counselling
Jericho Hill, Jericho Individual Compensation Program (JICP)	2-high	individualized, capped ($60,000)	oral hearing (hearing conducted by a person fluent in ASL)	counselling
Jericho Hill Class Action, Independent Compensation Fund (ICF) (must choose level)	4-very high	level 1: flat ($10,000) levels 2 and 3: individualized, lower maxima (not specified)	level 1: no hearing levels 2 and 3: oral hearing (ASL assisted) and medical tests	significant package of benefits and services
New Brunswick Institutions	1-low	individualized, capped ($120,000)	no hearing	counselling

Continued

Table 5.1 Continued

Case	Invest	Money logic (in local CAD or AUD currency)	Process used to validate and assess	Other outcomes (excludes legal costs)
Duplessis Orphans	0-low	time 1: equal (yrs in institution/s)	time 1: no hearing, unless requested	none
		time 2: flat ($15,000)	time 2: no hearing	
Indian Residential Schools (can apply to both levels 1 and 2)	4-very high	level 1: equal (yrs in residential school/s) (CEP)	level 1: no hearing	significant package of benefits and services
		level 2: individualized, higher maxima (IAP)	level 2: oral hearing	
Queensland Institutions (can apply to both levels 1 and 2)	1-low	level 1: flat ($7,000)	level 1: no hearing	counselling; small grants for household goods, dental expenses, wellness, and personal development (Forde Foundation Trust)
		level 2: individualized, capped ($33,000)	level 2: no hearing	
Tasmanian Institutions	2-high	phases 1–3: individualized, capped ($60,000)	oral hearing	counselling (reduced in phase 4)
		phase 4: individualized, capped ($35,000)		
South Australian Institutions	1-low	individualized, capped ($30,000)[18]	no hearing	counselling
Tasmanian Stolen Generations	1-low	equal: fixed pool of funds divided by eligible applicants[19]	no hearing	counselling (on request)
Redress WA	1-low	individualized, 4 bands, capped ($45,000)[20]	no hearing	counselling (limited to 3 sessions, but could request more)

services (*George Epoch, St John's and St Joseph's,* and *Grandview*), or they had an even more substantial set of outcomes (*Jericho Hill Class Action* and *Indian Residential Schools*).

To be fair to the Australian schemes, I note limitations with the 'invest' measure. Two states and the Commonwealth had spent considerable time and resources on public inquiries before redress schemes were introduced. Thus, the rationale for having an oral hearing in a redress scheme would be less strong in Australia than it would be in Canada, where just one case had a public inquiry preceding a redress scheme (*New Brunswick Institutions*). Public inquiries were held in Queensland and South Australia, and the Commonwealth's inquiries into the *Stolen Generations, Child Migrants,* and *Forgotten Australians* were relevant to the *Tasmanian Stolen Generations* and *Redress WA* schemes. Thus, redress schemes cannot be viewed in isolation from other government responses that take time and resources and can provide some degree of victim 'voice' in the justice process.

Application and assessment process

Appendix 2 lists the information claimants were asked to provide in an application and the process of assessment. Over time, five schemes changed their process or outcomes: *St John's and St Joseph's* (over time, oral hearings were less likely, and there was access to fewer benefits and services for post-group 2); *Grandview* (a second group applying after a January 1996 deadline was assessed by government lawyers, not independent adjudicators, and there was access to fewer benefits and services for group 2); *Nova Scotia Institutions* (a more stringent assessment of applications in phases 2 and 3); *Duplessis Orphans* (a lower financial payment in time 2); and *Tasmanian Institutions* (a more streamlined process in phases 3 and 4, and reduced counselling and a reduced cap in phase 4).[21] One inference is that claimants should apply early, and by the first deadline, when a redress scheme is announced.

File handling and approval

Some schemes had a more complicated process of receiving and gathering information, validating it, and subjecting the file to another round of review to determine a financial payment. This is evident in four Canadian cases (*Nova Scotia Institutions, Ontario Schools for the Deaf, Jericho Hill*-JICP, and *New Brunswick Institutions*) and one Australian case (*Tasmanian Institutions*, phases 1 and 2). The reasons are unique to each case, and no general pattern can be discerned.

As shown in Case Study 5.4, *Nova Scotia Institutions* was a complex case. The scheme's evolution was affected by some claimants, who alleged being abused by currently employed corrections staff; the staff, in turn, challenged the veracity of some claims. It was the only case that was subject to an outside review after it concluded, which reflects the controversies surrounding it. For *Ontario Schools for the Deaf* and *Jericho Hill*-JICP, there were added layers of receiving and processing information that can be explained, I believe, by the desire to gather accounts of Deaf claimants in an appropriate manner, but then to 'test' these with an independent decision-maker. The scheme in *New Brunswick Institutions* was implemented in-house by staff in the Department of Justice; however, because the final payment largely resulted from negotiations between lawyers, using a grid of injuries and damages, and arbitration was used if a decision was appealed, there were many levels of departmental review and approval.

Case example 5.4 *Nova Scotia Institutions*: a 'seriously flawed' redress scheme?

Government officials had hoped to implement a *Grandview*-like process with one lawyer working for a group of survivors; however, when negotiations were finalized in May 1996, over 60 lawyers represented victims. There are conflicting accounts of what was agreed to during the negotiations in the first part of 1996 (Kaufman, 2002, p. 133); ultimately, lawyers for victims had interpreted the government's desire for a summary process of review to mean that a claim should be accepted unless there was a concrete reason for doubting it. As the scheme evolved from May 1996 to the program's closure in 2000, the validation process tightened because there was a higher-than-expected number of claimants and a recognition that claims required more thorough investigation.

Concerns were raised that some claims were fraudulent (including an exchange of information by claimants, who were now in adult correctional settings). Corrections employees challenged some claimants' allegations of abuse as false. Early in 1997, employees began to take polygraph tests to disprove allegations. Employees who were investigated by the IIU for disciplinary misconduct felt a sense of 'embattlement' as officials and members of the public assumed that the allegations 'against [them] were certainly true' (Kaufman, 2002, pp. 301–2). In 1998, the government signed an MOU with the union, which provided employment support, financial benefits, and early retirement packages for those employees for whom allegations had wrongly been made by the IIU (pp. 320–1). Kaufman argues that justice for survivors and alleged abusers was compromised and the redress program was 'seriously flawed':

> So flawed that it left in its wake true victims of abuse who are now assumed by many to have defrauded the Government, innocent employees who have been branded as abusers, and a public confused and unenlightened about the extent to which young people were or were not abused while in the care of the Province of Nova Scotia. (p. 496).

What needed to be 'proved'?

Schemes varied in what claimants had to establish or 'prove' to receive a financial payment. For five, claimants did not need to show that abuse had occurred, but rather that they were placed in an eligible institution (*Duplessis Orphans* [times 1 and 2] and *Indian Residential Schools* [level 1, CEP]), removed from their family under certain *Acts* or without parental approval (*Tasmanian Stolen Generations*), or a class member in the *Jericho Hill Class Action* (level 1 payment). For the remaining 15 money outcomes, five were based on demonstrating sexual abuse while in state or church care, and ten, physical or sexual abuse while in care. These money outcomes were based on abuse and severity, or on abuse, severity, and resulting impact. For the five sexual abuse schemes, money outcomes were based on abuse and severity (*George Epoch* and *New Brunswick*), and for three, on abuse, severity, and impact (*Jericho Hill*-JICP, *Jericho Hill Class Action*, and *South Australian Institutions*). For the remaining ten that were for both physical and sexual abuse, four were based on abuse and severity (*St John's and St Joseph's*, *Nova Scotia Institutions*, *Ontario Schools for the Deaf*, *Queensland Institutions* [level 1]),[22] and six on abuse, severity, and impact (*Grandview*, *Indian Residential Schools* [IAP], *Queensland Institutions* [level 2], *Tasmanian Institutions* [phases 1–3 and phase 4] and *Redress WA*). (For ease of reference, what needed to be proved is shown in Appendix 3B on financial outcomes.) In Canada, the typical standard was 'on the balance of probabilities' or 'reasonable likelihood' of abuse. In Australia, 'balance of probabilities' was noted only in *South Australian Institutions* (although it could be waived). A claim was 'accepted unless there was evidence to the contrary' in *Redress WA*, but the standard of proof was not clear in published sources for the Queensland and Tasmanian schemes.

Who made the decisions?

For schemes with oral hearings, decisions on financial payments (and in a few cases, on allotments for counselling or significant medical and dental costs) were made in one of two ways: by the person who listened to and spoke with a claimant at a meeting (decision by the listener/adjudicator), or by another who received documents or a file, but had not listened to or spoken with a claimant (decision by another). Using 20 as the denominator for all types of money outcomes, 11 had the option of an oral hearing (nine Canadian, two Australian). Of the nine Canadian hearings, in five, outcome decisions were made by the listener/adjudicator at the meeting. In the two Australian schemes with a hearing (*Tasmanian Institutions*, phases 1–3 and phase 4), the decision was by another. In eight of the 11 schemes with oral hearings, claimants were permitted to bring a support person with them (for three, information was not available). The experiences of claimants in oral hearings was favourable in *St John's and St Joseph's* and especially so in *Grandview*, the latter being a model for its care and attentiveness to victims' concerns (see Case example 5.5).

Case example 5.5 *Grandview* process

The *Grandview* process is exemplary and unusual compared to the other cases. It was modelled on feminist principles and fashioned with strong levels of participation by the Grandview Survivors' Support Group. Close attention was given to the adjudication process and physical layout of the hearing room to ensure it had windows and that the setting was non-hierarchical. The process was designed to be non-adversarial and supportive. Female adjudicators were appointed, who were familiar with judicial processes and work on violence against women. Hearings occurred in a 'warm and friendly' environment (Leach, 1997, p. 21). Support person/s were allowed; and if requested, payment was made for a claimant's therapist to attend. Attention was given to employing administrative staff members who were sensitive and caring.

Whether a scheme should be designed to include a hearing is important for designers to consider with respect to resources and time. In *Redress WA*, the Guidelines note that except for 'clarifying details' with the applicant, there was no 'provision for hearings or negotiating an *ex gratia* payment' because 'the intention of the ... government is to avoid the expense, delay, and stress that any such processes necessarily involve' (Western Australia Communities, 2011, p. 22). Likewise, in *Tasmanian Stolen Generations*, the assessor said that 'the overall approach adopted was a non-adversarial and informal assessment process with the objective of conducting each assessment in an administrative manner without formal hearings' (Tasmania Premier and Cabinet, 2008, p. 9). However, if the assessor was concerned that an application may not succeed, an applicant was given an 'opportunity to meet with the Assessor ... and provide any further information ...' (p. 10).

Were assessors internal or external?

Who assesses an application is important for perceptions of decision-making 'objectivity'. Some schemes relied on department staff in-house (internal assessor) and others employed personnel at arm's length (external assessor). Using 20 as the denominator for all payment decision outcomes, external assessors were more likely in Canadian schemes (eight of 13 money outcomes) than those in Australia (two of seven, both in the *Tasmanian Institutions* scheme).[23] We might hypothesize that internal assessors would be more aligned with a scheme's underwriter than independent assessors. I explore this hypothesis below.

Were reasons for decisions provided? Could claimants appeal?

From a victim's perspective, another important element is whether reasons for decisions were provided. Using 20 as the denominator for money outcomes, reasons were provided as a standard practice in eight schemes; but for six, no reasons were given; and in five, it is unclear what information was conveyed, but it is likely no reasons were provided. In the remaining case, reasons were given on request. The Canadian schemes were more likely than those in Australia to provide reasons for decisions as a standard practice.[24] Examining the ability to appeal, and using 20 as the denominator, appeals could be lodged against eight of 13 Canadian money decisions, but in none of the Australian decisions. However, in three decisions in Australia (*Tasmanian Institutions* [phases 1–3 and phase 4] and *Redress WA*), review was possible if a claimant could show an error of fact, there were additional facts not brought to an assessor's attention, or there was an error of process.

When did the claimant sign a release?

For most, although not all redress schemes, claimants had to sign a 'release' form to receive a financial payment.[25] By signing the form, claimants acknowledged they could not sue government or church entities for similar claims of abuse in state care, although they could pursue claims against individuals. Using 15 as the appropriate denominator for *schemes*, the results are as follows. In two, claimants were required to sign a release when opting into the settlement agreement (*Indian Residential Schools*) or negotiated agreement (*St John's and St Joseph's*), and in three, claimants had to sign when submitting their application (*George Epoch*, *Grandview*, and *Jericho Hill Class Action*). In most (8 of 15), claimants signed a release only after being offered a payment amount. In two Australian cases (*Tasmanian Stolen Generations* and *Redress WA*), signing a release was not required.[26] For the Tasmanian case, the reason was that the payment was redress for a policy of wrongful child removal, not abuse; however, it is less certain why the Western Australian Government did not require claimants to sign a release before payment. Setting aside the class action cases, the three Canadian cases for which claimants had to sign a release before knowing the outcomes (*George*

Epoch, *St John's and St Joseph's*, and *Grandview*) were the earliest Canadian cases. As redress schemes evolved, release signage moved in claimants' favour.

Redress scheme constraints

Imagine you have been asked to design a compensatory mechanism for institutional abuse. You may have some idea of the number of potential claimants, although this can be expected to increase over time. Further, there is media pressure and victim group advocacy to do something. Countering these pressures are others: how much money can and should be spent on redressing institutional abuse and what types of processes are most efficient and effective in distinguishing valid claimants from others? From this perspective, it is important to place redress for institutional abuse within a reasonable fiscal framework.

I was interested to determine whether the 'invest' measure was associated with the expected (or actual) number of claimants. If scheme designers were rational economic decision-makers, they may limit the investment per claimant if a high number was expected to apply; conversely, schemes may be more generous if a low number was expected. I recognize, of course, that norms other than a simple economic calculus may guide the design of a redress scheme.[27] Nova Scotia is a good example: designers desired to 'assist victims... [to] regain control over their lives and integrate them back into society' (Simon and Scott, July 1995 memorandum to Cabinet, in Kaufman, 2002, Vol. 2, appendix E, p. 540).

To carry out this analysis, after inspecting the distributions on the relevant variables, I differentiated the 15 schemes with a lower number of claimants (less than 400, seven schemes) from a higher number (400 or more, eight schemes).[28] I then compared the level of 'invest' in each scheme, collapsing the five invest categories into two: 'lower invest' (score of 0 or 1, seven schemes) and 'higher invest' (score of 2 to 4, eight schemes). The results show that, in general, planners made rational decisions on time and resources: 'higher invest' was associated with a lower number of claimants; and conversely, 'lower invest' was associated with a higher number of claimants. The association is not perfect: five of the 15 schemes were incorrectly predicted.[29] Two (*Tasmanian Stolen Generations* and *South Australian Institutions*) had a low number of claimants and were low in 'invest'. Three schemes were unexpectedly generous in light of their numbers: *St John's and St Joseph's*, *Indian Residential Schools*, and *Tasmanian Institutions*.

Schemes varied in the degree to which services were provided to all claimants (such as counselling or interim counselling, once a response was underway), even if some claims were ultimately not validated or considered eligible for the scheme. However, validated claimants had access to longer-term counselling or other benefits and services. What, then, were the validation rates? Did these relate to 'invest', the number of claimants, or the type of assessor? In carrying out the analysis, I began with 20 as the denominator, but then excluded the two *Jericho Hill Class Action* outcomes (level 1, and levels 2 and 3), for which validation was not germane. Validation rates ranged from a low of 54 per cent (*Ontario Schools for the Deaf*) to a high of 97 to 98 per cent (*St John's and St Joseph's*, *Grandview*, and *Jericho Hill*-JICP). The average validation rate (mean) was 78 per cent; and the median, 77. The results show that higher validation rates were associated with a higher investment in claimants, but not with the number of claimants who applied to a scheme (and whose case was resolved), nor the type of assessor.[30] In light of the low sample sizes, these and other analyses must be viewed as exploratory.

Redress scheme structure and process: a wrap up

Redress for institutional abuse or related policy wrongs can take many forms. Of the 15 redress schemes, the design and concept of redress was forged in different contexts. In some cases, advocacy groups, working with legal representatives, participated in shaping the scheme and desired outcomes. For others, the schemes resulted from negotiations between each side's lawyers; and in others, they were decided by staff in a government office. Thus, I find a variable degree of participation – as one of several victims' justice interests – in the design of schemes. A scheme may be more or less generous to claimants depending on the bargaining power of victim advocacy groups, their lawyers, and the strength and number of pending litigation claims. Scheme elements were most generous in structured civil settlements, when a government (or church organization) decided that settlement was better than prolonged litigation. Differences are evident in the money logics used in deciding financial payments. Most common, however, was individualized and tiered according to abuse and severity, or abuse, severity, and impact. Application and assessment practices can be personalized, with oral hearings, decisions made by those attending the hearings, and reasons given for decisions. Or they can be impersonal, with a claimant completing a form, sending it to an office, and waiting to receive a response in the mail. Mid-way are practices in which claimants relied on lawyers to negotiate the best offer. Schemes varied in how much time, benefits, and services are offered to (or 'invested' in) claimants; this, in turn, was inversely related to the number of claimants. I found that in general, with a large number of potential claimants, there was less likelihood of oral hearings and less provision of benefits and services (other than counselling). I noted, however, that if redress schemes are preceded by public inquiries, there may be less reason to design a scheme with oral hearings. In the next chapter, I consider how the 'invest' measure relates to average financial payments.

There are many trade-offs to consider in planning a redress scheme. Resources are limited and must be spent wisely. At the same time, application and assessment processes should be claimant-friendly and treat individuals with dignity and respect. From claimants' perspectives, seeking redress includes interactions with all redress personnel, not just decision-makers or adjudicators. Survivors' experiences with redress are the subject of Chapter 7. I turn next to examine the outcomes from redress schemes, civil litigation, and public inquiries for the 19 cases.

6
Redress Outcomes

This chapter presents the outcomes from redress schemes, major civil settlements, and public inquiry cases without financial payments. Appendices 3 to 6 show redress payments and other outcomes, apologies, memorials and commemorative activities, and other media and memory projects associated with the cases. The money amounts are given in local currency, without continually using CAD or AUD. Adjustments for inflation and currency conversion, using 2012 as the reference year, are given in Appendix 3C.

Redress scheme outcomes

The structure of a redress scheme determines its elements and outcomes: and the major categories are financial payments, benefits and services, other elements, and apologies and memorialization. I first review benefits and services and other elements before turning to financial payments. I defer apologies and memorialization to the end of the chapter.

Benefits, services, and other elements in redress schemes

Benefits and services include *interim counselling* (available to all at the announcement of a scheme; or in some cases, during the period before a negotiated agreement is finalized); *longer-term counselling* (upon validation of a claim); *financial counselling* (to assist claimants in handling financial payments); support for *medical and dental* or *educational and vocational expenses*; and *legal costs*. By *benefits*, I mean a pool of funds that the scheme makes available for claimant application or reimbursement; and by *services*, I mean activities paid for by a government (or church) entity, which claimants can use. Appendix 3A itemizes the elements and outcomes for the 15 redress schemes.

All but two (*Ontario Schools for the Deaf* and *Duplessis Orphans*) had interim counselling, and all but one (*Duplessis Orphans*) had longer-term counselling. For Canada, a second group of *Grandview* claimants, who applied after the first deadline would not have received interim counselling after March 1997. For three Australian schemes, counselling services or benefits were reduced over time (*Tasmanian Institutions*, reduced in phase 4); limited to three sessions, unless requested by a claimant (*Redress WA*); or available only on request (*Tasmanian Stolen Generations*). Longer-term counselling was offered as a benefit in most of the Canadian schemes, but it was a service in most of the Australian schemes. When counselling is a benefit, claimants are allocated funds (or they apply for funds) to spend on counsellors of their choice. When it is a service, claimants use specified service providers. Financial counselling for those seeking advice in handling payments received was offered to all validated claimants in five schemes (and to special track claimants only in *Jericho Hill*-JICP). For the sole Australian case offering financial counselling (*Queensland Institutions*), one appointment with a financial advisor was offered, but 'no applicant accessed it', according to a department program officer (personal communication, 6 November 2013).

A handful of schemes had dedicated funds set aside in an Opportunity Fund (*George Epoch* and *St John's and St Joseph's*) or Contingency Fund (*Grandview*) to which validated claimants could apply for medical, dental, vocational, and educational benefits.[1] In one Canadian scheme, monies allotted to counselling could be used by the applicant to reimburse medical, dental, vocational, or educational expenses (*Nova Scotia Institutions*); and in another, tuition and book costs were factored into the financial payment (*New Brunswick Institutions*). *Jericho Hill Class Action* had a significant package of educational benefits for claimants and their families, including the establishment of the Jericho Hill Legacy Trust (renamed the BC Scholarship Trust in 2013), scholarships, American Sign Language classes for family members, and advocacy for the Deaf in colleges and universities in British Columbia.

In Australia, *Queensland Institutions* and *Tasmanian Institutions* had (and have) benefits. In Queensland, the Forde Foundation Trust was established in 2000, soon after the Forde Report (1999) was tabled, to provide small grants for 'basic life necessities', educational and self-improvement needs, dental and health care costs, and family reunion costs (Forde Foundation, 2008, p. 1). The Trust was established in lieu of a redress scheme, which the government did not want to implement at the time. As of 2014, the Trust continues to operate, having spent about \$810 per registered member since 2000. In Tasmania, the Abuse in Care Support Service was established when its redress scheme closed in February 2013. Eligible applicants cannot have received a payment from the redress scheme. Claimants can apply for 'up to $2,500 ... for goods and services...such as (but not limited to) education, employment, counselling, family connection, medical and dental services' (Tasmanian Health and Human Services, 2013). Having begun in 2013, the program continues to operate in 2014.

Research on the 'take up' of benefits was carried out by Shea (1999a) for *Grandview*. She found that the most widely used benefits were counselling and requests to the Contingency Fund (likely for dental expenses), with 90 per cent accessing these; after that, self-inflicted tattoo or scar removal (nearly 40 per cent) and vocational or educational assistance (34 per cent).[2] By comparison, few accessed financial counselling.

Support for legal costs was available to claimants in all but two schemes (*George Epoch* and *Duplessis Orphans*).[3] In one (*New Brunswick Institutions*), it was awarded as part of the financial payment and could be no higher than 20 per cent. No other scheme made this stipulation. What redress scheme designers had in mind in providing support for legal advice was to ensure that claimants knew the implications of accepting a financial payment (or opting into an agreement) for any future legal claims. However, the IHRD's (Institute for Human Resource Development) interviews with *Grandview* survivors found that some had wrongly assumed they had general access to legal advice: 'A common point of dissatisfaction of women from the first group...was that they understood that the government was going to pay their lawyers' fees in total, and they felt that it was not right that they should be billed as well' (IHRD, 1998, p. 90).

Some schemes had other benefit elements. In *Grandview*, for example, in addition to individual benefits, the agreement provided two general benefits: an evaluation of the agreement process (Leach, 1997) and a video with interviews of survivors, *Until Someone Listens* (1999). There were also group benefits for any former resident. These included access to a dedicated crisis line that was open for nearly 4 years, from May 1993 to March 1997, and the removal of self-inflicted tattoos and scars while at Grandview. This last item was significant because 'for many women, the existence of their tattoos, or the scars remaining from attempts to remove them, served as daily reminders of Grandview' (Graycar and Wangmann, 2007, p. 14).

Two schemes had Recorders, who assembled materials about the case, including interviews with survivors (*George Epoch* and *St John's and St Joseph's*). In *Jericho Hill*-JICP, the government donated $1 million to the

Deaf Foundation of British Columbia. *Indian Residential Schools* had a large set of other elements: continued funding of the Aboriginal Healing Foundation (which also received funds from the Catholic Diocese of Canada) and creation of a Truth and Reconciliation Commission (TRC) on the history and legacy of *Indian Residential Schools*. The TRC, initially established in 2008, and then re-established in July 2009 to run to 30 June 2015, is engaged in a broad program of activities. In addition to statement gathering and truth sharing, document collection, and research and report preparation, it established a National Research Centre (based at the University of Manitoba), sponsored national events, and with Aboriginal Affairs and Northern Development Canada, facilitated 145 commemorative projects (see Appendices 5 and 6).

Financial payments in redress schemes

'Compensation' is used loosely by many to refer to a financial payment that may be part of a redress scheme, when more precisely, compensation means an amount of money decided by a court for damages, where fault or liability for an injury has been or is likely to be established. Financial payments are a 'compensatory mechanism', and the more accurate term for a redress scheme is an *ex gratia* payment. This is understood to be an 'act of grace' or 'kindness' by state (or church) entities without an admission of liability. Because such payments are discretionary, eligibility criteria and payment levels may change. Although an *ex gratia* payment is the accurate term to use in all redress schemes, *Indian Residential Schools* had a level 2 payment (the IAP for Independent Assessment Process) that more closely aligned with a tort logic of damages and injury.

An important finding from my research is that governments (or church organizations) do not publish outcomes, including *ex gratia* payments, of redress schemes. Except for *Jericho Hill*-JICP and *Tasmanian Stolen Generations*, there was no final report of decision-making cesses and actual outcomes for the 15 redress schemes.[4] For some, this is reasonable because schemes continue or applications are being processed (as in *Duplessis Orphans, Indian Residential Schools*, and *South Australian Institutions*). For 13 of 15 redress schemes, I sought data on financial payments from relevant departments or people.

Appendix 3B shows the average payment for 19 money outcomes in each redress scheme. It also lists the number of claimants (for cases resolved), validation rate, money logic, what needed to be proved, the 'invest' variable and claimant numbers, potential payment range, average benefit (where relevant), and the estimated time to tangible result.

The comments section provides additional information on estimating payment amounts. For now, I present the findings without reference to currency differences or adjusting for inflation. Except for IAP (*Indian Residential Schools*), I have not taken into account legal fees that may have been deducted; and I focus on average financial payments, not both these and benefits paid.

First are the distributions for the 19 average payments, except for *Jericho Hill Class Action*, for which level 2 and 3 payments are not known. Average Canadian payments ranged from $10,000 to $100,530, and average Australian payments, from $7,000 to $58,333. These averages mask the range of payments that claimants received; however, I could not secure reliable range data for most cases. Table 6.1 shows the averages by type of money logic for the countries combined and separated. Drawing from Appendix 3B and Table 6.1, these observations can be made.

First, without adjusting for differences in currency or the year a payment was made, average payments in Canada are higher than Australia. One exception is the payment for *Tasmanian Stolen Generations* ($58,333), which was based on an equality formula. Second, among the Canadian payments, the average IAP payment in the *Indian Residential Schools* stands out as the highest ($100,530), after deducting 15 per cent in legal fees.[5] For the Canadian group of individualized, capped, or restricted cases, *New Brunswick Institutions*, *Jericho Hill*-JICP, *Grandview*, and *Ontario Schools for the Deaf* have higher average payments ($36,232 to $39,131), compared to two other Canadian cases, *St John's and St Joseph's* and *Nova Scotia Institutions*, which ranged from $22,319 to $28,583, respectively. In Canada, the average for flat payment schemes ($16,667) or other equality formula ($22,560) is generally lower than that for individualized schemes. Third, among Australian schemes, the *Tasmanian Stolen Generations* payment is the highest ($58,333); and for the group of individualized, capped, or restricted schemes in Australia, *Tasmanian Institutions* has the highest average payment ($33,906) for phases 1, 2, and 3. However, when its cap was reduced to $35,000 in phase 4, the average payment dropped to $14,136. The payment for *South Australian Institutions* is lower ($14,407) than that for *Queensland Institutions* ($19,894, when combining level 1 and 2 payments), and *Redress WA* ($22,465). The lowest payment is in *Queensland Institutions* (flat payment of $7,000 for level 1).

A fourth observation is the relationship between the average payment and the stipulated maximum: for the relevant individualized schemes, it is 24 to 65 per cent of the maximum. The average is about 50 per

Table 6.1 Average payment (mean) received by money logic (in CAD and AUD, unadjusted)

money logic	all (N = 19)	Canada (N = 12)	Australia (N = 7)
individualized, high			
mean		$100,530	
case name		Indian Residential Schools, IAP	
individualized, capped or restricted			
mean	$27,749	$33,404	$20,962
range		$22,319 to 39,131	$14,136 to 33,906
case names		St John's & St Joseph's, Grandview, Nova Scotia Institutions, Ontario Schools for the Deaf, Jericho Hill-JICP, New Brunswick Institutions	Queensland Institutions, levels 1& 2 combined; Tasmanian Institutions, phases 1–3, phase 4; South Australian Institutions, Redress WA
equal fixed or flat			
mean	$14,250	$16,667	$7,000
range		$10,000 to 25,000	NA
case names		George Epoch; Jericho Hill Class Action, level 1; Duplessis Orphans, time 2	Queensland Institutions, level 1
equal, other formula			
mean	$34,484	$22,560	$58,333
range		$19,412 to $25,707	NA
case names		Duplessis Orphans, time 1; Indian Residential Schools, CEP	Tasmania Stolen Generations

cent, which means that, on average, validated claimants received half the maximum cap. This is an important finding, and it helps to explain claimants' disappointment with the payments they received. For example in *Jericho Hill*-JICP, claimants were aware that payments could be 'up to $60,000'; and many assumed that this was the amount their abuse experience 'deserved' and what they were 'worth'. However, although about one-fourth received $60,000 (Morley, 2001, p. 43), the average was $36,462.[6] As I show in the next chapter, disappointment with the amount received is a common finding across all the schemes for which there is information.

I explored the relationship between 'invest' and the average amount of a payment, expecting to see an association between higher payments and a higher initial investment in claimants. However, there was no strong association.

Waiting for justice

From Chapter 4, we learned it took 37 years, on average, for a response to institutional abuse to begin, after there had been official knowledge of the problem. However, this is just the start of what can be a long process for survivors in achieving a tangible result. By *tangible result,* I mean monetary recompense for abuse, policy redress, or both, and depending on the scheme, its impact into adulthood. Other types of outcomes such as sincere apologies or counselling are important and may be considered 'tangible'. However, for now, I am interested to capture another type of subjectivity: once a response begins, expectations are raised that 'compensation' may follow. How much time does this take?

For this analysis, I first had to determine which year claimants would have received a payment. I estimated this from the year that the scheme opened and closed, together with other material, such as reports that indicated when payments were received by claimants. The receipt of payments could span several years, and in these cases, I chose the year when half the claimants would have received a payment. The 'year of tangible result' is shown for each money outcome in Appendix 3B. That year is important for another reason: I used it to calculate the value of the payment, adjusting for inflation, in different currencies (Appendix 3C). The 'time to tangible result' is the time from the response year to the 'year of tangible result' of receiving a redress scheme payment.

My analysis shows a range of 2 to 16 years, with an average (mean) of 8 years to achieve a tangible result. As we would expect, claimants in the two Australian redress scheme only cases (*Tasmanian Stolen Generations* and *Redress WA*) had the shortest time to the wait (2 to 3 years). By comparison, those in *Indian Residential Schools* had the longest time: 13 years (for the CEP, Common Experience Payment) and 16 years (for the IAP), from the 1996 response year. However, the latter is somewhat misleading because an estimated 4,134 claims had been resolved from the Alternative Dispute Resolution Process and settlements from 1999 to July 2006 (Russell affidavit, 2006, p. 16). Excluding the two residential schools outcomes, the average (mean) drops to 7.25 years. Other cases with a long time for claimants to wait are *Duplessis Orphans* (13 years for those applying to the 2007 program in time 2), and *Queensland Institutions* (11 and 12 years for level 1 and combined level 1 and 2 payments, respectively). Although Forde (1999) had recommended a financial payment scheme, the government was initially reluctant to do so, and did not announce a redress scheme until 2007. In Canada, negotiating agreements took time (up to 4 years); and in Australia, both the Queensland and South Australian governments delayed introducing redress schemes.

Civil settlement outcomes

Two cases had major civil settlements only as the outcome (*Mount Cashel* and *Alberta Sterilization*). In addition to *Indian Residential Schools* and *Jericho Hill Class Action*, whose outcomes I treat as redress packages, four other cases had civil settlements with 70 or more plaintiffs.

Major civil settlements

Mount Cashel and *Alberta Sterilization* had large civil settlements as the only outcome. Like redress scheme payments, I report money outcomes in the currency and amount in the year it was announced.

For *Mount Cashel*, Hughes (1991) recommended an *ex gratia* payment, but the government rejected the idea, saying that claimants would have to prove their claims in court. The first suit was filed by Shane Earle in April 1989, and he settled for a large, undisclosed sum with the Christian Brothers and the government in 1995. Three major sets of cases were lodged in 1989, 1997, and 1999. Settlements were announced in 1996, 2004, and 2013. The first group of 43 plaintiffs was paid in 1997; thus, it took about 7.5 years for them to receive a tangible outcome. The total settlement amount was $11.25 million, or on average $261,628 per person (before deducting legal fees).[7] In addition, the first group had services and benefits. The Christian Brothers funded interim counselling and education expenses for 3 years (IHRD, 1998, p. 36), and the government offered financial counselling for those requesting it (Kaufman, 2002, p. 372).

Interviews by the IHRD (1998, p. 74) of *Mount Cashel* survivors reveal a number of themes. Survivors thought the case took too long, and they blamed the Christian Brothers 'for prolonging the process and wasting money' on defending the case. The 'process went on so long that [they] were worn down and exhausted' by it and 'felt forced to settle'. Some believed the suit 'gave them a negative image', that they 'were portrayed as "money grabbing"', and the public did not understand the impact of the abuse. Different views were expressed by survivors in key areas: some felt they were well informed about the case, but others did not; some were pleased with the financial outcome, but others thought it was insufficient. The suit divided them for several reasons. Some wanted to hold out for a larger payment, but others wanted to settle earlier for financial reasons; and different levels of payment caused resentment. Some 'used the money wisely', and others 'wasted it and have nothing left'.

An estimated 209 unique individuals[8] have successfully sued the government and the Christian Brothers in three major settlements and other individual settlements. The third settlement, announced in May 2013, consolidated cases against the Christian Brothers in Canada and in 17 states in the United States. Some 100 plaintiffs in this settlement had been Mount Cashel residents before 1962. In February 2014, a retired judge determined the distribution of individual amounts in the third settlement (Sweet, 2014). The average payment was lower than the previous two settlements.[9] *Mount Cashel* has run for 25 years, since the government's response in 1989, and litigation continues.

For *Alberta Sterilization*, following the *Muir* judgment in January 1996, a significant number of claims was filed against the province, alleging involuntary sterilization, and when relevant, wrongful confinement. These were settled in four ways: by Public Trustee, negotiation, Settlement Panel, and the Stratton Agreement. The process began with the appointment of a Public Trustee in December 1996 to handle the claims of dependent adults, and it ended in November 1999 with the Stratton Agreement. Settlements were reached with an estimated 900 individuals, and published figures are reported for 881 individuals. I present all outcomes without deductions for legal fees and costs.

For the *Public Trustee*, 504 claims were settled at a total cost of 'about $48 million' (Alberta Government, 1998a). Payments ranged between $75,000 and $100,000. I estimate that each person received, on average, $95,000. For *negotiation*, by October 1998, 40 claims were settled at a total cost of about $4 million (Alberta Government, 1998b). I estimate that each person received, on average, $95,000. For the *Settlement Panel*, 91 claims were settled for an estimated cost of $8.4 million (Alberta Government, 1999).[10] I estimate that each person received, on average, $92,300. In light of what could have been paid (up to $150,000 and an additional $150,000 for more serious cases), this average seems low.[11]

In June 1999, the Honourable Joseph Stratton was retained by the province to resolve the outstanding cases with the Plaintiffs' Committee, which coordinated negotiations on behalf of 38 law firms, who represented nearly 250 clients. A total of 246 claims was settled at a cost of $82 million. The agreement also resulted in discontinuing 'one trial that had 17 test case plaintiffs selected by the court in consultation with lawyers for the plaintiffs and the government' (Faulds, personal communication, 16 July 2013). Based on the numbers reported, each litigant received, on average, $333,333. This average is higher than the previous settlements in this case because claimants were not considered 'dependent adults' and they had 'a greater awareness of the fact that they had been sterilized' (Faulds, personal communication, 16 July 2013), which would have translated to a higher injury award. Furthermore, these claimants had a stronger claim of having been wrongfully confined.

IHRD (1998, pp. 102–5) carried out interviews with *Alberta Sterilization* non-dependent survivors before their cases had been settled. The major themes were that survivors were not litigating for financial outcomes, but wanted the government to admit it had 'done wrong and that they shouldn't have been abused and institutionalized'. They wanted 'recognition and normalization' (p. 103). Almost all were 'upset by the delays', and blamed the government and court for these; most said 'the government cannot be trusted'. The litigation process 'stirred up old feelings and memories about their abuse', with 'recurring flashbacks and nightmares as memories surfaced'. However, none regretted participating in civil litigation (p. 104). Although many said they did not need counselling, they felt that the government should have offered free counselling. It would have been fascinating to know their views after their cases had been finalized.

Other civil settlements

In addition to the two cases above, along with *Jericho Hill Class Action* and *Indian Residential Schools*, four others had settlements of 70 or more plaintiffs: *George Epoch*, *Queensland Institutions*, *Child Migrants*, and *South Australian Institutions*.[12] For *George Epoch*, there were, at a minimum, 81 claims related to Epoch's offending that were settled in the 1990s and early 2000s. About half of the litigants had also received payments from the redress scheme (Donald McLean, personal communication, 30 April 2013). For *Queensland Institutions*, the Neerkol Action Support Group (St Joseph's Orphanage) settled with the Sisters of Mercy and Rockhampton Catholic Diocese in 1999. The number of former residents is variously given as 70 to 80, depending on the source. Payments ranged from $2,000 to $25,000 (Broken Rites, 2013). For *Child Migrants*, several hundred members settled with the Christian Brothers, who operated institutions in Western Australia. A Reconciliation Trust Fund was established in 1996; payments of $4,000 to $25,000 were made to those who alleged sexual abuse and 'could document serious psychological difficulties' (Senate Report, 2001, p. 224). Of 263 individuals, 223 agreed to the settlement (Gill, 1997, p. 659). The Senate Report (2001, p. 224) said that the Western Australian advocacy group, VOICES, 'encouraged its members to accept the settlement but without any sense of gratitude... One former Child Migrant stated that many felt betrayed by the... settlement and a justice system which proved unsympathetic'. For *South Australian Institutions*, the South Australia Attorney General (2013, p. 22) said that 158 civil cases had been filed on behalf of residents in state care for sexual, physical, and other abuses; and of these, 131 had been settled.

Adjusting payments for inflation and currencies

Most Canadian redress scheme payments were in claimants' hands during 1995 to 2006, whereas all Australian payments were received after 2006. Thus, payment amounts need to be adjusted for inflation. To assist readers familiar with other currencies, average amounts for redress scheme payments are shown in US Dollars, Euros, and British pounds in Appendix 3C. In Table 6.2, average payments, adjusted for inflation, are presented in the same manner as Table 6.1.

How adjustments and exchange rates were calculated

The Gross Domestic Product (GDP) price deflator was used to adjust for inflation. This measure is preferable to the Consumer Price Index (CPI) because it reflects the prices of all goods and services produced within a country, whereas the CPI reflects the prices of a representative basket of goods and services purchased by consumers. The computational steps were as follows. First, I brought the average payment values for Canada from the year they were received to 2012, using the GDP deflator for Canada. Likewise, I brought the average payment values for Australia from the year they were received to 2012, using the GDP deflator for Australia. Values in Canadian dollars were computed in Australian dollars, using the interbank exchange rate (bid rate) in 2012. Currency conversion was then carried out from Australian dollars to US Dollars, Euros, and British pounds, using 2012 exchange rates.

Adjusted money outcomes

Readers can inspect Appendix 3C for specific values. For redress schemes, the values of particular interest are those for which the money logic is individualized and capped. The average gap between the Canadian and Australian payments (unadjusted and in local currency) was more than $10,000 (CAD $33,404 and AUD $20,962) (see Table 6.1). However, the gap doubles when adjusting for inflation in 2012. The average gap in 2012 AUD dollars is just over $22,600. The relevant averages are AUD $45,766 for the six Canadian cases and AUD $23,130 for the five Australian cases (see Table 6.2). Thus, Canadian redress schemes have been more generous in their average financial payments. The highest average payment, adjusted and in 2012 AUD, is $97,474 for Canada (*Indian Residential Schools*, IAP) and $67,073 for Australia (*Tasmanian Stolen Generations*).

Not shown in Appendix 3C, I can report that the *Mount Cashel* settlement average, which was $261,628 in 1997 (before legal fees, in local currency) is $360,333, adjusting for inflation and in 2012 AUD. Likewise, for *Alberta Sterilization*, the settlement average for those in the Stratton Agreement, which was $333,333 in 2000 (before legal fees, in local currency) is $435,171, adjusting for inflation and 2012 AUD. These are likely to be among the highest publicly known average payments for group civil settlements in cases of institutional abuse (*Mount Cashel*) or policy wrongs and abuse (*Alberta Sterilization*).

Public inquiry cases

The three Australian Commonwealth cases – *Stolen Generations*, *Child Migrants*, and *Forgotten Australians* – had no financial payments to survivors. However, funds have been (and continue to be) directed to services, and for *Child Migrants*, travel benefits.

For *Stolen Generations*, the Commonwealth response to *Bringing Them Home* was to put forward a $63 million package over 4 years in 'practical assistance' measures. These were services to assist in family reunions and to provide counselling, health, and parenting services (detail of commitments by the Commonwealth and state governments is given in a 2003 report by the Ministerial Council for Aboriginal and Torres Strait Island Affairs [MCATSIA]). In addition, an oral history project was funded (1998–2002) that included the experiences not only of members of the Stolen Generations, but also of non-Indigenous people who worked in missions and homes. In 2001–02, $53.8 million was allocated over 4 years to support family tracing and reunion services, along with

Table 6.2 Average payment (mean) received by money logic: unadjusted in local currency and adjusted for inflation using GDP deflator and in Australian dollars 2012 bolded

money logic	all (N = 19)	Canada (N = 12)	Australia (N = 7)
individualized, high			
mean (unadjusted, local currency)		$100,530	
mean (adjusted, AUD 2012)		**$97,474**	
case name		Indian Residential Schools, IAP	
individualized, capped or restricted			
mean (unadjusted, local currency)	$27,749	$33,404	$20,962
mean (adjusted, AUD 2012)	**$35,477**	**$45,766**	**$23,130**
case names		St John's & St Joseph's, Grandview, Nova Scotia Institutions, Ontario Schools for the Deaf, Jericho Hill-JICP, New Brunswick Institutions	Queensland Institutions, levels 1& 2 combined; Tasmanian Institutions, phases 1–3, phase 4; South Australian Institutions, Redress WA
equal fixed or flat			
mean (unadjusted, local currency)	$14,250	$16,667	$7,000
mean (adjusted, AUD 2012)	**$17,357**	**$20,589**	**$7,662**
case names		George Epoch; Jericho Hill Class Action, level 1; Duplessis Orphans, time 2	Queensland Institutions, level 1
equal, other formula			
mean (unadjusted, local currency)	$34,484	$22,560	$58,333
mean (adjusted, AUD 2012)	**$39,892**	**$26,301**	**$67,073**
case names		Duplessis Orphans, time 1; Indian Residential Schools, CEP	Tasmanian Stolen Generations

education, training, counselling, and parenting services. From 2007, the Commonwealth continued to fund services, allocating $25 million per year in 2008 to 2010 for Bringing Them Home counsellors and family reunion services (National Sorry Day Committee, 2013). A joint federal–state initiative, *Closing the Gap*, which began in 2008, has created and consolidated many programs for promoting social and economic well-being of Aboriginal and Torres Strait Islander (see review by the Closing the Gap Clearinghouse [2013]); these programs are in addition to educational, housing, and employment programs.

For *Child Migrants*, three funds have been created over time to support reunion travel, each with differing criteria. The first, established by the British Government (1999–2002) with £1 million in funds, was highly restrictive. The travel had to be for a first-time visit to the United Kingdom; to a mother, father, or other close relative; and no reverse travel was permitted. The second, established by the Australian Government for 3 years (2002–05), with $5,500,000 in funds, had more relaxed criteria in that there was greater flexibility in who could be visited and carers' travel was supported. The third, the Family Restoration Fund, was announced by the British Government in 2010, as part of its apology to Child Migrants and their families, with a commitment of £6 million. The Child Migrant Trust (CMT) manages this scheme; it aims to create a more caring response, which is 'built around the psychological and medical needs of Child Migrants and does not re-traumatise' them (CMT spokesperson, personal communication, 15 March 2013). It has more relaxed criteria for travel than the previous two. For example, it does not matter whether a former Child Migrant has visited the United Kingdom before with support from previous schemes, they can visit from throughout the world, carers are again included, and there is more generous support for class of travel (if required). Between the end of the Australian travel scheme in 2005 and the start of the British scheme in 2010, there was no support for reunion travel.

In the decade preceding the Senate's Child Migrants inquiry, the CMT had received support from the British Government and local councils, and from the Australian Commonwealth and several states for specialist tracing services, counselling, and office staff support (see Gill, 1997, p. 502). In the Australian Government's response to the Senate Report (2001), an allocation of $125,000 was made for each of 3 years (2002–05), which increased to $150,000 in each of the next 7 years (2005–12), for a total of $1,425,000. From the CMT's perspective, the government's initial allocation was 'too half-hearted in tone and spirit' and 'did not seek to assume its full and proper responsibility for the many adverse consequences' of the federally approved policies (Senate Report, 2009, p. 8). In 2011, the Australian Government commitment to the CMT increased, with a total of $550,000 allocated in that year and in 2012. The annual allocation provides professional services as part of Find & Connect (described below). Except for the availability of travel funds to former Child Migrants, *Child Migrants* and *Forgotten Australians* are now viewed as one group with respect to government services.

For *Forgotten Australians*, in 2005, as part of the Commonwealth's response, $1.105 million was provided to Adult Learning Australia for adult learning; $100,000, to the advocacy group, Care Leavers of Australia Network (CLAN) for counselling support; $100,000 to other support groups; and up to $100,000 for memorials (Australian Government, 2005, pp. 10–17). The Alliance for Forgotten Australians, a national group of organizations and individuals, was established in 2006 with Commonwealth support. Funding became more generous, with a change of government in 2007. Find & Connect Support Services was established in 2010 with funding of $26.5 million. It provides information on family tracing, personal records, counselling, and other supports for all those placed in Australian orphanages, children's homes, and other institutions. As of September 2013, support services were available in all the states and territories. In addition, the Find & Connect web resource contains historical information on institutional care of children in Australia. First released in November 2011, the website was redesigned and launched in 2013. It was developed by 'a team of historians, archivists, and social workers from the University of Melbourne and Australian Catholic University' (Find & Connect, 2014) and will be 'enriched and expanded until the end of 2014'. This website contains 'information that is relevant to anyone who experienced out-of-home "care" in Australia, not only the Forgotten Australians and Former Child Migrants, but also members of the Stolen Generations, foster children, wards of the state and adopted children'. It is also an excellent resource for researchers.

Apologies and memorialization

Returning now to all 19 cases, Appendix 4 details public apologies that were given by governments and churches, and Appendix 5, memorialization and commemorative activities.

Public apologies vary in the depth and sincerity of the words used. Some government and church officials expressed 'sincere regret' and others gave a more fulsome apology. Analyzing apology texts is beyond the scope of my research. While I recognize that survivors 'hear' and receive apologies in different ways, I do not pursue this important line of analysis. For the 15 redress schemes, sincere public apologies were given by government officials in ten. There were two expressions of 'regret' in *Jericho Hill*.[13] For the remaining three cases, in one (*George Epoch*), the apology came from the church, and no government entity was responsible; and for two, I could find no evidence of a public apology (*Ontario Schools for the Deaf* and *New Brunswick Institutions*). In addition to public apologies, private apologies, in the form of letters written to survivors, were part of some schemes; but these are not listed in Appendix 4 because such information is not available for all the cases.

For the five cases without redress schemes, apologies were given by government officials in the three Australian cases (*Stolen Generations, Child Migrants, Forgotten Australians*); however, in the two Canadian cases, there was no government apology (*Mount Cashel*), or the government issued a 'statement of regret' (*Alberta Sterilization*). Apologies by churches were relevant for 13 of the 19 cases; and all gave sincere apologies. Of interest, churches were more quick to apologize than governments; in 11 cases for which there were government and church apologies (or a statement of regret), churches were the first to apologize in eight; and for two, the government and church apologized at around the same time; in just one case the government apologized before the church (*Duplessis Orphans*) (Appendix 3A).

Varied types of memorials (plaques, plinths, sculptures, statues, installations, garden designs) have been created (Appendix 5). Of the 15 redress schemes, two in Canada have memorials (*Jericho Hill Class Action* and *Indian Residential Schools*), as do four in Australia (*Queensland, Tasmanian,* and *South Australian Institutions*; *Redress WA*). For the five cases without redress schemes, all but one (*Alberta Sterilization*) have memorials. However, *Alberta Sterilization* has significant memory projects: a multi-sited university oral history project, *Living Archives on Eugenics in Western Canada*, and a documentary and play about Lelani Muir (see Appendix 6). In addition to commemoration, other types of memory projects feature in *Indian Residential Schools* (the TRC's document recovery and statement gathering, oral history projects, and a National Research Centre); *Stolen Generations* (oral history projects); and *Child Migrants* and *Forgotten Australians* (oral history project and museum installation). The latter four cases also hold annual remembrance days, typically marking the anniversaries of national apologies. Appendices 5 and 6 describe these and provide links to images of memorials and commemorative activities, which overlap with other media and memory projects.

Memorials, commemorative activities, and media and memory projects have a variety of objectives and functions. They seek to remember, validate, and vindicate victims. They encourage new formats for victim 'voice' and new ways to communicate experiences of institutional abuse. They promote new relational histories of institutional abuse and policy wrongs that include survivors, officials and carers, and societal 'on-lookers'. They bring an understanding of institutional abuse to a wider audience of new participants (family members of survivors and other society members), and they celebrate the potential for individual, communal, and societal change.

Redress outcomes: a wrap up

Redress is a broad and abstract term; but when learning about the actual outcomes of redress schemes, civil litigation, and public inquiries in these 19 cases, redress becomes more concrete. Redress schemes provide financial payments, benefits, and services to claimants, as well as apologies, memorials, and related activities that affect not only claimants, but also a wider public. Litigation provides financial payments, but unless it is a structured redress package with many elements, outcomes are limited largely to financial payments, although they may include apologies, memorials, and related activities. Public inquiry cases without financial payments instead provided services, as well as apologies, memorials, and related activities directed to survivors and a wider audience. These three outcome modalities emerge from the 19 cases.

Is one better than another? What would be the basis for deciding?

For litigation, reported financial outcomes were higher for successful civil litigants in Canada than in Australia. For redress schemes, financial payments were also higher in Canada than Australia. Among the Canadian cases, there is a substantial gap in financial payments from civil settlements and redress schemes, as we would expect. By contrast, among the Australian cases, the gap is small to non-existent. I cannot explain these differences, but observe that the average payments in the two Australian civil cases for which information exists (Neerkol in *Queensland Institutions* and *Child Migrants* in Western Australia) were low, with both no higher than $25,000. The outcomes were negotiated with church, not government entities. The two structured settlements arising from civil litigation, *Jericho Hill Class Action* and *Indian Residential Schools*, offered the largest package of outcomes. This suggests that when faced with significant civil liability, governments (and where relevant, church entities) will come to the negotiation table with a greater degree of responsiveness to survivors. This is not always the case, however, when we consider *Tasmanian Stolen Generations*, which did not arise from a significant press of civil litigation.

In Australia, redress for institutional abuse (and related policy wrongs) began with public inquiries. Government and victim advocacy groups seem to favour this start point; and it has produced a number of significant reports, which have gathered primary material on the memories and experiences of care leavers and survivors. The process of participating in an inquiry can also be cathartic for some. However, what happens after reports are tabled and recommendations are made? The trilogy of Commonwealth inquiries has produced services and supports for victims and a plethora of apologies, along with memorials, commemorative activities, and memory projects. For *Child Migrants*, family reunion travel grants have also been offered. However, there remains unfinished business: all advocacy groups for *Stolen Generations*, *Child Migrants*, and *Forgotten Australians* have argued for a national approach to redress, which includes financial payments.

Redress schemes in the four states vary in the level of average payments and eligibility criteria. Of the four, South Australia has been the least generous, especially when considering that *ex gratia* payments are for sexual abuse and the number of claimants is low. It is not surprising that South Australian survivors have been as likely to pursue redress by civil litigation (158 claims as of June 2013) as by the redress scheme (163 applications, 129 of which have been resolved as of 30 July 2014) (South Australia Attorney General, personal communication, 14 August 2014). Survivors are also rational actors! Peter Humphries, a lawyer representing many survivors, is opposed to the state's current redress scheme, saying 'it was doomed to fail and it did. There was no transparency…You simply put your documents into some office and eventually a number was spat out' (*The World Today*, 2012). In South Australia, civil litigation may be a better bet than the current redress scheme.[14] By comparison, the two Tasmanian schemes (*Tasmanian Stolen Generations* and *Tasmanian Institutions* [phases 1–3]) have been the most generous, with financial payments comparable to those in the Canadian individualized and capped schemes. If you were abused in state care in Tasmania, the *Tasmanian Institutions* scheme (phases 1–3) was a better bet (if money were the main criterion), compared to other Australian schemes.

The significant contribution of this chapter has been to show concretely what the average financial payments were in 15 redress schemes in two countries and the different types of money logics used. More generally, it shows what elements have been, and can be, part of redress schemes and packages. Without such evidence and clarity (which needs to be assembled for redress schemes in other countries), advocacy groups, policymakers, and other key actors will be groping in the dark to create redress schemes. At the same time, governments, churches, and insurers must provide detailed evidence on financial outcomes of redress schemes and civil settlements. Without a full picture of what has occurred (and is occurring), advocacy groups, members of the general public, among others, are ill-informed. Effective redress today requires not only 'truth' about past institutional abuse, but also 'truth' about what the past responses have been. Redress is, of course, more than outcomes. It is also about the processes of redress and the ways in which claimants, decision-makers, and responsible governments, churches, and charitable organizations participate in the process.

Public inquiries, civil litigation, and redress schemes all have a role in responding to institutional abuse, along with criminal prosecution. Thus, picking one of these justice mechanisms over another is not sensible. However, we may go some way to answering, 'what would be the basis for deciding which is better?' by using the construct of victims' justice interests in analyzing survivors' experiences seeking redress, which is the subject of the next chapter.

7
Redress and Victims' Justice Interests

Multiple realities

Reality 1

As part of the Forde inquiry in Queensland in 1998–99, witnesses were asked, 'what would you like to see come out of the inquiry'? Replies are listed for 79 individuals (Forde, 1999, appendix 12).[1] When reading them, I was struck that most replies were future oriented, for example:

- That it cannot happen today.
- I don't want to see any kid go through what I went through.
- A better deal for the kids. Changes in the homes – you know, a better life than what I had.
- I do believe that people need to be trained.
- I'd like to see laws passed that the individual be charged, not being able to hide behind who they work for or institutions they work for.
- One of the ideas I did have was something like... what I would call a preventative unit.

Over 60 per cent of the responses were like this. A smaller number (about 20 per cent) wanted 'recognition' of the abuse or 'the truth' to be known, for example:

- I'd like to see it all come out in the open.
- It's just to let everyone know that it did happen.
- Make it clear that these places did exist. People will know that it did happen.
- I'd just like people to know more about the truth, what happened in these institutions.

Another 11 per cent mentioned 'accountability' or 'justice':

- I want to know what will happen to the nuns and priest that are still alive from the home... I want to know if something can be done about that.
- I hope those people get charged, but some of them are probably 70- or 80-odd.
- Those people that knew they were doing wrong to face themselves... It won't be stopped until everyone is held accountable.
- I just want justice.

Five others mentioned things that would help them such as counselling, and one combined recognition, accountability, financial accountability, voice, and validation:

> I hope it achieves public recognition of the full extent, the treatment of us girls, and that they are held accountable, both publicly and financially to the girls... The Inquiry... [has] opened a door for us, that we don't have to keep the secret any longer... The girls who have come forward feel their efforts were heard and listened to, and validated,... and that alone has made a big difference for us.

Only one of 79 replies mentioned money, and the fact that the person said 'these victims are entitled' makes me think that s/he was not a former resident:

- I still do believe that these victims are entitled to compensation.

Reality 2

In December 2010, the Queensland Department of Communities commissioned a survey by RPR Consulting of Forgotten Australians, who had been residents in Queensland institutions for children. It focused on current circumstances, whether current services met their needs, and their priorities for future services. There were 603 completed surveys. One set of questions asked respondents to tick a box if 'any of the services or activities' on the list was helpful. The two most frequently ticked items were 'getting a payment from the government or past providers for past abuse' (59 per cent) and 'getting an apology from the government or past providers' (44 per cent) (Watson, 2011, p. 37). The next most frequently ticked item was 'seeing a counsellor face-to-face' (30 per cent). The author concluded 'the overall pattern is clear: what has been of central importance for Forgotten Australians is receiving a payment and an apology' (p. 40).

Reality 3

At the end of the RPR survey was an open-ended question that asked whether 'there are any other issues which are important to you about future services...' In reply, a dominant theme was that 'the redress system was unfair'. Except for one positive comment, all were negative about the redress scheme. The following examples are taken from Watson (2011, p. 76) and preserve the style of the writer:

- I am damaged and the Paltry sum of 20,000 doesn't provide a home. We should have received Millions for what happened to us. I will never improve. So what is your purpose.
- The compensation offered by the Qld Govt. was an insult that was not worth applying for. It forced applicants to relive the experiences for a paltry amount. I did not apply. Personally, I do not know how you repair a life or compensate for it.
- I think the redress was unfair I can't read + write good + didn't know about it.

The three realities suggest that no one 'reality' can easily capture care leavers' and survivors' experiences with and aspirations for justice, even when we restrict ourselves to a particular state, and its inquiry and redress scheme. Reality 1 suggests that most were interested in future outcomes, in particular, a better life for other children than theirs had been and ways to prevent abuse in residential care. The RPR survey shows that receiving a payment and an apology were by far the most helpful activities, but the survey's open-ended portion suggests a sense of injustice with the redress scheme. All of these are 'true', but they do not coalesce into one truth. Survivors' views may change over time, and they are sensitive to the questions asked, and to when and where the questions are asked (that is, to question context).

State of evidence

Social science research on institutional abuse and justice is scant. Few studies of survivors exist, and sample sizes are small and self-selected. This translates to an inability to generalize. Using the example above, we may be a bit more confident generalizing from realities 1 or 2 than reality 3. Reality 1 has 79 people replying to the same question, but we are not told how many could have been asked, nor the context of the question; reality 2 has a high number of respondents (although self-selected), but the data seem decisive. Reality 3 may reflect a self-selected set of claimants who chose to write negatively about redress payments.

Justice experiences evolve and change, and a redress process itself can mould claimants' accounts. For example, Rodney Hunt, who interviewed *Jericho Hill*-JICP claimants in a study with others (Battersby, Greaves, and Hunt, 2008) told me he observed a 'staggering consistency' in the responses. The interviews were carried out before the class action settlement was announced. Hunt said 'the language and processes of the JICP and the class action were central in shaping how claimants made sense of their experiences'(Hunt, personal communication, 28 March 2014); in particular, the legal construction of the case had created a 'standardized *victim discourse* [and] a consistent and uniform *story*' (Battersby et al., 2008, p. 114, emphasis in original). Another element is the degree of interaction and cohesiveness among claimants. When it is high, we may expect that their accounts will sound similar.

When a study is carried out is important. In some cases, research was conducted mid-way into a redress scheme. For example, Leach (1997) interviewed *Grandview* survivors from July 1996 to March 1997 before the adjudication process was completed; and Henton and McCann (1995) analyzed outcomes for *St John's and St Joseph's* up to mid-1995, when outcomes continued to 1997. Research by IHRD (Institute for Human Resource Development) was able to describe experiences of process and outcomes of survivors in *Mount Cashel, Grandview*, and *Nova Scotia Institutions*, but its interviews of those in other cases (*Alberta Sterilization* and *Duplessis Orphans*) were too early to capture outcomes.

More research on survivors' experiences of redress for institutional abuse comes from Canada than Australia; thus, for Australia, I summarize what is known from public inquiries, news stories, and other sources (for example, Hil and Branigan, 2011; Penglase, 2005). Within the limits of available evidence, I assess survivors' experiences with public inquiries and redress schemes through the lens of victims' justice interests.

Victims' justice interests: engaging all the elements

In Chapter 5, I introduced victims' justice interests and applied one element – participation – to advocacy groups' roles in designing redress schemes and desired outcomes. In this chapter, I analyze other activities associated with redress: public inquiries, the redress scheme application and validation process, and financial and other outcomes. Participation, voice, validation, vindication, and offender accountability may be present in one or more of these activities.

Participation

Recapping the modified definition of participation, it is being informed of options and developments in a case, including different types of justice mechanisms available; active participation in shaping the elements of redress, including optimal modes of implementation; being informed of negotiations and having a say (or vote) in ratifying a redress scheme (or settlement agreement); and understanding how the process works.

Voice

The *generic definition* of voice is telling the story of what happened and its impact in a significant setting, where a victim or survivor can receive public recognition and acknowledgement. Voice is also termed truth-telling and is related to participation in having a speaking or other physical presence in a justice process. To be relevant to institutional contexts of victimization and redress, I would *modify* this by adding the following: voice can be present in a range of texts and formats, but may be variably preserved and accessible.

The *generic* definitions of validation, vindication, and offender accountability can be applied without modification.

Validation

Validation is affirming that the victim is believed (that is, acknowledging that offending occurred and the victim was harmed) and is not blamed for or thought to be deserving of what happened. It reflects a victim's desire to be believed and to shift the weight of the accusation from his or her shoulders to others (family members, a wider social group, or legal officials). Admissions by a perpetrator, although perhaps desirable to a victim, may not be necessary to validate their claim.

Vindication

Vindication has two aspects: vindication of the law (affirming *the act* was wrong, morally and legally) and vindication of the victim (affirming a *perpetrator's actions* against the victim were wrong). It requires that others (family members, a wider social group, legal officials) do something to show that an act (or actions) were wrong by, for example, censuring the offence and affirming their solidarity with a victim or survivor. It can be expressed in symbolic and material forms of reparation (for example, apologies, memorialization, financial assistance) and standard forms of state punishment.

Offender accountability

Offender accountability is requiring that certain individuals or entities give accounts for their actions. It refers to perpetrators of offences taking active responsibility for the wrong caused, to give sincere expressions of regret and remorse, and to receive censure or sanction that may vindicate the law and a victim.

I turn next to three major activities: public inquiries, redress scheme process, and redress outcomes.

Public inquiries

Once an inquiry has been announced, survivors' oral and written testimonies can be brought forward and acknowledged, lending weight to claims for justice. The 'voices' of abuse experiences and impact are public stories, which survivors want to see placed on 'an official record' (Senate Report, 2001, p. 5). The goals of creating 'an official record' can be realized only if submissions to public inquiries are preserved and readily accessible.

Forgotten Australians and *Mount Cashel*: stark differences

Two years before the announcement of the Senate inquiry on Forgotten Australians, Leonie Sheedy and Joanna Penglase, co-founders of the Care Leavers Association Network (CLAN), participated in a hearing at the Child Migrants inquiry. They wanted the senators to know about their experiences and those of many others, who grew up in children's institutions in Australia. Penglase (National Museum of Australia, 2012) recalled:

> We were so nervous. Those five Senators looked at us expectantly, and we told them. It was extraordinary. They were glued to us. They didn't know the history. They kept asking these questions.... and Senator Andrew Murray, a Democrat from Western Australia, kept asking 'But how many people, thousands?' We looked at each other, 'tens of thousands, maybe hundreds of thousands'. That's how little we knew then.

Penglase recalls that by the end of the day, 'we were so high... We were so excited because that was an experience so unusual. We were heard. They listened. They believed us. That's what we're so used to not having: being believed'. *We were heard, they listened, they believed us*: these sentences crystallize voice and validation.

In January 2002, Senator Murray's policy advisor rang the CLAN office, saying that the Senator was 'determined to get up the third inquiry in the trilogy. We've had the Stolen Generation inquiry; we've had the Child Migrant inquiry; we will now have children in institutionalised care'. The Senator wanted to know, 'will you help us? Will you help me get that inquiry up?' Penglase and Sheedy were delighted to take up the offer. CLAN lobbied politicians to vote for an inquiry, and it passed in Parliament in March 2003. Here, then, is a clear illustration of victim group participation in the mobilization of a public inquiry.

Penglase continues. 'And so we had our inquiry. It reported 30 August 2004, a wonderful day. All of us who were there have an absolutely indelible memory of it' (National Museum of Australia, 2012). In 2005, Penglase had published a book on children's homes and adult survivors' memories of them. In it, she said,

> It would be impossible to exaggerate what *Forgotten Australians* means to care leavers. We have been waiting all our lives for this recognition, for something that would take the place of the denial and disbelief we are all so used to hearing. ... The Senate Inquiry marks a turning point: we can finally see and understand our individual histories within their social and political contexts. *Forgotten Australians* confirms what we have always felt and tried for so long to tell others: that our childhood in 'care' scarred us for life. (Penglase, 2005, p. 31)

In addition to 'this recognition' (which I interpret to mean both validation and vindication), Penglase points to a transformed understanding of care leavers' identities, when individual histories ('personal troubles') are made 'public issues' (Mills, 1959). This transformation affects not only care leavers, but a broader public, who becomes aware of the histories of institutional life and their impact. Penglase (2005, p. 339) concludes that the Senate's Report (2004) was significant because 'this history that we have experienced is *now on the public record*, for all to read and understand' (emphasis added).

By contrast, the Hughes inquiry in *Mount Cashel* was received less positively by survivors. It centred on investigating the police and prosecutorial handling of complaints of abuse in the 1970s; its terms of reference were more narrowly framed, and its practices seemed stacked against former residents. One survivor, Darren Connors, was not permitted to testify because he had not lodged a complaint in the 1975 investigation. This devastated him:

> I felt that I had the right to tell my story. They said that what I had to say was irrelevant. I felt that it was relevant. I felt I had to tell my story in order to get it off my chest, and this was the only chance I had to tell it. (Harris, 1990, p. 322)

Connors' situation arose when counsel for the defendants objected to former residents naming individuals, who were currently before the criminal courts. However, other former residents had been permitted to testify, who were in a similar situation as Connors; thus, there was a sense of unfairness to the proceedings. According to Harris (1990, p. 321), after Connors left the hearing room, 'he told reporters that his faith in the justice system had been destroyed for the second time'. Another problem was that although survivors were 'called time and time again to give evidence, senior members of the Christian Brothers and [justice department] were not asked to reappear'. Eight brothers whose cases were then before the court 'were never called as witnesses'; as a consequence, there was a 'sense of incompletion hanging over the proceedings, of dire and unfinished business that would only be cleared up' after the trials were concluded (pp. 365–6). Shane Earle said that the inquiry left him 'somewhat discouraged' because

> ...I don't know. I just figure some of the key witnesses were given an easy ride, and others weren't questioned enough, and others were there just for appearance and that was it. That was discouraging. The system is definitely not equal...(Harris, 1990, p. 379)

Connors was denied a chance to participate and to tell his story (voice); and for both Connors and Earle, the proceedings lacked fairness and offender accountability. Indeed, the former residents, not the Christian Brothers, seemed to be held to 'account'. IHRD (1998, p. 72) identified similar themes in their interviews with *Mount Cashel* survivors: some were denied voice ('victims told of being cut off by the judge, who said they were repeating themselves, and he had heard enough'), and there were general perceptions of unfairness ('victims felt that the inquiry treated others...in a different and better manner....They felt they were treated like offenders'). Some did not want to participate in the process, but 'felt they had no choice but to get involved...Some thought that if they did not agree to participate, they would get a subpoena' (p. 72).

The Hughes inquiry was televized, and this affected victims' experiences and relationships with members of the public. In his autobiography, Dereck O'Brien (1991) described how he was affected by taking the stand at the inquiry. Although Commission lawyers had given him a general idea of what to expect, he said, 'I really didn't know what I would say…Then the questions came and with them, my memories. It was like an out-of-body experience…Feelings and experiences came rushing back, and I was overwhelmed' (p. 159). It was after the hearings were over, when he began receiving phone calls and letters that he realized the enormity of what he had said. 'As soon as I hung up from one call, it would ring again':

> …People wanted to know how I ever got through it all without going crazy…Many phone calls were calls for help. People called to tell me things that they've never entrusted to another living soul. I heard countless tales of sexual, mental, and physical abuse. (p. 160)

He received letters 'from all over Canada, telling me that testifying was the right thing to do and that I should keep my head high. They said it was about time the system was stopped in its tracks…' He had no idea 'how important the whole event was to people, or how much impact it would have' (p. 163). O'Brien's participation in 'bringing the story to light' was a source of validation and vindication for him, which he had not expected. Others said, however, that the proceedings were 'too public. It should have been done privately between judges, victims and offenders.…The media blew it out of proportion and made into a circus' (IHRD, 1998, p. 15). The IHRD concluded that most survivors 'were dissatisfied with the outcome. They felt it changed very little except maybe public awareness. Many of them felt it put them on display' (p. 72). Two interviewees chose not to participate in the inquiry, and 'after the fact, they were glad they did not participate' (p. 72). In addition to O'Brien, another positive voice thought that 'some good' had come out of the inquiry:

> it seems as though progress is being made. Already it's out in the open now so it's something that the Catholic Church has to face and deal with, as well as the Congregation of Irish Christian Brothers, and Newfoundlanders for that matter. (Harris, 1990, p. 377)

To say that something is 'out in the open' means that survivors' claims were validated, and to say it is something the 'Church has to face and deal with' means a measure of offender accountability.

The differences between the two inquiries are stark, and they can be traced to the different purposes of each. Whereas the former invited and welcomed knowledge about the experiences of those in institutional care in Australia, the latter was investigating whether a government department interfered with a police investigation and whether the boys at Mount Cashel school had been physically and sexually abused. The former sought the participation and voice of survivors, and its published report validated their experiences. By contrast, the Hughes inquiry may have provided a degree of victim voice, and for survivors like O'Brien, validation and vindication from members of the Canadian public, but the process sought to 'test' victims' stories more than listen to them.

Redress scheme process

In seeking financial payments and benefits from a redress scheme, survivors typically go through two steps: complete an application form, and depending on the scheme, answer further questions about their claim.[2]

Application process: forms, feelings, and delay

Applying to a redress scheme requires an ability to understand what information is required and how the overall process works. The process of filling out a form can create emotional difficulties, when claimants relive memories of what happened to them. It may also strain relationships with family members or partners who 'do not want to stir up old issues' (IHRD, 1998, p. 90). Victims' justice interests of participation and validation can be undermined.

Grandview provides insight into temporal differences in claimants' knowledge of a scheme. According to IHRD (1998, p. 89) the second group of claimants, those who had applied after the first deadline, had 'clearer expectations' of the process, including that it would be 'less threatening' than a court process.[3] By comparison, those who were involved 'very early on in the agreement process were the most dissatisfied with the amount and clarity of information they received'. They wanted 'clear, consistent information about options to the agreement, the process itself, how to access benefits, and the limits of the agreement' (p. 91). In addition to clear information, the way it is conveyed was important. For example, *Grandview* survivors 'appreciated... [the] kindness, patience, and empathy' of the administrative staff (p. 90). *Jericho Hill*-JICP claimants had 'feelings of ignorance about what would transpire during the process and how decisions of compensation would be made', one saying 'they should have explained and clarified what the purpose of JICP is, and what our rights are and what we could do, and presented options'(Battersby et al., 2008, pp. 98, 96).

In *Grandview* and *St John's and St Joseph's*, claimants had to apply separately for each type of benefit from an Opportunity Fund, which meant they had to lodge multiple applications with appropriate documentation.[4] According to Leach (1998, p. 29), 'the administrative effort...was high, and the stress for the applicants significant'. In May 1994, the coordinator of Helpline resigned, saying that 'there were too many hoops, too many forms, too many delays'. It was 'proving too much for former wards [of *St John's and St Joseph's*], many of whom had barely a Grade 4 education' (Henton and McCann, 1995, p. 288). The process of implementing the Helpline agreement 'was filled with snags' as the 'other parties in the deal...were obsessed by the cost of the process and seemed to have forgotten what it was all about' (p. 289). The new Helpline leader, Patrick Healey, said 'it needs to be refined so there are less delays. It needs to acknowledge that it is dealing not with numbers but with human beings... [We are not] manufacturing cars here or fixing washing machines' (pp. 287, 289). Several former residents committed suicide because they 'could not cope with the delays in the compensation process' (p. 289).

The application form for *Grandview* attempted to strike a balance between 'elicit[ing] sufficient information to assess a claim [and] respecting the needs of applicants [such as] literacy level and possible impacts of completing the form' (Leach, 1998, p. 24). Despite this, 'some women stated that they found the form difficult to understand and that the process of completing it brought to the surface matters and events that they had not thought about for some time' (Graycar and Wangmann, 2007, p. 16). The following comment by a *Grandview* survivor was particularly incisive (IHRD, 1998, p. 92):

> Although the agreement process was...carefully thought out, it required a fairly high degree of understanding and ability to negotiate the system from survivors. *They treated survivors as if they had never been at Grandview.* All the skills Grandview took away from us were needed to get the most out of the process. (emphasis added)

Likewise, an applicant for the *Indian Residential Schools* Common Experience Payment (CEP) said, 'I can't even read or write. Some of these heavy words [in the CEP application] I couldn't even understand' (Reimer et al., 2010, p. 22). A person who assisted others to complete CEP applications said that

> the forms were difficult for people to complete. It was hard to get [records] because someone burnt [the residential school] down ... so a lot of records were burnt. And when you are in trauma and don't really remember a lot, it is hard to substantiate ... who was there. (p. 69)

Service Canada, who administrated CEP, worked with local Aboriginal Healing Foundation (AHF)-funded projects to assist claimants in completing applications. 'Having the forms notarized and completed at once and in person was helpful for applicants' (p. 65) more so than the CEP Response Centre toll-free lines, for which few participants had anything positive to say. The 'operators were perceived as giving rehearsed answers ... as unhelpful ... and as ill-equipped to provide any real information' (p. 64).

The difficulties completing CEP applications were compounded by the memories the application process evoked. 'Working through the application form was an emotional challenge' (p. 64), particularly without assistance and support. One female survivor wondered, 'Is it really worth it to apply? ... I am unemployed, I am retired, so I told myself it might help'. However, she continued,

> The process was long, very long. I had to write and make phone calls to prove I went to residential school. Nobody was helping and guiding me. Nobody would give me any detail on the type of documents needed ... I had a hard time getting proof of my registration at school ... I am angry about the whole process. It was them who came to get me to go to residential school, and now it was up to me to prove it. (Reimer et al., 2010, p. 64)

After the *Nova Scotia Institutions* redress scheme had been underway for a year, a lawyer for the claimants told government officials that 'their experiences and suffering are being demeaned and devalued by this process.... The participation in the process by itself is, for many survivors, churning up painful memories and the unresolved effects of the abuse' (Kaufman, 2002, p. 169). The same point is made in the Australian Senate Report (2010, p. 22): 'a recurring theme in the submissions related to the pain, shame, and humiliation involved in having to relive their experiences in order to apply for compensation'.

Summing up the redress scheme application process, several messages are clear. When it is 'self-help', without support and guidance, claimants become easily discouraged. Personalized, face-to-face assistance is preferable to a toll-free operator. Participation itself can create emotional turmoil and dredge up bad memories. Complex processes and delays compound the problem. For these reasons, the idea of 'active participation' in a redress scheme and 'understanding how it works' is as much a burden as a 'justice interest' for survivors. This is a point to reflect upon. The ability to participate takes time, resources, mental strength, and knowledge. Such 'knowledge' is not only about the process, but the existence of the redress scheme in the first place. The Senate Report (2010, p. 17) cites several Australian victim advocacy groups who said that survivors were unaware of redress schemes. Some may not be able to read, others were 'hard-to-reach people and families', who were 'socially isolated, [and] not part of community or support groups'. Another said that 'when [learning that] one has missed out on the opportunity for redress is devastating...and leaves victims of abuse feeling worthless'. Thus, to effectively participate, claimants need to be part of community and support groups, who can guide, advise, support, and provide realistic expectations and accurate information for what lies ahead.

Assessment process: investigation and validation

Victims' justice interests in validation – in being believed – are at odds with a 'validation process' that seeks to determine the claimant's eligibility for a redress scheme payment. The Law Commission of Canada (LCC) (2000, p. 112) suggests a need to 'balance interests', but in practice, this can be difficult to achieve. Morley (2001, pp. 31–40), who was chair of the *Jericho Hill*-JICP panel, has considered this dilemma at length, and I cannot do justice to her reflections here. She acknowledges that 'making an objective assessment of what occurred [and] respecting the needs of claimants for confidentiality and validation of their stories [was] a more complex task than was initially envisioned'. Ultimately, the JICP panel's aim was to 'balance its assessment function with the competing principle of minimizing the harm done to claimants' (p. 31).

Redress schemes are in the borderlands of administrative and legal decision-making, and some are more explicitly victim-centred than others. As a consequence, assessment processes varied, as did survivors' experiences with them. My examples come from cases that had oral hearings or where there was information on investigation processes.

Two redress schemes, *St John's and St Joseph's* and *Grandview*, had a great deal of input from advocacy groups, who worked closely with the Ontario Government. According to Kaufman (2002, p. 356), a Ministry of the Attorney General senior staff member said that the 'direct involvement of the advocacy groups with the government promoted a degree of trust and facilitated reconciliation'. Moreover, the advocacy groups 'recognized the detrimental effect that false claims would have on the overall credibility and success of the program...and engaged in some self-regulation or screening of claims brought forward, as did counsel on their behalf'. Validation rates in these schemes were very high: 97 to 98 per cent,[5] and survivors' reports of the oral hearings were uniformly positive. One St Joseph's survivor said:

> The experience of the hearing itself, the fact that I could finally say out loud what I had experienced as a boy and suffered all my life, to a group of people who not only believed what I said, but listened with deep compassion, acted as a tremendous release for me. From that day forward, I began to look at life from a different perspective. I had gained a greater sense of my own worth as a human being and acquired a new sense of self confidence. (Hoffman, 1996, p. 239)

Hoffman, as Recorder for *St John's and St Joseph's*, sat in on many hearings. He made these observations:

> ...When asked by a claimant if the Board is likely to find them valid, an informal indication is sometimes given. When the Board gives such an indication, and throughout the hearing as claimants see they are being listened to with care and objectivity, the experience of 'validation' of a claimant can be observed...To be heard, free of any recrimination, without prejudice, in a supportive manner. This impressed the Recorder as a moment of healing for many claimants. (Hoffman, 1996, p. 259)

The hearings for *St John's and St Joseph's* were held before a 'victim-friendly' Criminal Injuries Compensation Board (CICB), and those for *Grandview* were conducted in a victim-centred manner. The *Grandview* adjudication process was designed to accomplish several goals: a traditional legal goal of 'assessing evidence relating to "validation" and the assessment of quantum of damages', but importantly, from a victim's perspective:

> to offer...an opportunity to describe their experiences in their own words to someone in authority..., to define the wrong that was done to them, to explain the repercussions on their lives, to demand accountability and the restitution of their dignity, and to claim official recognition of injustice. (Grandview Adjudicators, 1998, p. 10)

These goals encapsulate voice ('describe their experiences in their own words [and] define the wrong that was done to them'), vindication ('restitution of their dignity and…claim official recognition of injustice'), and accountability ('demand accountability'). From the perspective of victims' justice interests, they are an ideal script for an oral hearing. As we shall see next, survivors felt validated during the process.

There are many positive quotes from *Grandview* survivors about their experiences with the adjudication process. In studies by Dubinsky (2007), Feldthusen et al. (2000), IHRD (1998), and Leach (1997), the consistency of praise for the adjudication process (with perhaps one or two exceptions) is remarkable. In their comparison of sexual assault survivors' experiences of civil litigation, CICB, and the *Grandview* process, Feldthusen et al. (2000, p. 89) concluded that 'what distinguishes' *Grandview* was 'reactions to the adjudication itself':

> The overwhelming majority…85 per cent, reported feeling comfortable, calm, 'listened to', and 'believed'. Adjudicators were consistently described as respectful, considerate, empathetic, patient, fair, and sincere.

From Leach (1997, p. 31):

> We were allowed to speak freely about what happened. We were able to express our feelings totally without being looked down upon.
>
> I finally felt that I had been acknowledged. I was not bad. There had been something very wrong – this was finally confirmed.

These quotes show respectful and attentive listening by an adjudicator, the ability to tell one's story (voice), being believed (validation), and confirmation that 'something was very wrong' (vindication of the law).

Other aspects of the process were important: all the adjudicators were women, one of whom was Aboriginal, and detailed written reasons were provided for the decision. A high share (88 per cent) of claimants said that having a female adjudicator was very important because most abuse was perpetrated by men; they believed a female adjudicator would 'understand their experiences and feelings', and they would have been uncomfortable discussing offence details with a man (Leach, 1997, pp. 31–2). Aboriginal survivors could use an 'eagle feather instead of a bible as the basis for an oath' and a smudging ceremony at the start of the proceeding, both of which were 'comfort-making to the Aboriginal women' (Aboriginal Adjudicator, 1998, p. 9). The sole Aboriginal adjudicator said that 'some Aboriginal claimants may have been reluctant to tell a non-Aboriginal adjudicator about all of their experiences, especially those involving racism' (p. 3). She also noted that 'initial investigations and written applications portrayed reluctant understatement...when compared to the detail described when they had a full opportunity to speak orally to an Aboriginal adjudicator' (p. 9).

Having written decisions was important because it ratified the claimants' experiences in some detail, using their own words. Written reasons gave a 'detailed narrative account of the incidents of abuse' and their impact, although the adjudicators spent more time on the former because they wanted 'to avoid "freezing" the survivors' lives...or "labelling" a survivor in stereotypical terminology' (Grandview Adjudicators, 1998, p. 16). According to Leach (1997, pp. 35–6) 87 per cent of survivors said that receiving written reasons was very important; one said, it 'was validating and supportive'; and another, 'it was an acknowledgement by the government. It helped me understand why my whole life had gone so wrong'. Written reasons provided vindication of the law; however, as we shall see in the outcomes, *Grandview* survivors were relatively less positive about the level of the financial payment. The full force of vindication may be weakened when a payment is perceived to be too low.

Compared to these generally positive experiences were more negative ones from *Nova Scotia Institutions*. Many claimants had been interviewed three times: first, as part of the Stratton investigation, which was conducted in a victim-friendly manner; second, as part of the Royal Canadian Mounted Police's (RCMP) investigations of accused employees, which was viewed as 'courteous and professional'; and third, by the Internal Investigations Unit (IIU), which survivors judged negatively (Kaufman, 2002, p. 297). About 6 months into the redress program, the more relaxed criteria of assessing applications had given way to closer scrutiny and testing by the IIU of survivors' accounts. The tightening of criteria continued when employees (and their union) said that some claimants were making fraudulent claims. In his review of *Nova Scotia Institutions*, Kaufman (2002, pp. 295–8) interviewed some claimants. One admitted knowing a person who had made a false claim and received a large settlement, which she said, 'ruined the process for people like me who could prove their claim. They weren't listening anymore'. Kaufman (2002, p. 297) said that claimants were 'presumed to be guilty of fraud and not treated with respect. The IIU investigators sought to trip them up on trivial matters'. The interviews of claimants by IHRD (1998, pp. 84–5) were generally negative:

- The ADR [alternative dispute resolution] process was disrespectful ... I felt dirty all over again.
- The ADR was a crock. The politicians were in control, the victims were railroaded, and the lawyers were bullied.
- Government should stick to their commitment and stop changing the rules to suit themselves ... They just did want they wanted.
- One investigator says 'maybe you asked for it'. What 11 year old boy asks to be fondled by a pervert?
- No amount of money would take away the pain and humiliation suffered during this investigation. We didn't get justice. They treated us like shit.

In July 1996, about a year into the process, a lawyer for the victims wrote to the government, saying she was 'gravely concerned about the potential for this process to compound the harm ... on survivors'. She argued that 'the process of resolving ... the claims must be governed ... by the principle of ensuring that survivors feel they are believed, respected, and acknowledged' (Kaufman, 2002, p. 169).

For *Indian Residential Schools*, the validation rate for the CEP was 77 per cent, and Reimer et al. (2010, p. 32) say that over a third of those in their sample 'felt they were not believed in their first application'. Survivors were asked to produce school records, which may have been lost by the government; and the process of proving attendance by alternative means was 'complicated and time-consuming'. Compounding this was the large number of applicants (over 100,000), which meant that claimants had to deal with a large bureaucracy and an impersonal handling of their claims.

Redress outcomes

Of the major outcomes of redress schemes – financial payments, benefits and services, and other types of outcomes (apologies and memorialization) – the largest volume of material is on financial payments. That does not mean that the most important element of redress for survivors is a money payment. Indeed, the available evidence suggests that counselling is as, if not more, important. (In addition, evidence suggests that it should be available early, when redress scheme negotiations begin or a scheme is announced.) When a redress scheme has other types of benefits such as medical and dental costs, or educational benefits, these are rated highly. Most *Grandview* women (80 per cent) said that benefits such as education and counselling helped them to 'make concrete changes in their lives' and that 'while the financial payment may go, education and counselling benefits last' (Leach, 1997, p. 41).

The meaning and significance of 'healing'

In Canada, terms such as 'healing' and 'reconciliation' were part of the name and the expressed goals of many (not all) redress schemes, although the terms were rarely defined. One exception is Reimer et al.'s (2010) study of the CEP (*Indian Residential Schools*), a payment calculated according to the number of years a claimant spent in an eligible Indian residential school. In this context, 'healing' and 'healing journey' were (and are) salient dimensions of identity and aspiration for Canadian Aboriginal people; and the terms were relevant to evaluating the CEP. Although healing is intensely personal, its general dimensions are, in the words of one Aboriginal survivor, 'to find yourself within, emotionally, physically, spiritually, culturally, mentally' (p. 78). Other characterizations are 'facing memories, dealing with the emotions, forgiving yourself and others'; a 'spiritual journey in which [one] learns to deal with the anger and sadness rooted in the school experience and to live in peace', 'finding answer to questions about [one's] past, learning from them, and continuing on with life "in a new light, like a new day"'; and simply, 'unloading a big chip from [one's] shoulder' (p. 80). All of this suggests a significant personal transformation from an unsettled 'past' of disturbing and destructive thoughts towards improved self-understanding and self-acceptance. The 'towards' is a key word: most would say that healing is a life-long journey. No justice mechanism should be expected to accomplish significant personal transformation, although it may contribute to it.

In evaluating *Grandview*, Leach (1997) asked whether the agreement contributed to healing, and 30 per cent said that it did 'a lot' (p. 51). However, many said that calling the agreement '"a healing package" may have contributed to unrealistic expectations':

> Healing from abuse is neither short nor linear, and no 'package' of awards and benefits could ever provide healing...Neither the process nor the package of benefits will ever undo what happened to them as girls at Grandview. (p. v)

Naming justice practices is important, and the *Grandview* experience suggests that calling the agreement 'a healing package' may have been misleading and premature.

In Australia, healing has been a salient dimension to Indigenous redress for forcible child removal. In their joint submission to a Senate inquiry into the *Stolen Generation Compensation Bill 2008*, the Public Interest Advocacy Centre (PIAC) and the Australian Human Rights Centre (AHRC) (2008) say that addressing the experiences of members of the Stolen Generations must be done in a way that 'recognizes and validates trauma if the process of healing is to be executed effectively' (paragraph 29). Healing blends Aboriginal or Indigenous spirituality with Christian principles and general therapeutic aims. The restorative justice advocacy literature ('a healing justice' or a 'justice that heals') exemplifies this syncretism (Sullivan and Tifft, 2006; van Ness and Strong, 2010). While respecting other belief systems and worldviews, my position is that healing should not be an explicit goal or outcome of justice activities, for the same reasons that 'therapeutic outcomes' should not be a goal. These terms refer to positive mental, emotional, and spiritual states of mind and a sense of well-being. The processes and outcomes of justice activities may promote or produce such states of mind, but such states of mind should not be the principal goal of justice activities. Otherwise, the justice process is viewed largely as a mental health or rehabilitative activity for victims. The goal should be to identify victims' *interests* in a justice activity, that is, the principles of a victim-focused justice or the entitlements that victims as citizens should expect from justice. Such interests are separate from the *effects* of justice activities, which may (or may not) improve one's well-being. In the design of redress schemes, careful attention must be given to these justice interests, how they will be addressed, and the words used in defining goals and activities.

Financial payments

> No amount of money can adequately compensate victims for the pain and suffering experienced while in institutions and other forms of care, [but it can go] some way towards acknowledging past abuse and affording a sense of justice and closure for many victims. (Senate Report, 2004, p. 226)

The Senate Committee's words, which are common in the literature, demonstrate the antinomy of denial and support at the heart of redress payments:[6] first, there is *denial* that money can compensate for pain and suffering; but second, there is *support* for money as accomplishing some good. The problem with money is that unlike other outcomes of redress schemes (counselling, educational benefits, apologies, and memorialization), it has a market meaning. Sunga (2002, p. 40) argues that 'unless there is a clear articulation that a monetary award does not signify a market transaction, money will tend to indicate some form of exchange for abuse injuries'. The consequences are that money payments may 'alienate abuse survivors and objectify injuries that are personal and psychic in nature', leaving them to feel that 'their worth has not been understood or acknowledged by the party responsible for the abuse' (p. 41). This is precisely why many claimants in the Canadian and Australian cases were angry and disappointed with the payment they received.

To address this problem, Sunga outlines what scheme planners need to consider in fashioning redress payments. One must articulate a clear relationship of meaning to accompany an award. In addition, money must be viewed as symbolic: as 'a form of recognition for injury and as solace for pain' (p. 60). Jane Wangmann (2010), who appeared as a witness to a Senate inquiry on compensation payments, made the same point: 'money... [must have] some sort of symbolic meaning and provide recognition of the harm that is done and is not seen as a payoff... ' (Senate Report, 2010, p. 32). A 'clear relationship of meaning' of *ex gratia* payments to recognition or solace was not apparent in most redress schemes; and as a consequence, problems arose. Indeed, the tiered schemes carefully 'calibrated' money payments to injury and impact (Winter, 2009, p. 55). Little wonder, then, that claimants did the same.

In theory, a money payment should be associated with vindication of the law and of the victim, as articulated by Australian care leaver Frank Golding:

> Compensation is a tangible means of *acknowledging the wrongfulness of the abuse* [vindication of the law] and the harm that was done; it can close an unhappy chapter in a person's life and be the start of a healing process. Compensation is also a form of vindication: in acknowledging *the truth of the matter, the victim is set free from the suffering* [vindication of the victim] caused by abuse all those long years ago. (Senate Report, 2010, p. 32; emphasis added)

This is an ideal way to think about money, but was it realized? The cases suggest there were positive responses to money payments, but the recurring message from the available research, all from Canada, is 'mixed' (that is, qualified positive responses, or both positive and negative).

Positive responses

For *Grandview*, Leach (1997, p. 35) learned that 40 per cent of the women were 'very satisfied' with the financial award,[7] with three saying:

- It made my life somewhat easier; gave me a sense of retribution and validation.
- Besides the recognition, I can now make plans for the future and an education.
- It has been very positive because it gave me hope for the future. (pp. 44–5)

Feldthusen et al. (2000, p. 97) found that 34 per cent of *Grandview* survivors were satisfied with the financial payment, one saying, 'the adjudicator heard me, believed me. It gave me something I thought I would never have. It gave me "someone believed me"'. These positive responses centre on the money payment as validation.

For *Indian Residential Schools*, Reimer et al. (2010, p. 44) found that of those with positive, negative, or mixed experiences, 31 per cent were fully positive.[8] The most frequently mentioned positive was pragmatic: it 'relieved financial stress and worry…it was good to pay off debts, which in turn was good for self-esteem, or the money helped to improve everyday life' (p. 48), one recipient saying,

> I just went totally crackers! But I enjoyed it. I thought, well thank you, thank you for the thought of us. At least they are trying, the government is trying, and that is what I am looking at.

Another frequently mentioned positive was the ability to share the money with family and friends. This was seen as 'symbolically important…the money helped some families to reconnect by covering travel expenses for gathering'. In other cases, recipients gave the money away to those who needed it and to family members, which accorded with 'cultural ideas of sharing' (p. 49). Whereas 60 to 90 per cent of positives fell into these two categories, 15 per cent said it was 'symbolically important':

> as a tangible recognition by Canada of the Aboriginal experience…an admission by the government of the fundamental wrong-doing in forcibly removing…children from families and enforcing an assimilation policy through schooling. (p. 50)

'The government is trying' and 'tangible recognition' are examples of vindication and government accountability; however, a victim's justice interest in vindication is most strongly evident when a survivor believes it is absent.

Negative responses

Negative responses had these themes: the payment did not reflect the abuse and suffering experienced, it devalued a survivor's worth, and other people received more money than a survivor did. All of these can be traced to the problems identified by Sunga (2002): the payment was interpreted as monetary exchange for abuse or injuries suffered, and a survivor's 'worth' was not recognized. Here are some examples. For *St John's and St Joseph's* (all taken from Henton and McCann, 1995):

- This is hard to swallow... It's a slap in the face. It is like saying, 'We don't believe you again'. (p. 262)
- The assessment panel had awarded him just $8,000 for the beatings, the anal sex, the forced fellatio. He wasn't happy with the amount, but he was not going to go through the rest of his life complaining about it. (p. 269)
- The first fourteen decisions of the Criminal Injuries Compensation Board wounded me deeply. While I do not envy them the job of putting a price on a man's pain, their awards were insulting. (quoting McCann, p. 294)

The examples demonstrate that survivors equated money with their injuries, suffering, and value as a person. But this is precisely what scheme designers did, and it was a recipe for re-victimization.

For *Grandview*, Feldthusen et al. (2000, pp. 97–100) found that most survivors were not satisfied with the payment they received, using terms such as 'angry', 'outraged', 'disappointed', 'heartbroken', and 'devastated'.[9] One said, 'it doesn't compare to the hurt, suffering, misery. It doesn't even give me $20,000 for every year I was there'. Another's brother said, 'at least you got something for being in there', to which she replied 'Do you think that everyone has a price?' (p. 98). Leach (1997, p. 35) learned that some *Grandview* women were dissatisfied because they believed their award was lower than other women's, or lower than that received by *St John's and St Joseph's* survivors. (The *Grandview* average financial payment was, in fact, higher than that for *St John's and St Joseph's*.) Leach also discovered that the *Grandview* matrix 'led to animosities between women' about payments received, and may have fostered a perception of a "hierarchy of pain"' (p. 58). A sense of unfairness was registered when survivors felt 'they got less than women who had experienced less abuse' (IHRD, 1998, p. 40). Although *Grandview* and *St John's and St Joseph's* survivors decided to use an individualized, tiered model when negotiating their agreements, after implementation, some wondered whether a flat payment would have been better.

For *Nova Scotia Institutions*, IHRD (1998, p. 83) found that many survivors 'objected to the use of categories to define and rate their childhood abuse experiences', one saying 'it's like they were labelling beef'. Another said, 'the abuse affected me badly. Money won't change that' (p. 84). For *Jericho Hill*-JICP, with one exception, all the survivors had negative views about the financial payment. The positive survivor said she had 'never really thought about the money aspect':

> ...I think, if anything, I wanted them to understand it's not about money, it's about me as a human being and being a proud Deaf individual. (Battersby et al., 2008, p. 104)

In the following quote, a *Jericho Hill*-JICP said he wanted 'at least' the maximum:

> When I started in the process, I wanted to get money, and *I'd heard that $60,000 was the maximum, so I wanted at least that*...A few people I knew had been there only a couple of years had gotten the maximum...I'm not sure what made their abuse worse. (p. 102, emphasis added)

Again, we see comparisons drawn with amounts received by other claimants and not understanding why one's experience of abuse was not judged as worthy. Another survivor made a similar point about the 'worth' of abuse, and also asked why sexual abuse alone was the basis for the money payment:

> My wife was only given $30,000, and she'd grown up her whole life there. That doesn't seem fair. And then other people are getting $60,000, and they've only been there 2 years. It didn't seem to matter how much abuse you'd experienced and how much suffering you'd gone through, the sexual abuse was all. (p. 105)

Equating one's suffering and 'worth' with money is clearly shown in the following comment:

> It was not as much as I expected to cover the suffering I went through, but money doesn't solve everything either.... You know how much you feel...you're worth. And when the span is from $3,000 to $60,000,...I thought that $40,000 wasn't enough. Perhaps $60,000 was too much for me, but $40,000 wasn't enough. (p. 103)

The following example demonstrates the emotional impact of a lack of vindication, which arose from a low payment and absence of 'justice':

> I was upset. I was very upset. Angry. Mostly I was just angry, mad, upset. And I'm not sure if it was because – it was very confusing for me. I had the two things, I'm not sure, and it probably was both. I had very low compensation. I didn't feel like it was sufficient for what I'd gone through. But also, there'd been no justice. (p. 103)

For this survivor, 'justice' meant a broad understanding of vindication that was not confined to a money payment alone.

For *Indian Residential Schools*, the basis for negative responses to the CEP was the 'injustice of the 10-plus-3 formula' (that is, it was too low). Here is what two former residents said:

- I think the '10–3' was just a drop in the bucket – it was an insult... (p. 52)
- They thought they could just give us a couple of bucks, pat us on the back and say move on. (p. 51)

For *Indian Residential Schools* and *Grandview*, what some viewed as a low level of payment was interpreted as 'hush money' and 'shut up' money, that is, not representing recognition, but bad faith by the government.

Other effects of financial payments

The range of experiences with financial payments cannot be fully captured by 'positive' or 'negative' responses, nor by validation and vindication as justice interests. Some *Grandview* survivors internalized a symbolic meaning for the money received. One said that with part of the redress payment, she 'ended up buying this couch':

> It's totally different from my other furniture. This couch is what I suffered for. The couch has to make up for the childhood I missed, the pain and suffering, and the family I lost. And it doesn't. It never will. (Feldthusen et al., 2000, p. 100)

Another said,

> I invested in a home. My home is like Grandview. It's like sitting in Grandview. You get this feeling that everything you have is because of Grandview. (p. 99)

Feldthusen et al. (2000, pp. 98–9) suggest that the first example shows that money cannot really 'compensate' for past abuse, and the second shows that it can be difficult to 'accept and enjoy' a financial award. I have another interpretation. Just as Sunga (2002) proposes, each woman created a symbolic meaning for the money: as a couch and a house, which stood as memorials to *Grandview* and their experiences there. However, in each case, the memorials did not commemorate them or transcend their *Grandview* experience. My inference is that having a symbolic meaning for money is not sufficient: money needs to be tied to the 'right' sort of meaning.

For *Indian Residential Schools*, Reimer et al. (2010, p. 55) argue that there was 'a lack of planning by those implementing CEP [by not preparing for] triggered emotions, self-destructive reactions, and predatory behaviours'. One CEP recipient said, for example, 'the things I have forgotten have come back. Things that I had tried to forget' (p. 47). Some spent the money right away because they were 'not at ease keeping' it; others did 'not want to look' at the cheque, and one 'did not open his CEP envelope for 3 months because he hated his time at school' (p. 53). In some communities, CEP was associated with a rise in 'accidental deaths, suicides, and homicides', which contributed to a 'general demoralization' in some communities (p. 44). Two factors were responsible: increased alcohol and drug use, and 'pressure and abuse by a survivor's inner circle', which included taking advantage of Elders (p. 54). These outcomes were fully anticipated in a study initiated by the AHF before the *Indian Residential School* redress scheme began; it investigated the impact of lump sum payments that had been made previously in Aboriginal communities. The AHF recognized that 'the wave of [CEP] payments would represent a massive and sudden influx of money into Aboriginal communities across Canada' (Dion Stout and Harp, 2007, p. 6), and the report identified a range of negative effects. I do not know why the findings and recommendations of the 2007 report were not taken up with the care they deserved.

Developments in Australia

In Australia, news stories and book chapters contain individuals' experiences with redress schemes and payments. However, except for the questions asked by RPR Consulting of Forgotten Australians in Queensland

(Watson, 2011), no research has explored care leavers and survivors as a group with respect to redress schemes. Advocacy groups have criticized redress schemes on these grounds: payments are too low (with reference to payments in *Queensland Institutions*); caps should not be lowered after a program is announced (as occurred in *Redress WA*); payment amounts are not explained adequately ('lack of transparency'); and the four states' redress schemes vary with respect to eligibility, type of abuse considered, and payment maxima. Thus, there is a lack of consistency among states with redress schemes, as well as inequality between states with and without such schemes. The Senate Report (2010) concluded that states with redress schemes review them, and those without, provide them. It recommended that schemes be a state, not federal responsibility, but that federal consideration be given to abuse in institutions or foster care in the Australian Capital Territory or Northern Territory.[10] The Supplementary Submission by PIAC and the AHRC (2008) to the *Stolen Generation Compensation Bill 2008* presents the most detailed proposal for redress to date. It uses a reparations framework, drawing on international human rights law and the van Boven principles (restitution, compensation, rehabilitation, satisfaction, and guarantees of non-repetition). Its proposed Reparations Tribunal combines a range of benefits, services, cultural and educational programs, memorials, and financial payments.

Other outcomes

Public apologies, memorials, commemorative activities, and other media and memory projects can be significant outcomes, not only for survivors, but also for members of the general public, who may have little understanding of the histories and practices associated with institutional abuse. Apologies vary in sincerity, attention to ceremony, and engagement with and participation by survivors on the day. However, depending on what is said and how it received, they may provide vindication, and perhaps also, accountability. Memorials and commemorative activities have the potential to provide a wider communicative and cultural platform, engaging survivors and many others, to remember and reflect upon the past and to celebrate positive movement for change. These activities were especially prevalent in *Indian Residential Schools, Stolen Generations, Child Migrants*, and *Forgotten Australians* (Appendix 5). Other media (books, film, and television) and memory projects (oral histories, statement gathering, museum installations, and plays) have an even broader audience. In addition to informing members of the general public, these media and memory projects can explore the complexity of abusive relationships in institutions, and different perspectives on what occurred and why by residents, staff, and others (Appendix 6).

Presence and preservation of victim voice

Care leavers and survivors participate in redress processes in varied ways: some give public or confidential accounts to public inquiries; others give explanations in oral hearings; and others write books, participate in other media, or participate (or are represented) in other types of memory projects. Essential to this activity is the creation of a public record.

For the 19 cases, victim voice was present in 14 as part the process: in public inquiries (seven cases), oral hearings when seeking financial payments (eight), or Recorders' reports (two). (Three cases had more than one voice element; thus, the number adds to greater than 14.) All the public inquiry reports are preserved; but in just two, survivors' submissions are readily accessible (*Child Migrants* and *Forgotten Australians*). Victim voice is typically brought into the reports by directly quoting witness testimony or submissions (*Mount Cashel, Stolen Generations, Forgotten Australians, Child Migrants, Queensland Institutions, South Australian Institutions*); but in one, there was no direct victim voice (*New Brunswick Institutions*). The texts of the oral hearings were treated as confidential, and some were destroyed after the hearing; for the rest, I suspect that none has been preserved. The two Recorders' reports (Mussell, 1995, for *George Epoch*; Hoffman, 1996, for *St John's and St Joseph's*) are preserved, but not accessible to the public.

In nine of 19 cases, victim voice and experiences were registered in other media: in books by journalists, in biographies of or autobiographies by survivors; and in film, television, or DVDs; or as part of oral history projects, museum installations, and plays. In addition, for Australia, the oral history and museum projects in the three Commonwealth cases (*Stolen Generations, Child Migrants*, and *Forgotten Australians*) included material relevant to the five state cases or redress schemes. Victim voice was also present in academic research. A public record of victims' and survivors' experiences of abuse, and of direct victim 'voice', which has been preserved and remains accessible, exists for 12 of 19 cases. Importantly, in just two of these was the public record generated from official activities alone. Thus, other media play a significant role in putting abuse on an official or public record that is available and accessible to the general public.

Victims' justice interests: reprise and reflection

The response to institutional abuse is recent, and researchers are searching for ways to analyse redress processes and outcomes and how these relate to other legal and administrative justice mechanisms. 'Victims' justice interests' provides one way to grasp the strengths, limits, and variability of redress schemes, and redress more generally, from a victim's perspective. I highlight and reflect upon the key findings in this chapter.

Participation in applying for a payment (or benefits) and in understanding how a redress scheme works can be as much a burden as a 'justice interest' for survivors. It is difficult to imagine a redress process without an application or intake process of some type. Problems in the application process include having to remember past experiences, which had been buried or forgotten; difficulties filling out forms and finding records, and delays in receiving information on decisions. Survivors should not participate in the application process as a 'self-help' activity; they must have support, information, and guidance from advocacy groups or community organizations.

By comparison to problems that can arise with participation, 'voice' appears to be a clear justice interest, but with one significant caveat. In the Mullighan inquiry in geographically remote Aboriginal Lands, despite concerted outreach efforts, no one disclosed 'that he or she had been sexually abused as a child ... on the Lands'. This arose due to 'difficulties of victims and survivors and their families of reporting ... to authorities' and '... women [being] placed under pressure in a variety of ways not to talk to the Inquiry' (Mullighan, 2008b, p. 22). Thus, in some contexts, it is not safe to tell a public victim story.

I found that what victims have said orally or in written submissions to public inquiries has not been preserved in ways that are readily accessible to the public. I recognize the importance of confidential submissions; however, consent can be requested before making any submission public. Otherwise, victims' voices, as part of the official redress process, will be lost; and there will be no 'official record'. This point is especially important to underline because survivors who come forward to participate in public inquiries want to see their involvement as having a larger purpose, not just for themselves, but for others. This was evident in the Forde inquiry (opening page of this chapter) and the Mullighan inquiry (2008a, city/town component):

- [I want to give evidence because] there are so many kids whose lives have been utterly screwed up, and if I can add a little to that and something is eventually done to stop it, so be it. (p. 61)
- [I want to tell my story] to help other kids... If I can see an end result, that will be all I ask. (p. 250)

Final reports from inquiries are not reader-friendly for survivors or members of the general public: their size alone is daunting. Victim voice texts (and analyses of them) need to be assembled in other formats as an 'official record' that can have broader impact. We would know little of victims' experiences of abuse, were it not for other media, memory projects, and academic research.

Validation is not only a victim's justice interest, but also an interest of a scheme's gatekeeper, the authority who determines eligibility and payment levels in a redress scheme. This sets up a potential conflict between a survivor who wants to 'be believed' and a gatekeeper who tests the veracity of the claim, although redress schemes varied in their standards of proof. Self-regulation by advocacy groups, as occurred in *St John's and St Joseph's* and *Grandview*, was beneficial in screening out weak claims and achieving high validation rates. However, of 20 money outcome decisions, nine had no option for an oral hearing, and paperwork was mailed to an office; reasons for decisions were not given as a standard practice in 12. Such practices may be administratively efficient; but from a claimant's perspective, the process of deliberation and decision-making seems to occur within a black box. As a consequence, some survivors questioned the legitimacy of the validation process.

Vindication of the law and of the victim can occur by sincere apologies, benefits, and services to individuals and groups, memorials and commemoration, and state punishment. Here I confine my discussion to money payments, which are termed 'a contentious, and possibly the most contentious, issue of all the possible reparation measures' (Senate Report, 2004, p. 225). What strikes me more in reading material by survivors, advocacy groups, and government (or church) officials is not contention over how to establish or fund a money scheme, but more fundamental matters. There is *confusion* in the use and meaning of key terms; and there are *disparate goals* for money payments and *different meanings* attached to money. Some advocacy group members do not understand why *ex gratia* payments are relatively small compared to amounts received in civil settlements (although these too can be small), or amounts received when the government admits liability in major civil cases.[11] The problem is the term 'compensation', which has a precise meaning, but is used loosely and inaccurately when discussing redress schemes. For *disparate goals*, in Australia, some are seeking to rectify the 'past', by relating payments to abuse injury and its impact; others seek 'to assist with the healing process' (Tasmanian Ombudsman, 2004, p. 1); still others identify amounts that are tied to wage loss, which can provide economic support for older survivors (Senate Report, 2010, pp. 18–20). These are different goals: some are linked to injury, others to mental health, and others to social security. What they all have in common is that money amounts need to be 'appropriate' (that is, higher than $35,000 to $40,000, one may infer from the Senate Report, 2010). For *different meanings,* most victims may relate a money payment to 'recognition' or acknowledgement of the harm (vindication of the law and the victim) in the abstract; but in practice, after receiving a money payment, a symbolic meaning may shift to a market meaning: the money amount is viewed as the measure of the 'worth' of one's abuse and one's self.

Accountability for institutional abuse may be achieved through criminal prosecution and successful litigation, when culpability or liability is admitted. It may be harder to achieve in public inquiries or redress schemes. When it is achieved in the latter contexts, it is indirect. For example, officials of high status in government and churches may give sincere apologies for the previous actions of their officials and staff, but they are not directly held accountable. *Ex gratia* payment schemes are explicit that a government or church does not accept liability for abuse. For some survivors, money payments were equated with establishing trust between themselves and government or church organizations, trust that had been lost as a result of policy wrongs, institutional abuse, or both. Thus, money payments may be viewed as a measure of accountability.

The construct of victims' justice interests does not fully capture other goals that survivors had in engaging a response to institutional abuse. By participating in public inquiries, some hoped that the next generation of children would not suffer as they did. Some wanted to see a 'public dialogue' on the multiple causes of male violence against women and children that included having been victimized as a boy. Thus, by participating in redress activities, outcomes did not solely benefit themselves, but had larger social objectives.

8
Summary and Implications

As a new field of knowledge, redress for institutional abuse confronts many questions. What is institutional abuse? What is redress? What kinds of redress processes and outcomes are optimal? What do survivors want? How does money matter? What theorizations help us to understand this multi-faceted phenomenon? I address these questions by summarizing the book's main points and reflecting on their implications.

Defining institutional abuse

Institutional abuse is defined differently, depending on what is considered 'institutional' and 'abuse'. My analysis of historical institutional abuse centred on residential institutions, not community-based institutions. As such, I sought to reclaim Goffman's insights on care regimes and day-to-day life in total (and not-so-total) institutions. Adult survivors seeking redress today for historical institutional abuse lived in these institutions, although some were also placed in foster care. Thus, in general, 'total institutions' as a concept has relevance to their experiences and desires for redress. Another reason for reclaiming Goffman is political. The research literature on residential care has focused on institutions for children in affluent nations. Because large residential care facilities declined over the 20th century in affluent nations, it is assumed by some writers that residential institutions for children are a less relevant focus of analysis. I disagree. Such institutions remain in affluent nations, and they are growing in other parts of the world (central and eastern Europe, the former Soviet Union, Sri Lanka, Indonesia, Zimbabwe, Ghana, among others; see Czáky, 2009). The reasons given for placing children in institutions today are similar to those more than a century ago: poverty, social exclusion, and disability, to which today we would add family displacement caused by conflict and environmental disasters. These children will be among the next generation of historical institutional abuse survivors. (I recognize that some children today are in especially vulnerable circumstances with no place to live, living and sleeping on the streets.) In affluent nations, increasing attention is given to contemporary institutional abuse in community-based institutions; but in broadening the sites of abuse, the focus often narrows to sexual abuse. I cannot explain why this has occurred except to say that sexual abuse has a privileged status. In light of survivors' memories of abuse, an unfortunate consequence is that some public inquiries of historical (or contemporary) institutional abuse may focus solely on sexual abuse.

Historicizing institutional abuse and responses to it

Changing concepts of childhood in the 1960s softened the ground for the 'discovery' and diffusion of new concepts of child physical abuse in the 1960s and child sexual abuse in the 1970s. Institutional abuse built upon these ideas and began to emerge as a social problem in the 1980s. Celebrated cases of clergy sexual abuse in the 1980s gave the impression of a widespread prevalence of sexual abuse of children, albeit mainly in community-based settings. A catalyst for change in official responses to institutional abuse was the 'sexual turn' in reporting abuse, that is, when accounts of sexual abuse were put forward, they were 'more disturbing' than simply 'harsh punishment'. Not only was sexual abuse more disturbing, but it was the subject of extensive media coverage and thus 'observable'. Key to its observability were the 'public stories' by survivors. This was new, having only begun in the 1970s with accounts by feminist survivors of intra-familial sexual abuse. Public stories of institutional abuse began in the late 1980s, when adult male survivors described being sexually abused in boyhood by religious men. Analysts write of the 1980s as a time of a 'moral panic' about child sexual abuse. Heightened concerns with child sexual abuse in the 1980s may have 'jumped' to institutional settings, although there is little evidence that claims were exaggerated. A moral panic analysis does not explain responses to institutional abuse. Most cases in my sample had a history of alleged police or department cover-ups or failed investigations, which was as significant to the media story as accounts of abuse; furthermore, the five core-plus cases came to public attention for reasons in addition to abuse in institutions.

Different types of cases

For all 19 cases, the response sought to address a failure of government or church authorities to protect children (the core response), and five had an additional policy or practice layer (the core-plus cases). The latter came into the public arena and sparked a response because of advocacy group campaigns or the threat of significant civil litigation, not allegations of sexual or physical abuse alone. Such allegations of abuse were relevant, but secondary to a moral claim of policy or practice wrongs against children (the core-plus-one cases) or policy or practice wrongs against children that were embedded in a more general discrimination against a minority group (the core-plus-two cases). We must pay attention to variability in institutional abuse cases, and in particular, the differences between the core and core-plus cases. Such variation has implications for the meanings of 'redress' and how justice responses are theorized.

Defining redress

I defined redress broadly to include all the activities, processes, and outcomes that recognize and provide a compensatory mechanism for harms or wrongs against an individual or group. One question is whether 'redress' or 'reparation/s' is the better term. The former is more likely used in the institutional abuse literature, and the latter, in the international human rights and criminal justice literature. However, both terms are used to describe redress schemes, and victim redress is featured in international criminal justice (McCarthy, 2012). For these reasons, I do not see a bright line between the two terms; however, I do see a brighter line between what is considered to be the subject of redress or reparation/s. If a policy wrong against children or discrimination against a group (or other type of 'historical wrong') has occurred, responding to it is not the same as responding to institutional abuse alone. We need then to consider the justice theorizations that have been applied to date in understanding and responding to historical institutional abuse: restorative justice, therapeutic jurisprudence, and transitional justice.

Justice theorizations

I offer a brief exploration of justice theorizations, but intend to develop the ideas in future work. Restorative justice is defined in many ways and used in different social, political, and legal contexts (Daly and

Proietti-Scifoni, 2011). It was applied to historical institutional abuse cases in Scotland in the Time to be Heard Forum (Johnstone, 2011; Sacro Restorative Justice Services, 2011). A survivor could attend a restorative justice meeting, with a professional facilitator and a representative of the home where the abuse had occurred. The aim was for survivors 'to be heard, receive an apology and feel vindicated, and for organizations to recognize and own their responsibility' (Sacro Restorative Justice Services, 2011, p. 6). In the pilot project, financial payments were excluded as a potential outcome. In addition, Studsrød (2012) has considered the potential of restorative justice processes in responses to historical institutional abuse in some Norwegian jurisdictions. Applied to these cases, restorative justice principles may be used in several ways: to devise face-to-face meetings between survivors and representatives of relevant government entities or care providers, or to structure oral hearings between survivors and decision-makers or adjudicators. Outcomes that meaningfully relate to the abuse would also be part of restorative principles.

Therapeutic jurisprudence shares much in common with restorative justice in its focus on socio-legal processes; however, it centres on the ways in which such processes and outcomes can achieve therapeutic effects (not only for victims, but also offenders). Positive effects are defined as improved states of 'psychological or physical well-being' (Feldthusen et al., 2000, p. 68). Both restorative justice and therapeutic jurisprudence assume that procedural justice is part of the process, that is, a survivor is 'treated with respect, politeness and dignity, and…their rights as citizens are acknowledged' (Tyler, 1992, p. 440). One difference is that a restorative justice meeting may not be facilitated by a legal actor (police officer, tribunal adjudicator, judicial officer), whereas therapeutic jurisprudence assumes a formal process with a legal decision-maker, even if the process may take a more relaxed form (as in *Grandview*). However, like restorative justice, analysts using a therapeutic jurisprudence framework anticipate that processes and outcomes will assist 'with the healing process by receiving an acknowledgment of the harm [which is]…a way of holding the perpetrator accountable while being treated with respect' (Graycar and Wangmann, 2007, p. 6). These theorizations focus on victims' experiences of process and outcome. They can be used to devise optimal redress schemes, but they are not well-suited to assess them or to compare different justice mechanisms (criminal prosecution, civil litigation, public inquires, and redress schemes) in responding to institutional abuse. My construct of victims' justice interests – for participation, voice, validation, vindication, and offender accountability – is designed precisely to assess and compare justice mechanisms. What it relies upon, however, is research evidence on victims' and survivors' participation in and experiences of varied justice mechanisms. Such evidence for institutional abuse is in short supply.

The application of transitional justice frameworks to responses to institutional abuse in Ireland (McAlinden, 2013) and to the policy and practice wrong against Aboriginal children and people caused by the Canadian Indian residential school system (Jung, 2011) has a different purpose. In these analyses, justice for victims and survivors is not in the frame of reference. Rather, authors focus on how responses to historical institutional abuse have the potential to transform state–church relations (McAlinden, 2013) or post-colonial relations (Jung, 2011). Those using a transitional justice framework are adapting ideas and practices from one societal context to another. The original context was societies in transition from conflict to peace or from authoritarian to post-authoritarian states, and the more recent context is 'transition in contemporary settled democracies' (McAlinden, 2013, p. 211), that is, in affluent democratic nations. The value of this approach is drawing connections between justice mechanisms that are used in both contexts, for example, truth commissions (in post-conflict societies) and public inquiries (in settled democracies). A second is employing a socio–political analysis of the potential for change in state–church–citizen relationships, which is at the heart of the Irish case of historical institutional abuse. McAlinden argues that truth recovery, particularly the uncovering of enmeshed power relations between the church and state in running the industrial school system, has not been achieved in several Irish public inquiries. However, she is silent on the role of the Irish Residential Institutions Redress Board, whose average payment to survivors, as reported in its 2013 Newsletter, was €62,500 (AUD $80,490 in 2012). How might a transitional justice framework analyse the Redress Board's activities?

In Canada, Jung (2011) analyzes the ways in which redress of the policy wrong against Aboriginal children and discrimination against Aboriginal peoples has the capacity to re-configure post-colonial relations. A transitional justice framework seems apt for the 'core-plus' cases (and especially core-plus-two) – cases that may be considered 'historical wrongs' – more so than the core cases. Historical institutional abuse in Ireland is not a core-plus case, as I define it, although arguably what occurred was an 'historical wrong'. The focus of McAlinden's transitional justice analysis is on the limits of one type of justice mechanism ('truth seeking' via public inquiries). She sees this activity as being comparable to 'truth seeking' in post-conflict contexts. Yes, there are affinities, but as

Sköld (2013, p. 12) points out, there are important differences. Inquiries into historical institutional abuse are typically not concerned with 'a dissociation from or settlement with a former regime', and survivors' memories are not of 'historically specific events or memories of a certain era'. What is clear is that scholars are searching for theoretical toe-holds to understand institutional abuse and justice.

Need for multiple theorizations

Historical institutional abuse and responses to it is a large and multi-faceted problem; thus, scholars must be open to varied theorizations. No one overarching theoretical framework can contain it all. It cannot be grasped solely in structural socio–political terms, nor in social–psychological measures of the impact of justice processes and outcomes on survivors. There are, in addition, other relevant theorizations and foci of analysis such as social construction, accounts, and social problems (as I show in Chapters 3 and 4); normative arguments on corrective justice mechanisms (Winter, 2009); the impact of litigation on organizational change (Lytton, 2008); and social constructions of sex and gender (Keenan, 2012). Sköld (2013, p. 7) is right to say that responses to historical institutional abuse 'may constitute a new interdisciplinary field'; and thus the challenge will be to take that observation seriously by working across different levels of analysis, facets of the problem, and disciplinary and theoretical languages. Not only is the field interdisciplinary, but it is also international. The challenge will be for researchers to 'see' the problem not only from the history, politics, policies, and practices of a familiar 'home' country, but also from that of others.

My contribution has been to compare justice mechanisms that have been used in responding to historical institutional abuse in Canada and Australia, with a focus on redress schemes. I have given some attention to the perspective of redress scheme designers, but my attention has centred on how the processes and outcomes of redress are apprehended from survivors' perspectives. I turn to consider these questions: is there an optimal process, and how does money matter? With limited information on civil litigation and public inquiries, I address the questions largely with respect to redress schemes.

Is there an optimal process?

To the question, is there an optimal process?, the answer depends on what 'the process' is *for*. Is it for a *survivor* to tell his or her story to someone in authority who listens and does not challenge it? Or is it for a *claimant* to tell his or her story to a decision-maker as part of a validation process and a determination of a money payment or other outcome? If the latter, other questions arise about the process. Redress scheme processes can range from a personalized face-to-face oral hearing for a claimant to an exchange of paperwork with little or no social interaction. Moreover, 'the process' includes many other types of interactions and activities that are part of any redress scheme, including learning how it works, completing application forms, determining one's eligibility for benefits and services, among other activities. The message from my research and that of others (Feldthusen et al., 2000; Law Commission of Canada, 2000; Leach, 1998) is the need for clear information about the existence of a scheme, how it operates, who is eligible, and what steps a claimant will go through. These are pre-requisites for 'participation' as a victim's justice interest. What also comes through is that it takes particular skills and competencies to participate, which some claimants may lack. Finally, the process of seeking redress may itself cause emotional upset and difficulties for survivors and claimants. All of this suggests that government- (or church-) stipulated approaches, without the involvement of victim or survivor advocacy groups, are not recommended. Even with strong victim advocacy in the design of a redress scheme, as occurred in *Grandview* and *St John's and St Joseph's*, some survivors were distrustful of the scheme, and others identified problems with implementation. No redress scheme, however optimally designed, will be without some degree of distrust or complaint.

How does money matter?

From a government (or church) perspective, the question of money looms large. Money is also important to lawyers. I shall not dwell on these two groups for long, but wish to make several observations about them before turning to the perspectives of survivors or claimants.

Drawing on what occurred in *Indian Residential Schools* and *Alberta Sterilization*, Jacobs (2007, p. 151, 153) suggests, there is 'an almost inherent mistrust that a victim and others, including the general public, may feel when [a government, who is the] *author of the wrong* turns into the *master of the compensation process*' (emphasis added). Furthermore, when a government (or another) entity introduces a method for determining financial payments, there is a suspicion that 'cost efficiency' is being favoured 'over a genuine attempt to compensate individuals fairly' (p. 153). Winter (2009) makes a similar point for Australian *ex gratia* payments offered by governments. He suggests that the level of *ex gratia* payments may be justified in light of 'financial constraints on public finances' and 'making costs predictable'. However, without an explicit justification for the rationale and level of an *ex gratia* payment, a government may appear to be 'offering a defective form of redress' (p. 53). My analysis shows that with some exceptions, there is no explicit justification by government (or church) entities for the level of *ex gratia* payments or of negotiated payments that use a 'grid of damages'. This must be addressed in any future redress scheme and is relevant to constructing a symbolic meaning of money as recognition and solace for pain.

Information is sparse on legal fees gained from civil litigation and settlements, redress schemes, and where relevant, criminal injuries boards or tribunals. Some redress schemes structure legal fees into the financial payment (*Indian Residential Schools*, level 2, Independent Assessment Process; *New Brunswick Institutions*); in the former, a lawyer is not permitted to charge more than 30 per cent, and in the latter, 20 per cent. Other redress schemes provide modest amounts for claimants to seek legal advice before deciding to opt into an agreement or sign a release. With the exception of some survivors' experiences in *Grandview*, it is uncertain whether claimants have paid lawyers additional fees when participating in redress schemes. The secrecy surrounding fees paid to lawyers in civil settlements (or other redress contexts) is not in the interests of redress claimants, plaintiffs, consumers of legal services, or members of the general public. Greater transparency should be possible without compromising ethical relationships between lawyers and clients.

For victims and survivors, a recurring theme, both in these cases and other research, is that 'it's not the money that matters' to them. Instead, their initial motives are to be heard and believed (*validation*) and for the abuse to be recognized and acknowledged (*vindication*). In addition, when provision is made for counselling, or there are medical, dental, or vocational–educational benefits, these may matter more than a lump sum payment (Death, 2013; Leach, 1997). However, in time, a payment may come to matter because it is linked to a survivor's sense of validation (being believed) and vindication (recognition by an authority that a wrong has occurred). The sparse evidence suggests that Sunga's (2002) advice to articulate a clear relationship of meaning for a money payment has not been taken up by redress scheme designers. Most survivors did not see the payment as symbolic, as recognition for injury and solace for pain. Instead, they equated the amount received in an individualized scheme to the level of abuse and injury they had experienced and to their 'worth'. They did not understand why others received more money than they did.

An important dimension to the meaning of seeking redress is time. Balboni and Bishop's (2010) analysis of Boston survivors' experiences with civil litigation for clergy abuse finds that over time, their initial desires to have the 'truth' of the abuse recognized and to provide mutual support for each other gave way to being only 'about the money'. This occurred when the attorneys 'had "monetized" the negotiations into a language of currency' (p. 151). The authors suggest that 'attorneys could look "outside the check"' and that 'non-pecuniary objects were the most meaningful' (p. 152). Boston survivors 'detested' the sense that they were in competition with other survivors for a fixed pot of money, which was awarded based on a ranking of who was most 'damaged'. Similar sentiments were registered by *Mount Cashel* plaintiffs who resented differences in settlement payments. For redress schemes, similar problems emerged when the 'money logic' was individualized and based on combinations of abuse, severity, and impact. Feldthusen et al. (2000, p. 109) call attention to the problems using 'a sliding scale/matrix', and they propose it be reconsidered.

In redress schemes for historical institutional abuse, an equality formula based on the number of years in residential care has much to commend. It centres on a regime of 'care', or in the policy cases, on policies of wrongful placement (*Duplessis Orphans*) or forcible assimilation (*Indian Residential Schools* and as proposed for *Stolen Generations*). However, unless the amount of money per year in residential care has a symbolic meaning, the idea runs into potential problems of not being viewed as 'sufficient' redress. In addition to an equality formula based on years in residential care, scheme designers may wish to consider a second level, which focuses on acts of physical or sexual abuse that uses individualized criteria. Key to discussions on redress schemes is that survivor groups and members of the general public must be better informed about the varied types of compensatory mechanisms, and especially why amounts in civil settlements are normally higher than *ex gratia* payments in government- or church-based redress schemes. Without a basic understanding of what is possible, expectations will be unrealistic. A good starting point is to remove the word 'compensation' entirely from the conversation on *ex gratia* payments. Ultimately, whatever money logic (or logics) is used in a redress scheme, the meaning of a financial payment must be symbolic, and not tied to a market value meaning. Further, such payments must be viewed as part of a larger redress package, not in isolation.

Government (or church) experience and accountability

Canadian and Australian jurisdictions have had considerable experience with redress schemes for historical abuse, but the wisdom that might have been gained has not been fully realized. To date, of the 15 redress schemes analysed in this book, there are reports or relevant information for seven (two complete and five partial) by officials, panel chairs, adjudicators, journalists, or evaluators on the processes and/or outcomes of redress schemes. However, reports are lacking for eight schemes. One would think that analysis and reflection on what occurred and lessons learned would be a requirement for all redress schemes. In addition, I found a lack of government (or church) accountability in reporting the outcomes of schemes, including validation rates, range in payments made, expenditure on benefits and services, other outcomes, and administrative costs. The overall expenditure on a scheme was not publicly available for any of the 15 redress schemes, although validation rates and average payments were publicly available for four (two of which I sought assistance to update or interpret the numbers). If we are to build knowledge about redress for historical institutional abuse, reflective reports on processes and clear analyses of outcomes are necessary. These should be joined with reports of outcomes of civil litigation between survivors and government, church, charitable, or other organizations; and such reports should include average deductions for legal fees. Information on the role of insurers is also required. Unless there is greater transparency on the range of monetary outcomes, the discussion about monetary redress is without an evidentiary foundation. In addition to financial payments, other types of outcomes should be recorded.

Looking forward

In 1993, Canada was the first country to commence a redress scheme for historical institutional abuse of children. Ireland and Australia followed a decade later with schemes in 2002 and 2003. Since that time, many inquiries, redress schemes, and related responses have been launched or concluded in other countries, and we are likely to see more in the future. I have sought to create an authoritative record of what occurred in Canada and Australia, including the actual outcomes of redress schemes and litigation. Others are now doing the same, and in time, our collective efforts will create a larger international picture. My contribution has been to depict redress for institutional abuse from survivors' perspectives, but there are many more avenues to explore. As our research develops and contributes to current responses to institutional abuse, we would do well to remember that residential institutions for children are not a thing of the past. According to United Nations data, at least 8 million children (conservatively) were in residential care in 2006 (Csásky, 2009). The next generation of institutional abuse survivors is growing up today. What will we be saying some decades from now, when they come of age and begin to tell their public victim stories?

Appendix 1: The Cases

Case id; does case continue?	Short case name; type of case	Long case name and previous names, dates of institutional opening and closure, or dates that policy or legislation spanned	Location	Types of institutions or places	Types of abuse and groups included*	Number of institutions and children affected	Number of unique individuals as validated claimants in redress schemes, and where relevant, civil settlements
(1)	(2)	(3)	(4)	(5)	(6)	(7)	(8)
CA1 continues	*Mount Cashel* (core)	Mount Cashel Boys' Home and Training School, 1969–90 (formerly Mount Cashel Orphanage for Boys, 1892–1968).	Newfoundland and Labrador, CA: St John's	One training school.	Physical and sexual abuse. Male orphans, those from broken or poor families, or wards of the state.	One school.	Estimated 209 in three major and smaller civil settlements: 1996 (43), 2006 (50 unique and relevant individuals), and 2013 (100 unique and relevant). In addition, there were 16 individual settlements (Shane Earle, his brother, and others).

Continued

Case id; does case continue?	Short case name; type of case	Long case name and previous names, dates of institutional opening and closure, or dates that policy or legislation spanned	Location	Types of institutions or places	Types of abuse and groups included*	Number of institutions and children affected	Number of unique individuals as validated claimants in redress schemes, and where relevant, civil settlements
(1)	(2)	(3)	(4)	(5)	(6)	(7)	(8)
CA2	*George Epoch* (core)	Jesuit Fathers of Upper Canada (George Epoch, a Jesuit priest, 1946–86). Civil suits centre on offending in 1969–83.	Ontario, CA: Wikwemikong, 1959–60, 1969–71, 1983–86; Cape Croker and Saugeen, 1971–83	Three Aboriginal reserves.	Sexual abuse. Male and female children in three Aboriginal communities.	One offender in three communities.	Estimated 124 to 156, but not all civil settlements are known. There were several groups: Appropriate Assistance (AA) in 1993–94 (40), Reconciliation Agreement (RA) in 1995–96 (83), and civil cases settled (81, at a minimum). All those receiving AA could apply for the RA or sue, but not both, although some sued after participating in the RA (40).
CA3	*St John's and St Joseph's* (core)	St John's Training School for Boys, 1895–77 (Toronto, 1895–57; relocated Uxbridge, 1957–77); St Joseph's Training School for Boys, 1933–73.	Ontario, CA: Uxbridge and Alfred	Two training schools.	Physical and sexual abuse. Male orphans, truants, delinquents, those with physical or mental disabilities, 'difficult' boys from Indian residential schools, or those from broken or poor families. Abuse by residents not explicitly excluded.	Two schools.	580 validated claimants in groups 1 and 2. In addition, 430 claimants in post-group 2 (validation and outcomes unknown).

CA4	*Grandview* (core)	Grandview Training School for Girls, 1967–76, Cambridge (formerly Ontario Training School for Girls, 1933–66, Galt). (Cambridge was a change of name, not relocation.)	Ontario, CA: Cambridge	One training school.	Physical and sexual abuse, including by residents. Female delinquents or those 'incorrigible'.	One school.	329 claimants participated (257 in group 1 and 72 in group 2), but no information for the number validated. Estimated 320 (250 in group 1 and 70 in group 2), using the same validation rate as CA3.
CA5	*Nova Scotia Institutions* (core)	Shelburne Youth Centre, 1985–2004, Shelburne (formally Nova Scotia School for Boys, 1947–85, Shelburne; Halifax Industrial School for Boys, 1865–1947, Halifax); Nova Scotia School for Girls, 1967–85 (formerly Maritime Home for Girls, 1914–67); Nova Scotia Youth Training School, 1929–97. (Two schools, Sydney Children's Training Centre and Dartmouth Children's Training Centre, were considered in the Stratton Investigation, but dropped.)	Nova Scotia, CA: Shelburne, Truro, and Bible Hill	Three training schools or youth detention centres.	Physical and sexual abuse, including by residents (only in early phase of redress scheme). Delinquent, neglected, or dependent boys; young men serving sentences. Homeless, disadvantaged, or delinquent girls. Emotionally disturbed male and female children.	Three schools or detention centres.	1,101 validated claimants (number is sourced from a Freedom of Information request to the Nova Scotia Government, Oct 2013; it is lower than that reported in Kaufman, 2002).

Continued

Case id; does case continue?	Short case name; type of case	Long case name and previous names, dates of institutional opening and closure, or dates that policy or legislation spanned	Location	Types of institutions or places	Types of abuse and groups included*	Number of institutions and children affected	Number of unique individuals as validated claimants in redress schemes, and where relevant, civil settlements
(1)	(2)	(3)	(4)	(5)	(6)	(7)	(8)
CA6	*Ontario Schools for the Deaf* (core)	Sir James Whitney School for the Deaf, 1870–present; Ernest C. Drury School for the Deaf, 1963–present; Robarts School for the Deaf, 1973–present. Convictions of staff in three institutions, but negotiated agreement is with former students of Sir James Whitney School.	Ontario, CA: Belleville, Milton, and London	Three schools for Deaf and hard-of-hearing children.	Physical and sexual abuse, including by residents. Male and female Deaf and hard-of-hearing children and youth.	Three schools.	86 validated claimants.
CA7	*Jericho Hill* (core)	Jericho Hill Provincial School, 1955–93 (formerly British Columbia School for the Deaf and Blind, 1922–55).	British Columbia, CA: Vancouver	One school for Deaf students; before 1979, for Deaf and blind students.	Sexual abuse, including by residents. Male and female Deaf children (Deaf and blind children before 1979) or young adults.	One school.	359 validated claimants; in addition, 175 other individuals in class action. (Total 350 in class action, but about half also applied to the JICP redress scheme.) Estimated total 534.

CA8	*New Brunswick Institutions* (core)	New Brunswick Training School, 1962–98, Kingsclear (formerly Boys' Industrial Home, 1893–1962, Saint John); Dr. William F. Roberts Hospital School, unknown start year to 1985, Saint John.	New Brunswick, CA: Kingsclear and Saint John	Two training schools for males and a school for children with mental disabilities.	Sexual abuse by staff (no residents). Male delinquents or wards of the state awaiting foster placement (Saint John and Kingsclear). Male and female children with mental disabilities and wards of the state (Roberts).	Two training schools, and one for those with mental disabilities.	345 validated claimants.
CA9	*Alberta Sterilization* (core-plus)	Alberta sexual sterilization of those with mental disabilities, 1928–72. Four feeder schools (99 per cent of cases): Alberta Hospital (Ponoka), Provincial Training School in Red Deer (also called Michener Institute), Alberta Hospital (Oliver), and Deerhome (Red Deer). Travelling guidance clinics referred 1 per cent of cases.	Alberta, CA: Ponoka, Red Deer, and Oliver	Four institutions for those with mental disabilities.	Policy: involuntary sterilization of males and females (children and young adults) with mental disabilities (eugenics policy). Physical and sexual abuse.	Four major feeder schools; 2,834 sterilizations carried out of the 4,739 approved by the Eugenics Board.	Estimated 900 after *Muir* judgment. Four settlement groups: group 1 (504 by Limited Trustee), group 2 (40), group 3 (91 by negotiation and Settlement Panel), and group 4 (246, by Stratton Agreement), plus an additional 'less than 20' other individuals (Alberta Government, 1999, p. 2).

Continued

Case id; does case continue?	Short case name; type of case	Long case name and previous names, dates of institutional opening and closure, or dates that policy or legislation spanned	Location	Types of institutions or places	Types of abuse and groups included*	Number of institutions and children affected	Number of unique individuals as validated claimants in redress schemes, and where relevant, civil settlements
(1)	(2)	(3)	(4)	(5)	(6)	(7)	(8)
CA10 continues	*Duplessis Orphans* (core-plus)	Duplessis Orphans, 1930–65.	Québec, CA	Nurseries, orphanages, training schools, farm schools, and psychiatric institutions.	Policy: children falsely classified as mentally defective or wrongly placed in psychiatric institutions (income generation policy). Physical and sexual abuse, and medical experimentation.	Minimum 26 institutions (17 psychiatric and 9 non-psychiatric institutions), plus farms. Estimated 5,000 affected children.	4,493 validated claimants in two programs (as of 30 Sept 2013).
CA11 continues	*Indian Residential Schools* (core-plus-two)	Indian Residential Schools, under government authority, 1867–1996; explicit government policy of funding schools for assimilation, 1883–1996, although earliest schools were formed in 1831 and 1848–51.	Canada wide (except Prince Edward Island, New Brunswick, and Newfoundland and Labrador)	Training, boarding, and residential schools for male and female Aboriginal children.	Policy: Aboriginal male and female children compelled to attend Indian residential schools (forced assimilation policy). Physical and sexual abuse, including by residents.	139 schools recognized. Estimated 150,000 affected children.	79,179 validated claimants for level 1 payment (as of 31 Dec 2013). Of this group, 18,190 validated for level 2 payment. Latter process continues with more applications (14,213) to be resolved (as of 30 Sept 2013). As of 17 Jul 1996 before the IRSSA was implemented, 4,134 civil claims had been resolved.

AU1 continues	*Stolen Generations* (core-plus-two)	Separation of Aboriginal and Torres Strait Islander Children from Their Families, 1900–1969. Start year is average of relevant legislation; end year is last year in place (HREOC, 1997, p. 225). (HREOC inquiry gives 1910–1970 as indicative.)	Australia wide	Orphanages, settlements, missions, and training schools; includes foster or adoptive family placements.	Policy: removal of Indigenous male and female children, termed 'half-caste' or 'white appearing', from families to state care (institutionalized or not) (forced assimilation policy). Physical and sexual abuse.	Number of institutions unknown. Estimated 20,000 to 25,000 affected children.	Public inquiry and services only.
AU2 continues	*Queensland Institutions* (core)	Queensland Institutions for Children, 1865–1999. (Forde inquiry time span is 1911–99.)	Queensland, AU	Orphanages, homes, training schools, and youth detention centres; excludes foster care placements and institutions for children with disabilities or acute health problems.	Physical and sexual abuse, including by residents, and neglect. Male and female children in institutionalized state care or detention.	159 institutions.	7,453 validated claimants for level 1 payment; of this group, 3,492 validated claimants for level 2 payment. Forde Foundation Trust has 2,222 members on file as of 16 May 2013. Estimated 70 to 80 former Neerkol residents settled in 1999 with Sisters of Mercy and Rockhampton Catholic Diocese.

Continued

Case id; does case continue?	Short case name; type of case	Long case name and previous names, dates of institutional opening and closure, or dates that policy or legislation spanned	Location	Types of institutions or places	Types of abuse and groups included*	Number of institutions and children affected	Number of unique individuals as validated claimants in redress schemes, and where relevant, civil settlements
(1)	(2)	(3)	(4)	(5)	(6)	(7)	(8)
AU3 continues	*Child Migrants* (core-plus)	Australian Institutions receiving Child Migrants, 1912–70. (Senate Report, 2001, defines Child Migrant as a person 'under the age of 16 brought to Australia under an approved scheme during the 20th century', p. 13).	Australia wide, except the two territories.	Orphanages, homes, training schools, and farm schools receiving children sent from the UK and Malta.	Policy: removal of male and female children in UK and Malta to Australian institutions (rural development and population growth policy). Physical and sexual abuse.	52 institutions. Estimated 7,000 affected children, half pre-WW II and half post-WW II. Half sent to Western Australia; 310 sent from Malta.	Public inquiry, benefits, and services only. Estimated 1,700 trips taken for family reunification with UK and AU funds (as of Apr 2013). Civil settlement in 1996 accepted by 223 residents in Christian Brothers' homes in Western Australia (most, not all, were former Child Migrants) and the Christian Brothers.
AU4 continues	*Forgotten Australians* (core)	Australian Institutions for Children, 1895–2003. Start date is when most Australian jurisdictions had established child protection legislation, although the first orphanage was established on Norfolk Island in 1795. (Senate inquiry timespan is 1920s to 1970.)	Australia wide	Orphanages, homes, industrial or training schools, youth detention centres, and homes for children with disabilities. Foster care considered in separate Senate Report (2005)	Physical and sexual abuse and neglect. Male and female children in institutionalized state care.	334 institutions. Estimated 500,000 affected children in institutional and out-of-home care.	Public inquiry and services only.

AU5 continues	*Tasmanian Institutions* (core)	Tasmanian Institutions for Children, 1873–1999.	Tasmania, AU	Orphanages, homes, training schools, and youth detention centres; includes foster care placements.	Physical and sexual abuse and neglect. Male and female children in state care (institutionalized or not). Abuse by residents not explicitly excluded.	38 institutions.	1,836 validated claimants in four phases of the program (as of Sept 2013). Program closed 15 Feb 2013, but a benefit scheme was then established (Abuse in State Care Support Service).
AU6 continues	*South Australian Institutions* (core)	South Australian Institutions for Children and Indigenous children in geographically remote communities, 1895–2004. (Mullighan inquiry timespan is 1940–2004.)	South Australia, AU	Orphanages, residential and group care units, youth detention centres, homes for children with disabilities, and homes for Indigenous children; includes foster care placements and family homes (latter while on probation).	Sexual abuse only, including by residents. Male and female children in state care (institutionalized or not).	56 institutions (19 state and 37 other types of state care); foster or family placements in addition.	242 (validated by Mullighan) and 141 (inferred by Mullighan) in the APY Lands. Claimants (validated or not by Mullighan) apply to Victims of Crime Fund, Abuse in State Care. 91 validated (as of 30 Jul 2014). 158 civil cases lodged against the government; most (131) resolved by negotiation (as of Jun 2013).
AU7	*Tasmanian Stolen Generations* (scheme only; redress of core-plus-two case)	*Stolen Generations of Aboriginal Children Act 2006*, 1935–75. (First Indigenous reserve was established in Tasmania in 1912.)	Tasmania, AU	Homes (group, family, and foster care), institutions, settlements, and missions.	Policy: removal of Indigenous male and female children, termed 'half-caste' from families to state care (institutionalized and not), part of assimilation policy. Includes biological children of those removed if the individual was deceased.	Number of institutions and affected children unknown.	106: 84 validated claimants as members of Tasmanian Stolen Generations, and 22 validated claimants as biological children of Stolen Generations members (since deceased).

Continued

Case id; does case continue?	**Short case name; type of case**	**Long case name and previous names, dates of institutional opening and closure, or dates that policy or legislation spanned**	**Location**	**Types of institutions or places**	**Types of abuse and groups included***	**Number of institutions and children affected**	**Number of unique individuals as validated claimants in redress schemes, and where relevant, civil settlements**
(1)	(2)	(3)	(4)	(5)	(6)	(7)	(8)
AU8	*Redress WA* (scheme only; redress for abuse arising from core and core-plus cases)	Western Australian Institutions for Children, 1886–2006. Start year is legislation in respect of Indigenous people; end year is eligibility criteria for scheme.	Western Australia, AU	Orphanages, homes, training schools, youth detention centres; includes foster care placements.	Physical and sexual abuse and neglect. Male and female children in state care or detention (institutionalized or not). Abuse by residents not explicitly excluded.	156 institutions.	5,345 validated claimants. Redress scheme analysis is of 5,212 validated claimants, who were not in special categories of interim payment, deceased person, or unclaimed monies.

* Information about whether abuse by residents was included in the scheme is provided when it is known. When no information is given, it is not relevant to the case, not known, or highly unlikely.

Appendix 2: Redress Scheme Application and Assessment Process

Case id and name	Information required in application	Government and/or church entity and how application is assessed
CA2 *George Epoch*	• personal information • medical treatment received • sexual abuse experienced • psychological injuries that resulted • supporting documentation	Church: Jesuit Fathers of Upper Canada • Claimant sends application and request for apology to Reconciliation Implementation Committee (RIC), composed of a representative for the victim, the Jesuits, and an independent chair. • RIC sends documents to assessor. • Assessor interviews claimant and determines validity of claim. • Claimant applies separately to Vocational Opportunity Fund for other benefits.

Continued

Case id and name	Information required in application	Government and/or church entity and how application is assessed
CA3 *St John's and St Joseph's*	• abuse experienced • injuries suffered • treatment received • detail of statements to police	Ontario Government: Ministry of the Attorney General Church: Ottawa Brothers and Roman Catholic Church (Archdioceses of Ottawa and Toronto) **groups 1 and 2** (statement to police before 1 April 1993) • Claimant sends application to Reconciliation Process Implementation Committee (RPIC), composed of two representatives from Helpline, a representative of each of the government and church groups, and a chair. • RPIC reviews, comments on, and forwards file to Criminal Injuries Compensation Board (CICB). • CICB-designate holds hearing with claimant (group 2, if requested by claimant). • CICB-designate determines if abuse occurred; and if so, the amount to award; also awards benefit for counselling. • Government pays amount to RPIC, who distributes it to claimant (additional monies came from Ottawa Brothers of the Christian Schools). • Claimant applies separately to Opportunity Fund for other benefits. **post-group 2** (statement to police after 1 April 1993 to 1 June 1996 deadline; more streamlined process and reduced benefits and services; no information on outcomes) • Claimant sends form to CICB. • CICB-designate determines whether abuse occurred; and if so, the amount to award. Oral hearing held only by request of one of the parties. • Claimant does not apply to Opportunity Fund but automatically receives $3,000, if validated.

CA4 *Grandview*	• personal information • abuse or mistreatment experienced • harms that resulted	Ontario Government: Ministry of the Attorney General (MAG) **group 1** (application received by 2 January 1996 deadline) • Claimant sends application to MAG, Abuse in Provincial Institutions Office. • Investigator from the CICB reviews application and relevant files for evidence or inconsistencies, and checks that claimant attended Grandview and for how long (uncertain if claimants can be dropped at this point). File is sent to adjudicator. • Claimant attends oral hearing with adjudicator. • Adjudicator decides if alleged abuse or mistreatment occurred and resulted in substantial and prolonged injury; and if so, determines award. May also award funds for medical treatment. • Second adjudicator reviews decision and may suggest changes. • First adjudicator makes final determination. • Claimant applies separately to Opportunity Fund for other benefits. **group 2** (application received after 2 January 1996 to 17 October 1997) • Claimant sends application to MAG, and it is reviewed by an investigator. • Application is assessed by counsel for the province (uncertain if there is an oral hearing). • Reduced level of services (counselling hot-line ended 31 March 1997) and benefits (not specified)
CA5 *Nova Scotia Institutions*	**phases 1 and 2** 'demand' (claim) on province contains • payment sought • statement that describes abuse and alleged perpetrator(s) **phase 3** • payment sought and rationale for request • statement that describes abuse and alleged perpetrator(s)	Nova Scotia Government: Department of Justice (DOJ) **phases 1 and 2** (revised MOU in phase 2 has more careful investigation of claim) • Claimant gives notice of intention to make a demand to DOJ • Claimant sends demand. • If DOJ is satisfied abuse occurred, it accepts the demand or negotiates with claimant and lawyer to reach agreement on payment. **phase 3** (November 1997, Guidelines introduced, which have more strict procedures than those in previous phases to address potential for fraudulent claims by claimants) • Claimant sends statement to Internal Investigation Unit (IIU)[1] and demand to DOJ. • IIU investigates statement. • If accused employee has taken a polygraph test, DOJ notifies claimant and asks if s/he also wants a test; if yes, DOJ arranges a test. Both are used in DOJ's assessment. • If DOJ is satisfied abuse occurred, it accepts demand or negotiates with claimant and lawyer to reach agreement on payment.

Continued

Case id and name	Information required in application	Government and/or church entity and how application is assessed
CA6 *Ontario Schools for the Deaf*	Sources are unclear on what information was sought, but at a minimum: • personal information • details of abuse experienced	Government: Ministry of Education and Training (MET) • MET sends application pack to claimant, who completes forms and returns them to MET. • Research consultant meets claimant to record abuse and its effects (with sign language interpreter). • Research consultant prepares investigation report and submits it to project coordinator. • Project coordinator determines eligibility; and if validated, submits file to independent adjudicator. • Independent adjudicator determines level of award, with reasons, and informs project co-ordinator, who advises claimant.
CA7 *Jericho Hill,* Jericho Individual Compensation Program (JICP)	• personal information • statement of sexual abuse experienced • names of people to whom abuse was disclosed	Government: Ministry of Attorney General • Claimant meets compensation consultant (CC), who explains the process and determines eligibility. • CC obtains and reviews claimant's records. • Claimant tells story in 'hearing' (signed) with CC. • CC writes claimant's story and provides this and other material in a file that is passed to the Compensation Panel. • Panel members read file and meet as a group to review, discuss, and make decision on claim. • Claimant receives decision and meets with CC to have the decision explained.

CA7 *Jericho Hill Class Action,* Independent Compensation Fund (ICF)	Sources are unclear on what information was sought.	ICF Trustee (Canada Trust Company) **level 1** • Claimant tells ICF Trustee of decision to apply to level 1. • Claimant sends application, release, and acknowledgement of process and outcome. **levels 2 and 3** • Claimant tells ICF Trustee of decision to apply for level 2 or 3. • Claimant sends application, release, and acknowledgement of understanding the process to ICF Trustee. • If applying for level 2, claimant undergoes standardized assessment with an administrator; if applying for level 3, claimant has clinical assessment with a psychologist or psychiatrist. The tests are scored to rank severity of abuse. • Scores sent to ICF Trustee, who notifies claimant. • Individual amounts determined after all claimants' scores are determined. • Final award reduced by the amount received, if any, from the JICP.
CA8 *New Brunswick Institutions*	Statement of claim[2] that describes abuse.	Government: Department of Justice (DOJ) • Claimant sends statement of claim to DOJ. • DOJ lawyer reviews claim and decides if claimant suffered harm. • DOJ lawyer interviews claimant, and when relevant, seeks response from named alleged abuser. • DOJ lawyer makes decision on claim; if accepted, makes an offer to claimant's lawyer. • If offer is accepted, DOJ forwards draft recommendation to DOJ policy advisor, who determines whether the amount falls within the scope of the program. • If so, policy advisor forwards recommendation to higher level DOJ official to approve.

Continued

Case id and name	Information required in application	Government and/or church entity and how application is assessed
CA10 *Duplessis Orphans*		Government: Ministère des Relations avec les Citoyens et l'Immigration (MRCI) (time 1), Ministère de l'Emploi et de la Solidarité sociale (MESS, time 2)
	time 1 • personal information • placement history • why claimant believed s/he was placed in an institution, and why the placement was not justified	**time 1** (2001 program) • Claimant sends application to MRCI. • Claimant can request hearing with Comité Multipartite in person or by phone. • Comité Multipartite makes decision.
	time 2 • personal information • placement history • experiences in institution or placement • if available, institutional record of psychological assessment(s) that concluded claimant was 'intellectually handicapped or mentally retarded and thus unsuitable for adoption…' (MESS, 2007, application form, p. 3).	**time 2** (2007 program) • Claimant sends application and relevant documents to MESS. • MESS determines validity of application; and if further information is required, contacts claimant.

CA11 *Indian Residential Schools,* Common Experience Payment (CEP) and Independent Assessment Process (IAP)	Claimant can apply for one or both. **CEP** • personal information • date of placement and school/s attended **IAP** • personal information • placement history • details of abuse and harm caused • treatment (medical, counselling, traditional healing) sought or received • work and education history • any opportunities lost because of abuse • future care needs	Government: Aboriginal Affairs and Northern Development Canada (AANDC) **CEP** • Claimant requests, completes, and sends CEP application to Service Canada. • Service Canada requests AANDC to verify claimant's residential school history. **IAP** • Claimant sends application to IAP Secretariat. • IAP Secretariat reviews application to determine eligibility. • IAP Secretariat determines if claim is standard, complex, or exceptional.[3] • If a standard claim, claimant attends a hearing with adjudicator or the Secretariat resolves claim without a hearing. If a complex claim, claimant attends a hearing with an adjudicator, with expert evidence generally required. If the claim is exceptional, the matter goes to court, and a judge makes a determination.

Continued

Case id and name	Information required in application	Government and/or church entity and how application is assessed
AU2 *Queensland Institutions*	Claimant can apply for level 1 or levels 1 and 2. **level 1** • personal information • placement history • non-detailed account of abuse or neglect **level 2** • more detail about abuse and harm suffered • assistance sought in relation to the harm • whether claimant had reported abuse or neglect to police or had sought legal advice	Government: Department of Communities (DOC) **level 1** (abuse) • Claimant sends application to DOC redress services. • DOC reviews application and advises claimant of outcome. • If payment is offered, claimant can defer receiving it until after a level 2 payment decision is made; or advise DOC of intention to apply for level 2 payment. **level 2** (more serious abuse and harm) • Decisions are made only after all level 1 payments are finalized. • Expert panel reviews and makes decisions.

AU5 *Tasmanian Institutions*	In phases 1 and 2, claimant provides initial information by phone contact; in phases 3 and 4, by written application • personal information • details of the abuse • details of placement	Government: Office of Ombudsman (Omb, phases 1 and 2), Department of Health and Human Services (DHHS, phases 1–4), Department of Premier and Cabinet (DPAC, phase 3) **phases 1 and 2** (2003–6) • Claimant calls Omb and has phone interview. • Omb seeks information from department records to determine eligibility; prepares file for interview team. • Claimant has interview with two interviewers (can request telephone interview). • Interviewers prepare summary of claim and recommendations on its strength, and send summary to coordinator, who completes an assessment report for the Omb to ratify. • Assessment report sent to independent assessor (an external lawyer), who reviews it and makes determination of payment level. **phases 3 and 4** (2007–13) • Claimant sends application to DHHS After Care Support Service. • With assistance of assessment team, independent assessor determines if a claim is eligible. • Member of assessment team carries out interview and makes recommendations to independent assessor. • Independent assessor makes determination of whether any payment should be made; and if so, payment level.
AU6 *South Australian Institutions*	• personal information • names of relatives and carers at the time of abuse • placement history • details and effects of sexual abuse • medical treatment sought • debts owed to state	Government: Attorney General's Department (AGD) • Claimant sends application to AGD Victims of Crime Fund, Victims of Abuse in State Care. • Assessment team, composed of legal advisors, decides whether further investigation or interview is required; it decides claimant's eligibility and severity of harm suffered; and it makes a recommendation to the AG on payment level. • AG makes final decision.

Continued

Case id and name	Information required in application	Government and/or church entity and how application is assessed
AU7 *Tasmanian Stolen Generations*	Sources are unclear on what information was sought, but at a minimum: • personal information • details of removal or placement	Government: Department of Premier and Cabinet, Stolen Generations Office (SGO) • Claimant submits application to SGO. • Assessor gathers documents (e.g. birth certificates and adoption files) from government departments. • Office manager prepares a summary of facts and preliminary advice for the assessor. • If assessor thinks an application may not succeed, claimant is given opportunity to meet assessor. • Assessor makes final decision.
AU8 *Redress WA*	Sources are unclear on what information was sought, but at a minimum: • personal information • statement of abuse or neglect	Government: Department of Communities (DOC) • Claimant sends application to DOC, Redress WA. • Redress WA reviews claim. • If satisfied that the abuse or neglect occurred and resulted in injury, harm, or loss, senior redress officer determines which level[4] and recommends offer. • If level 1 or 2, a team leader decides whether to approve. If level 3 or 4, senior redress officer gives a report to an internal member who assesses the application; then an independent review panel decides whether to approve the amount.

[1] Statements in phases 1 and 2 could have been given to the Stratton investigators, the Royal Canadian Mounted Police, or the Internal Investigations Unit (IIU). However, with the introduction of the Guidelines in November 1997, a new claimant had to give a statement to the IIU.

[2] Sources are not clear on the definition of 'statement of claim'; however, the same term is used for the document a plaintiff files to commence a civil suit.

[3] A complex claim is for a wrongful act, other than sexual or physical abuse, with serious psychological consequences. An exceptional claim is when loss of income (or opportunity for income) or physical harm are beyond the IAP maxima, or the matter is sufficiently complex that court is most appropriate.

[4] These are as follows: level 1 (moderate abuse or neglect); level 2 (serious abuse or neglect, with some continuing effects); level 3 (severe abuse or neglect, with ongoing effects); and level 4 (very severe abuse or neglect, with ongoing effects).

Appendix 3A: Redress Scheme Elements and Outcomes

case id	case name	interim counselling	counselling (service)	counselling (benefit)	financial counselling (service)	medical/ dental (benefit)	voc/ed (benefit)	legal advice (service or benefit)	other	other includes	govt apology	church apology	which apology first?	memorial	other memory projects
(1)	(2)	(3)	(4)	(5)	(6)	(7)	(8)	(9)	(10)	(11)	(12)	(13)	(14)	(15)	(16)
CA2	George Epoch	yes	yes	yes (had to apply, no maximum set; offered in addition to counselling as service)	yes	no	yes (had to apply to max of $4,000 in Fund)	no	yes	Recorder	NA	yes	NA	no	no
CA3	St John's and St Joseph's	yes	no	yes (had to apply to max of $10,000 for counselling)	yes	yes (had to apply to max of $3,000 in Fund)	yes (had to apply to max of $3,000 in Fund)	yes ($450 service)	yes	Recorder; wage loss	yes	yes	same time	no	no

Continued

case id	case name	interim counselling	counselling (service)	counselling (benefit)	financial counselling (service)	medical/ dental (benefit)	voc/ed (benefit)	legal advice (service or benefit)	other	other includes	govt apology	church apology	which apology first?	memorial	other memory projects
(1)	(2)	(3)	(4)	(5)	(6)	(7)	(8)	(9)	(10)	(11)	(12)	(13)	(14)	(15)	(16)
CA4	Grandview	yes, but access reduced for group 2	no	yes (had to apply, to max of $10,000 for counselling)	yes	yes (had to apply to max of $3,000 in Fund); adjudicator could award up to $10,000 for exceptional medical or dental costs	yes (had to apply, to max of $3,000 in Fund)	yes ($1,000 benefit)	yes	general benefits (dedicated crisis line, scar/ tattoo removal; evaluation of Grandview; video of survivors); other individual benefits (short-term residential program to max of $5,000)	yes	NA	NA	no	no
CA5	Nova Scotia Institutions	yes	no	yes (allotment made based on abuse severity, $5,000, $7,500, or $10,000)	no	partly (could use the counselling benefit for medical or dental)	partly (could use the counselling benefit for medical or dental)	yes (paid by govt to lawyers)	no	NA	yes	NA	NA	no	no
CA6	Ontario Schools for the Deaf	no	no	yes (had to apply, to max of $10,000)	no	no	no (facilitated referrals only)	yes ($1,000 benefit)	yes	interpreter costs for legal advice or other scheme process activities	no	NA	NA	no	no

CA7	Jericho Hill, JICP	unlimited access to RHAP*	unlimited access to RHAP*	no	no (regular claimants); yes (special track claimants)	no	no	yes ($1,000 benefit)	yes	special track claimants: counselling and legal services provided; govt donated $1m to Deaf Community Foundation	regret	NA	NA	no	no
CA7.1	Jericho Hill Class Action	unlimited access to RHAP*	unlimited access to RHAP*	no	no	no	yes (as part of Legacy Trust)	yes (included in settlement)	yes	Jericho Hill Legacy Trust; scholarships, ASL classes for family, educational advocacy in the province's colleges and universities	regret	NA	NA	yes	no
CA8	New Brunswick Institutions	yes (allotment of $5,000)	no	yes (part of initial allotment; could seek more funds)	yes	no	yes ($800 tuition and books, included in financial payment)	yes (included in financial payment not to exceed 20%)	no	NA	no	NA	NA	no	no
CA10	Duplessis Orphans	no	no	no	no	no	no	no	no	NA	yes	yes	govt	no	no
CA11	Indian Residential Schools	yes	yes	no	no	no	no	no CEP; yes IAP (15% included in financial payment; overall legal costs not to exceed 30%)	yes	Aboriginal Healing Foundation; TRC's activities (statement gathering, document collection, national events, National Research Centre)	yes	yes	church	yes	TRC commemorative and related projects

Continued

case id	case name	interim counselling	counselling (service)	counselling (benefit)	financial counselling (service)	medical/ dental (benefit)	voc/ed (benefit)	legal advice (service or benefit)	other	other includes	govt apology	church apology	which apology first?	memorial	other memory projects
(1)	(2)	(3)	(4)	(5)	(6)	(7)	(8)	(9)	(10)	(11)	(12)	(13)	(14)	(15)	(16)
AU2	Queensland Institutions	yes	yes	no	yes (one appt)	no	no	yes ($500 benefit)	yes	Forde Foundation Trust (small grants for household, dental, personal development, and wellness; est $811 per registered member of Trust)	yes	yes	church	yes	no
AU5	Tasmanian Institutions	yes, but limited in phase 4 to 3 sessions	no	yes, but limited in phase 4 to 3 sessions	no	no	no	yes (phases 1–2, one consultation benefit; phases 3–4, $300 benefit)	no	NA	yes	yes	church	yes	no

AU6	South Australian Institutions	yes	yes	no	no	no	no	yes ($750 benefit)	no		yes	yes	church	yes	no
AU7	Tasmanian Stolen Generations	yes, on request	yes, on request	no	no	no	no	NA (no release)	yes	assist in documentating application; learn more about family history	yes	yes	same time	no	no
AU8	Redress WA	yes, limited to 3 hours, but could request more	Dnk	no	no	no	no	NA (no release)	no	NA	yes	yes	church	yes	no

*RHAP: Residential Historical Abuse Program, which also includes specialist services to the Deaf, hard of hearing, and DeafBlind, is a service provided by the province to any individual sexually abused in an institution.

Appendix 3B: Financial Payments, Validation, and Other Case Data

case id	case name and scheme	number of claimants (cases resolved)	per cent validated	number validated	money logic	based on proving	invest and number of claimants	potential range, flat amount, or other formula	average payment in CAD or AUD	benefit (excludes legal costs)	year of tangible result	time to tangible result (yrs)	comments on estimates and outcomes
(1)	(2)	(3)	(4)	(5)	(6)	(7)	(8)	(9)	(10)	(11)	(12)	(13)	(14)
CA2	George Epoch	97	86	83	flat equal	sexual abuse and severity	high invest-low N	$25,000	25,000	est $2,700 per person	1996	6	Actual benefits were not reported and had to be estimated; uncertain whether planned benefit of $4,000 was received by all claimants; re-estimated based on information in Kaufman (2002).
CA3	St John's and St Joseph's, groups 1 and 2	595	97.5	580	individualized, lower	abuse and severity	high invest-high N	not stipulated, but govt contribution to a max of $25,000	22,319	est $2,328 per person (N=580); plus $3,356 per person (N=468) for counselling	1995	5	Average payment was interpolated from Hoffman (1996) and Kaufman (2002). Average benefit ranges from $2,328 (Opportunity Fund, but no counselling sought) to $5,684 (those who sought the counselling benefit).
CA4	Grandview	329	97.5	320	individualized, lower	abuse, severity, and impact	high invest-low N	$3,000 to $60,000	37,700	est $8,130 per person (individual benefit)	1998	7	Leach (1998) reports $37,700 average financial payment, but Kaufman (2002, p. 338) suggests it was lower. Actual individual and general benefits were not reported; individual benefit estimated.

CA5	Nova Scotia Institutions	1,222	90	1,101	individualized, lower	abuse and severity	low invest- high N	no min to $120,000	28,583	est $7,281 per person	1998	7	Counselling benefit was estimated by dividing total costs for counselling by the number of validated claimants; costs for interim counselling were not included. In the 1997 Guidelines, counselling benefit could also be used for voc/ed and medical/dental expenses..
CA6	Ontario Schools for the Deaf	160	54	86	individualized, lower	abuse and severity	high invest- low N	$3,000 to $60,000	39,131	$10,000 plus interpreter costs	2000	9	Actual benefits for counselling and interpreter costs were not reported.
CA7	Jericho Hill, JICP	365	98	359	individualized, lower	sexual abuse, severity, and impact	high invest- low N	$3,000 to $60,000	36,462	NA	1999	7	
CA 7.1	Jericho Hill Class Action (level 1)	350 class members	NA	NA	flat equal	valid member of class	high invest- low N	$10,000	10,000	in settlement package	2006	8	About half of the 350 class members had received a JICP payment. Start year for time to tangible result is the year the litigation began (1998).
CA 7.1	Jericho Hill Class Action (levels 2 and 3)		NA	NA	individualized, no cap; distributed from residual pool of funds, using points from medical/ psychological assessment	sexual abuse, severity, and impact	high invest- low N	level 2, no min to $75,000; level 3, no min to $125,000	dnk	in settlement package	2007	9	Start year for time to tangible result is the year the litigation began (1998).

Continued

case id	case name and scheme	number of claimants (cases resolved)	per cent validated	number validated	money logic	based on proving	invest and number of claimants	potential range, flat amount, or other formula	average payment in CAD or AUD	benefit (excludes legal costs)	year of tangible result	time to tangible result (yrs)	comments on estimates and outcomes
(1)	(2)	(3)	(4)	(5)	(6)	(7)	(8)	(9)	(10)	(11)	(12)	(13)	(14)
CA8	New Brunswick Institutions	443	78	345	individualized, lower	sexual abuse, severity, and impact	low invest-high N	no min to $120,000	36,232	$5,000 (higher if more counselling sought)	1998	6	Actual benefits for counselling were not reported. Financial payment includes tuition benefit ($800) and legal costs (not to exceed 20%). If 15% for legal fees is deducted from the average financial payment, the amount is $30,797.
CA10	Duplessis Orphans (time 1)	1,507	67	1,012	equal (other formula)	no abuse had to be established	low invest-high N	$10,000 plus $1,000 for each year	25,707	NA	2003	6	
CA10	Duplessis Orphans (time 2)	5,025	69	3,481	flat equal	no abuse had to be established	low invest-high N	$15,000	15,000	NA	2010	13	Figures as of 30 Sept 2013; program continues.
CA11	Indian Residential Schools (CEP)	102,993	77	79,179	equal (other formula)	no abuse had to be established	high invest-high N	$10,000 plus $3,000 for each additional year	19,412	NA	2009	13	Figures as of 31 Dec 2013; 98% of applications resolved.
CA11	Indian Residential Schools (IAP)	23,661	77	18,191	individualised, lower, distributed from residual pool of funds	abuse, severity, and impact	high invest-high N	$5,000 to $275,000, or up to $430,00, depending on income loss	100,530	NA	2012	16	Figures as of 30 Sept 2013; 62% of applications resolved. Legal fees of 15% have been deducted from average payment.

AU2	Queensland Institutions (level 1)	10,218	73	7,453	flat equal	abuse and severity (declaration)	low invest-high N	$7,000	7,000	NA	2009	11	Began with pool of $100m. All level 1 payments distributed; then allocated residual to validated level 2 claimants.
AU2	Queensland Institutions (level 2)	5,416	64	3,492	individualized, lower, distributed from residual pool of funds	abuse, severity, and impact	low invest-high N	no min to $33,000	12,894	NA	2010	12	Recipients of level 2 payments received on average $19,894 (levels 1 and 2 combined).
AU5	Tasmanian Institutions (phases 1–3)	1,873	78	1,454	individualized, lower	abuse, severity, and impact	high invest-high N	no min to $60,000	33,906	NA	2007	4	Financial payment may include a counselling component in phases 3 and 4.
AU5	Tasmanian Institutions (phase 4)	541	71	382	individualized, lower	abuse, severity, and impact	high invest-high N	no min to $35,000	14,136	NA	2012	9	Counselling reduced in phase 4 to 3 sessions.
AU6	South Australian Institutions	129	71	91	individualized, lower	sexual abuse, severity, and impact	low invest-low N	max $30,000 (exceptional $50,000)	14,407	NA	2011	7	Figures as of 30 Jul 2014; 79% of applications resolved. Average payment is of those accepting the offer
AU7	Tasmanian Stolen Generations	128	66	84	equal, other formula	no abuse had to be established	low invest-low N	pool of funds distributed equally to eligible claimants	58,333	NA	2008	2	Began with pool of $5m. Of 23 family members who applied, 22 validated; $100,000 awarded for average of $4,545 per person. Residual of $4.9 allocated equally to 84 validated members of Stolen Generations.
AU8	Redress WA	5,768	90	5,210	individualized, four fixed bands	abuse, severity, and impact	low invest-high N	max $45,000	22,465	NA	2010	3	An additional 135 validated claimants of 149 who applied were in special categories (interim payment only, deceased person, or unclaimed monies)

Appendix 3C: Financial Payments, Adjusted for 2012, in Different Currencies

case id	case name and scheme	avg per person in local currency AUD/CAD	yr tangible result (yr used to adjust payments)	adjusted GDP deflator for Canada 2012 $	adjusted GDP deflator for Australia 2012 $	CAD to AUD (0.9696) 2012	AUD to USD (0.9933) 2012	AUD to Euros (0.7765) 2012	AUD to British Pounds (0.6227) 2012
(1)	(2)	(3)	(4)	(5)	(6)	(7)	(8)	(9)	(10)
CA2	George Epoch	25,000	1996	35,939	–	34,847	34,614	27,059	21,699
CA3	St John's & St Joseph's (groups 1 and 2)	22,319	1995	32,604	–	31,613	31,401	24,547	19,685
CA4	Grandview (groups 1 and 2)	37,700	1998	53,781	–	52,146	51,797	40,491	32,471
CA5	Nova Scotia Institutions	28,583	1998	40,775	–	39,536	39,271	30,700	24,619
CA6	Ontario Schools for the Deaf	39,131	2000	52,688	–	51,086	50,744	39,668	31,811
CA7	Jericho Hill, JICP	36,462	1999	51,123	–	50,100	49,765	38,903	31,198
CA7.1	Jericho Hill Class Action, level 1	10,000	2006	11,652	–	11,297	11,221	8,772	7,035
CA7.1	Jericho Hill Class Action, levels 2 & 3	dnk			–				

CA8	New Brunswick Institutions	36,232	1998	51,687	–	50,116	49,780	38,915	31,207
CA10	Duplessis Orphans, time 1	25,707	2003	32,783	–	31,787	31,574	24,683	19,794
CA10	Duplessis Orphans, time 2	15,000	2010	16,114	–	15,624	15,519	12,132	9,729
CA11	Indian Residential Schools, level 1 (CEP)	19,412	2009	21,467	–	20,815	20,676	16,163	12,962
CA11	Indian Residential Schools, level 2 (IAP)	115,610 less 15% in legal fees = 100,530	2012	100,530	–	97,474	96,821	75,689	60,697
AU2	Queensland Institutions, level 1	7,000	2009	–	7,662	7,662	7,611	5,949	4,771
AU2	Queensland Institutions, levels 1 & 2 combined	19,894	2010	–	21,644	21,644	21,499	16,807	13,478
AU5	Tasmanian Institutions, phases 1–3	33,906	2007	–	40,791	40,791	40,518	31,674	25,400
AU5	Tasmanian Institutions, phase 4	14,136	2012	–	14,136	14,136	14,041	10,977	8,802
AU6	South Australian Institutions	14,407	2011	–	14,718	14,718	14,619	11,428	9,165
AU7	Tasmanian Stolen Generations	58,333	2008	–	67,073	67,073	66,624	52,082	41,766
AU8	Redress WA	22,465	2010	–	24,361	24,361	24,198	18,916	15,170

Appendix 4: Public Apologies and Statements

Appendix 4 presents the public or official apologies, and where relevant, public statements of regret or acknowledgement that do not reach the status of a complete or 'real' apology, for the 19 cases. Some cases also gave personal or individual apologies to validated claimants, but these are not shown. With considerable range in the words used and their meanings, the texts can be generically termed 'apology responses'. Precisely how survivors have interpreted the words (that is, as a 'real' apology or not) cannot be known. Some statements are more heartfelt than others and contain elements associated with 'real' apologies, but survivors may interpret the same apology differently (see Alter, 1999; Senate Report, 2009, pp. 21–33).

In gathering material, I noted some inaccuracies in Kaufman (2002), Political Apologies and Reparations (<www.political-apologies.wlu.ca>), and the Senate Report (2001). Although I may not have sourced all apology responses, I believe that this compilation is the most accurate to date for the 19 cases.

In general, when there are multiple government responses, they are ordered by date within government level (federal, then province or state). Church responses are listed by church name (alphabetically) or by date, depending on the material available. All quoted material preserves the original text and spelling.

In Australia, information on apologies is also available at the Find & Connect web resource, <http://findandconnect.gov.au>.

CANADA

Mount Cashel (CA1)

Government (province)

On 2 December 1996, the Newfoundland Minister of Justice and Attorney General Chris Decker read a statement to the legislature, advising that the government had taken steps to reach settlement (first large civil settlement only) 'to provide reasonable compensation ... to end the distress caused to the victims by the prolonged proceedings to date'.

There was no mention of apology or regret in the statement (see <http://www.assembly.nl.ca/business /hansard/ga43session1/96-12-02>).

Church

Catholic Church

Two apologies were made by church officials: one, for abuse by clergy members who worked in the St John's Diocese, but outside the Mount Cashel School; and the second, for abuse by Christian Brothers or staff who worked at Mount Cashel. The latter is relevant to this case, but I list both to show a wider context.

On 18 July 1990, Archbishop Alphonsus Penney, speaking for the St John's Diocese, apologized to victims and their families. At the time, four priests had been convicted, and two were awaiting trial (Winter, 1990, p. 1). According to a news story (Ulbrich, 1990), Penney's apology said, in part, 'We are sorry for the times you were not believed, were not supported or were ostracized in any way in our community... For every word and action which may have deepened your pain, we are profoundly sorry'.

On 5 April 1992, the Christian Brothers of Ireland formally apologized to Mount Cashel survivors, but no further detail could be sourced on the apology.

George Epoch **(CA2)**

Church

Catholic Church

Two apologies were made by church officials. In August 1992, Jesuit Provincial Supervisor, Father Eric MacLean apologized. MacLean said, 'the healthiest way to achieve healing and wholeness in your own lives may well be to focus your anger on his [Epoch's] actions, realizing that he was the one who did something wrong, not you the victims' (Mussell, 1995, p. 14).

As part of the Reconciliation Agreement in 1994, the Jesuits published an apology that expressed their 'sorrow, regret, and humility' for Epoch's behaviour. The apology was given to the Chiefs of the Band Councils at Cape Croker, Saugeen, and Wikwemikong and provided to the major newspapers.

St John's and St Joseph's **(CA3)**

Government (province)

On 25 June 1996, Attorney General Charles Harnick apologized in the legislature, on behalf of the people of Ontario, for abuse at the two schools from the 1940s to the 1970s. His resolution was passed unanimously, and a minute of silence was held. The Helpline agreement had stipulated that a premier was to 'apologize for and condemn the abuse', but Premier Mike Harris refused to do so. David McCann, who established Helpline, sued Harris and successive premiers, without success, until 2004 when the premier 'agreed... to apologize and pay [McCann's] legal fees' (Henton, 2004). On 2 June 2004, in the legislature, Premier Dalton McGuinty apologized to survivors.

Church

Catholic Church
In 1996, Ottawa Archbishop Marcel Gervais and Toronto Archbishop Aloysius Ambrozic issued a statement of apology and invited school survivors to attend special Masses in Ottawa and Toronto. On 21 April 1996, during the Mass in Ottawa, Gervais' apology was interrupted by a survivor, who said 'I don't want an apology from you. I want an apology from the brothers who ruined my life, those dogs...' (Alter, 1999, p. 8).

Grandview **(CA4)**

Government (province)

On 16 November 1999, Member of Parliament Jim Flaherty moved that 'this House, on behalf of Ontario and pursuant to the 1994 Agreement with the Grandview Survivors Support Group, apologizes and expresses sincere regret for the harm caused by the physical, sexual, and psychological abuse at the school... between the 1930s to 1970s' (see <http://gateway .ontla.on.ca/web/house-proceedings/house_detail.do?locale=en&Date=1999-11-16&detailPage=/house-proceedings/transcripts/files_html/1999-11-16_L012A.htm#P116_31487>). It took 5 years for the government to apologize because their position was to wait until criminal proceedings had concluded, which occurred the year before, in 1998.

Nova Scotia Institutions **(CA5)**

Government (province)

On 3 May 1996, Minister of Justice William Gillis apologized in the legislature to survivors of five Nova Scotia institutions. The apology formed part of his announcement of a compensation package (Alter, 1999, p. 11).

Ontario Schools for the Deaf **(CA6)**

No apology response was sourced.

Jericho Hill (CA7)

Government (province)

On 28 June 1995, when tabling Special Counsel Thomas Berger's report (1995), Attorney General Colin Gabelmann made a ministerial statement to 'recognize the victims and survivors'. He said, 'we regret that they were exposed to... terrible experiences...' His statement announced a compensation package to begin in 1996. Present were members of the Deaf community (see <http://www.leg.bc.ca/hansard/35th4th/h0628pm1.htm>).

Distinct from the compensation package was a class action, settled in April 2004. One component of the settlement was an acknowledgement of abuse that occurred in Jericho Hill School and the importance of the settlement in furthering the public interest. On 12 May 2004, British Columbia Premier Gordon Campbell, on behalf of the province, announced in the legislature his 'deepest regret' for the abuse. A DVD of the event, with American Sign Language interpretation, was sent to each class member (Anne Sheane, lawyer for the plaintiffs, personal communication, 9 January 2014).

New Brunswick Institutions (CA8)

Although Kaufman (2002, p. 369) reports that 'the Minister of Justice later decided to issue apologies on behalf of the Departments of Justice and Solicitor General and the province', this was likely in the form of personal apology by letter. I contacted former officials from the relevant department, and none recalled a public apology or statement.

Alberta Sterilization (CA9)

Government (province)

In announcing the last major civil settlement (the Stratton Agreement), the government published a 'statement of regret', which quotes Premier Ralph Klein as saying 'we are doing the best we can... to make things right and to correct, as much as possible, the wrongs of many years ago' (Alberta Government, 2 November 1999). In a CBC News story (9 November 1999), Klein is quoted as saying, 'We extend regrets for the actions of another government, in another period of time. It's unfortunate' (see <http://www.cbc.ca/news/canada/alberta-apologizes-for-forced-sterilization-1.169579>).

Duplessis Orphans (CA10)

Government (province)

On 14 March 1999, as part of the government's financial payment offer, the Québec Premier, Lucien Bouchard apologized. On 30 June 2001,

COOID accepted a revised government offer, along with an apology by Québec Premier Bernard Landry.

Church

Catholic Church
In September 1991, Québec's Catholic bishops refused to make an apology. On 22 November 2007, Marc Cardinal Ouellet, the Catholic Church's senior bishop in Québec, 'issued a sweeping apology for historical wrongs, [but] ... the apology made no mention of the Duplessis Orphans', which attracted criticism that it 'lacked credibility' <http://www.thecanadianencyclopedia.com/articles/duplessis-orphans>.

Other

Québec College of Physicians
Despite COOID's requests, an apology from this peak medical body has not yet been made.

***Indian Residential Schools* (CA11)**

Government (federal)

On 7 January 1998, in a Statement of Reconciliation, the Minister of Indian Affairs, Jane Stewart, said that the 'Government of Canada ... formally expresses ... our profound regret for past actions ... The Government of Canada acknowledges its role [in the schools] ... and to those ... who suffered [sexual and physical abuse] ..., we are deeply sorry'. The statement was made when the government announced its response to the Royal Commission on Aboriginal Peoples (Minister of Indian Affairs and Northern Development, 1997).

On 11 June 2008, Prime Minister Stephen Harper, offered a Statement of Apology to former students of Indian Residential Schools in the House of Commons. Attending the televized event were church representatives, hundreds of former students, and many Aboriginal leaders. In addition to 'overflow crowds' in a room outside the House of Commons and on the lawn of Parliament Hill, 'more than 30 events were staged across the country' to view the apology live. Background material is at <http://www.cbc.ca /news/canada/pm-cites-sad-chapter-in-apology-for-residential-schools-1.699389>. The order of proceedings, apology text, and responses are at <http://www.atns.net.au/agreement .asp?EntityID=4657>. Analysis from an Aboriginal perspective is at <http://www.ammsa.com/publications/windspeaker/govt-canada-apologize-100-years-atrocities>.

Church

Anglican Church
On 6 August 1993, Primate Michael Peers apologized on behalf of the Anglican Church to the First Nations people of Canada at the National Native Convocation in Minaki, Ontario. The text of the apology has been translated into ten First Nations languages, in addition to French and English, at <http://www.anglican.ca/relationships/trc/apology>. In 2008, the 15th anniversary of the apology was commemorated; a video was produced with clips from the original apology and response, and with comments by the Primate Fred Hiltz (see 'The living apology' at <http://vimeo.com/25669733>).

Catholic Church
The Canadian Conference of Catholic Bishops (CCCB) (2013) lists the following three apologies, in addition to statements and healing initiatives.

On 15 March 1991, a statement was given at the National Meeting on Indian Residential Schools by 'Canadian Catholic Bishops and leaders of men and women [sic] religious communities' that said 'we are sorry and deeply regret the pain, suffering, and alienation that so many experienced'. The text is at <http://www.cccb.ca/site/images/stories/pdf/apology_saskatoon.pdf>.

On 24 July 1991, the Rev. Doug Crosby, on behalf of the Missionary Oblates of Mary Immaculate, apologized to the First Nations people of Canada for 'the existence of the schools themselves ... The biggest abuse is not what happened in the schools, but that the schools themselves happened. ... We wish to apologize ... for the instances of individual physical and sexual abuse'. The text is at <http://www.cccb.ca/site/images/stories /pdf/oblate_apology_english.pdf>.

In 1995, the CCCB presented a brief to the Royal Commission on Aboriginal Peoples, 'Let justice flow like a mighty river', part of which addressed the Indian Residential Schools. The text, which is more of a statement than an apology, is at <http://www.cccb.ca/site/images/stories/pdf/justice_flow_residential_schools.pdf>.

Other responses are listed by the Archdiocese of Vancouver (press release 13 September 2013) with links to the texts (see <http://rcav.org/uploadedFiles/News _Events/Statements_Letters/TRC%20press%20release%20Sept%2013%20v.2.pdf>).

In April 2009, Pope Benedict XVI expressed 'sorrow' in a private audience with a delegation from the Assembly of First Nations (AFN) for the experiences of those in Catholic-run residential school (see <http://www.cbc.ca/news/world/story/2009/04/29/pope-first-nations042909.html>).

Presbyterian Church

On 8 October 1994, a Confession on the church's role in the Indian residential school system was presented formally by the Rev. George Vais at the Forks National Historic Site of Canada (Winnipeg), where it was received by Phil Fontaine, Grand Chief of the Assembly of Manitoba, on behalf of First Nations people. The church views the text as an apology, although variants of the word 'apology' are not in it. The text of the Confession and other activities aimed at healing and reconciliation are available at <http://presbyterian.ca/resources-hr/>.

United Church

On 31 October 1986, the Rt. Rev. Robert Smith, on behalf of the United Church of Canada, acknowledged that the church 'tried to make you be like us and in so doing we helped to destroy the vision that made you what you were' and sought forgiveness. Statement texts are at <http://www.united-church.ca/beliefs/policies/1986/a651> (Smith's apology) and <http://www.united-church.ca/aboriginal/relationships/response> (the All Native Circle response by Memnook).

On 27 October 1998, the Rt. Rev. Bill Phipps, on behalf of the United Church of Canada, offered 'our most sincere apology'... 'for the pain and suffering' caused by the church's involvement in the Indian residential school system, a 'cruel and ill-conceived system of assimilation'. The text is at <http://www.united-church.ca/beliefs/policies/1998/a623>. The year before, in May 1997, the St Andrew's United Church (Alberni, British Columbia) apologized to First Nations People.

Other

University

On 27 October 2011, University of Manitoba President, David Barnard, apologized to the University's Aboriginal students and faculty for the institution's not challenging 'the forced assimilation of Aboriginal peoples and consequent loss of their language, culture and traditions'. See news story at <http://www.cbc.ca/news/canada/nova-scotia/u-of-m-president-apologizes-for-residential-schools-1.1027554>.

AUSTRALIA

Stolen Generations (AU1)

Government (federal)

Motions of Reconciliation and of Apology were introduced in the Australian Parliament in 1999 and 2008, respectively.

On 26 August 1999, Prime Minister John Howard moved a Motion of Reconciliation, expressing 'deep and sincere regret' and a commitment to reconciliation between Indigenous and non-Indigenous Australians. The Leader of the Opposition, Kim Beazley, moved to amend the motion to include an unreserved apology to Indigenous Australians for past injustices, and to establish processes to provide justice and restitution. The Opposition's amendments were not accepted, and the motion carried in its original form. The text of Howard's motion is at <http://parlinfo.aph.gov.au/parlInfo/search/display/display.w3p;query=%28Id:media/pressrel/23e06%29;rec=0> and the amendments proposed by Beazley's motion are at <http://parlinfo.aph.gov.au/parlInfo/search/display/display.w3p;db=CHAMBER;id=chamber%2Fhansardr%2F1999-08-26%2F0031;query=Id%3A%22chamber%2Fhansardr%2F1999-08-26%2F0030%22>.

On 13 February 2008, at the first session of federal parliament, Prime Minister Kevin Rudd moved a Motion of Apology to Australia's Indigenous Peoples. The Leader of the Opposition, Brendan Nelson, responded by supporting the motion; it passed both houses of Parliament.

Video and text of the 2008 apology are at <http://australia.gov.au/about-australia/our-country/our-people/apology-to-australias-indigenous-peoples>. Background to the apology and subsequent activities are described at <http://www.dss.gov.au/our-responsibilities/indigenous-australians/programs-services/recognition-respect/apology-to-australias-indigenous-peoples>.

Government (state and territory)

All state and territory apologies were moved as motions in parliament. The following excerpts draw from the start of the apology and do not include other elements (the introduction and full text are provided in Dow, 2008, appendix 2, <http://www.aph.gov.au/About_Parliament/Parliamentary_Departments/Parliamentary_Library/pubs/BN/0708/BringingThemHomeReport>).

Western Australia

On 27 May 1997, Leader of the Opposition, Geoff Gallop, moved that 'this House apologises to the Aboriginal people on behalf of all Western Australians for the past policies under which Aboriginal children were removed from their families...' Premier Richard Court supported the motion.

South Australia

On 28 May 1997, Minister for Aboriginal Affairs, Dean Brown, moved that the 'South Australian Parliament expresses its deep and sincere regret at the forced separation of some Aboriginal children from their families and homes...[and] apologises to these Aboriginal people for these past actions...'

Queensland

On 3 June 1997, the Queensland Minister of Families, Youth, and Community Care moved to express 'sincere regret' for Indigenous children removed from families. On 26 May 1999, Premier Peter Beattie moved that 'this House apologises to Aboriginal and Torres Strait Islander people on behalf of the people of Queensland for the past policies under which Indigenous children were forcibly separated from their families...'

Australian Capital Territory

On 17 June 1997, Chief Minister Kate Carnell moved that 'this Assembly apologises to the Ngunnawal people and other Aboriginal and Torres Strait Islander people in the ACT for the hurt and distress inflicted upon any people as a result of the separation of Aboriginal and Torres Strait Islander children from their families...'

New South Wales

On 18 June 1997, Premier Bob Carr moved that 'this House, on behalf of the people of New South Wales, apologises unreservedly to the Aboriginal people of Australia for the systematic separation of generations of Aboriginal children from their parents, families, and communities...'

Tasmania

On 13 August 1997, Premier Tony Rundle moved that 'this Parliament, on behalf of all Tasmanians, expresses its deep and sincere regrets at the hurt and distress caused by past policies under which Aboriginal children were removed from their families and homes [and] apologises to the Aboriginal people for those past actions...' A video is available at

<http://www.sbs.com.au/news/video/17713731796/Tasmanias-apology-to-Stolen-Generations>.

Victoria
On 17 September 1997, Premier Jeff Kennett moved that 'this House apologises to the Aboriginal people on behalf of all Victorians for the past policies under which Aboriginal children were removed from their families...'

Northern Territory
On 24 October 2001, Chief Minister Claire Martin moved that 'this Assembly apologises to Territorians who were removed from their families under the authority of the Commonwealth Aboriginals Ordinance and placed in institutional or foster care...'

Analyses of the 1999 Commonwealth motion and response, as well as the state apologies, are at <http://www.humanrights.gov.au/publications/bringing-them-home-apologies-state-and-territory-parliaments-2008>.

Church

Church submissions to the Human Rights and Equal Opportunity (HREOC) inquiry contained apologies or statements of regret. They are itemized in HREOC (1997) as follows.

- Centacare Catholic Community Service, on behalf of the diocesan welfare agencies of the New South Wales Catholic Church.
- Three national groups of the Catholic Church (Society of the Catholic Apostolate [Pallottines], Kimberly Sisters of St John of God, and the Roman Catholic Church of the Diocese of Broome). These were prefaced with a 'statement of sincere regret' from three Catholic social welfare agencies (Bishops' Committee for Social Welfare, National Aboriginal and Torres Strait Islander Catholic Council, and Australian Catholic Social Welfare Commission).
- Anglican Church Social Responsibilities Committee, which offered an 'unreserved apology', joining other apologies that had been offered by parts of the Anglican Church in Australia.
- National Assembly of the Uniting Church, whose resolution in September 1996 acknowledged 'the trauma and on-going harm caused to individuals', saying that the church was 'blind to the racist assumptions that underlay the policy and practice'.
- Federal Aborigines Board of the Churches of Christ.
- Anglican Church of Australia, Diocese of Perth.

- Baptist Churches of Western Australia.
- Doomadgee, Inc., the successor of the Aborigines Mission at Doomadgee in Queensland.

In addition, an 'expression of regret' from the Australian Association of Social Workers was noted. After publication of HREOC's *Bringing Them Home* in 1997, more church responses expressed sorrow or regret or gave an unreserved apology. The *Social Justice Report 1998* (Australian Human Rights Commission 1999, pp. 48–52) lists a selected set of Christian church responses, which are as follows.

- 11 June 1997, 'heartfelt and unreserved apology' by the Religious Orders of Australia.
- 20 November 1997, apology by the Seventh-Day Adventist Church.
- 14 December 1997, 'sorrow' by the Canberra Baptist Church.
- January 1998, 'heartfelt apology' expressed in the Quaker Sorry Statement.
- 13 March 1998, 'apologise unreservedly' from the Baptist Union of Victoria.
- Month unknown, 1998, 'apologise unreservedly' from Rosanna Baptist Church, Victoria.

In addition, there were responses by the Anglican and Catholic Churches.

Anglican Church

On 15 February 1998, the General Synod, on behalf of the Anglican Church of Australia, unanimously passed resolution 27, which 'apologises unreservedly and seeks forgiveness for any part played...by the unjustified removal of Aboriginal or Torres Strait Islander children from their families...' This was affirmed in resolutions on 26 July 2001 and 2 July 2007 (<http://www.anglican.org.au/content/home/about/social_issues/Reconciliation_and_other_Indigenous_Issues.aspx>).

Catholic Church

On 26 May 1998 (National Sorry Day), the Australian Catholic Bishops Conference issued a statement of 'deepest sorrow', and asked victims for 'their forgiveness for any part the church may have played...' On the same day, the Australian Catholic Social Justice Council of the Catholic Church of Australia issued a statement of 'sincere regret'.

On 20 November 2001, Pope John Paul II issued an apology, on behalf of the Vatican. It was contained in a message apologizing for injustices to Indigenous people in Australia, New Zealand, and the South Pacific Islands, which was issued by email from a 'lap top in the Vatican'. It was termed the Pope's first 'virtual apology' (BBC News, 23 November 2001, <http://news.bbc.co.uk/2/hi/europe/1671540.stm>).

Queensland Institutions **(AU2)**

Government (state)

On 25 August 1999, Premier Peter Beattie and other officials apologized to children who were abused and neglected in Queensland's institutions (see Case AU4).

Church

- October 1997, the Rockhampton Sisters of Mercy apologized 'unreservedly' for abuses at St Joseph's Home in Neerkol.
- 24 February 1998, a 'sincere apology' published in a letter from Bishop Heenen on behalf of himself and the Diocese of Rockhampson for abuses at St Joseph's Home in Neerkol.

Federal apologies and where relevant, church apologies, extend to children in Queensland institutions (see Cases AU1, AU3, and AU4).

Child Migrants **(AU3)**

Government (federal)

Australia

On 16 November 2009, Prime Minister Kevin Rudd, for the Australian Government, apologized to the Forgotten Australians and Child Migrants. The Opposition Leader Malcolm Turnbull also apologized. The ceremony took place in the Great Hall in Parliament House, with hundreds of care leavers in attendance. The text of Rudd's apology is at <http://www.theaustralian.com.au/archive/politics/apology-by-prime-minister-kevin-rudd-to-the-forgotten-australians-and-child-migrants/story-e6frgczf-1225798266181>, and Turnbull's is at <http://www.theaustralian.com.au/archive/politics/malcolm-turnbull-apology-to-forgotten-australians/story-e6frgczf-1225798266117>.

United Kingdom

On 24 February 2010, Prime Minister Gordon Brown, for the UK Government, apologized in the House of Commons for the government's role in the child migration scheme. The text of the Prime Minister's and Opposition leaders' statements is at <http://www.publications.parliament.

uk/pa/cm200910/cmhansrd/cm100224/debtext/100224-0004.htm>. The Prime Minister then gave an apology in person to former Child Migrants at the Palace of Westminster with a commitment of £6 million for a Family Restoration Fund. Videos of the apology and response in the Palace of Westminster are at <http://www.childmigrantstrust.com/news/uk-apology-to-former-child-migrants--3rd-anniversary--24022013>.

Malta

On 10 March 2010, Prime Minister Lawrence Gonzi and Opposition Leader Joseph Muscat apologized to the 315 Maltese Child Migrants, who had been sent to Australia.

Government (state)

Of the six Australian states participating in child migration schemes, only Western Australia and South Australia have made apologies or statements specific to Child Migrants.

Western Australia

On 13 August 1998, Opposition Leader Geoff Gallop moved 'that this House apologise to the former Child Migrants on behalf of all Western Australians for the past policies that led to their forced migration and the subsequent maltreatment…' The text is at <http://www.parliament.wa.gov.au/hansard/hans35.nsf/3e8095c2de81a3b048256c6b002e9930/220f4130def869ad4825668f0028ce8f?OpenDocument>.

South Australia

In February 2001, Minister for Human Services, Dan Brown, made a 'public statement' (its context is unclear), acknowledging the 'experiences of physical, emotional, and sexual abuse' of Child Migrants as a result of being sent to Australia. The text is in the Senate Report (2009, p. 15).

Church

The Senate Report (2001, pp. 229–31) cites responses by Catholic Church organizations that were directed to former Child Migrants (the texts are given in different parts of the report or in the Committee's Hansard). I note that two apologies cited (Rockhampton Sisters of Mercy and the Diocese of Rockhampton) were not directed to former Child Migrants; these are listed in Case AU2.

- July 1993, 'unreservedly apologise' from the Christian Brothers of Western Australia.

- 1997, apology on behalf of the Catholic Church in Britain, during a visit by former Child Migrants (Senate Report, 2001, p. 230, submission by the Child Migrant Friendship Society), although this appears to have been a private event.
- 1999, apology by the Salesians of Don Bosco for abuse at St John Bosco Boys' Town in Glenorchy, Tasmania.
- 22 March 2001, apology by the Catholic Church's Joint Liaison Group on behalf of the Australian Catholic Bishops' Committee for Migrants and Refugees and the National Executive of the Australian Conference of Leaders of Religious Institutes (Senate Report, 2001, p. 230).

In March 2010, soon after the Prime Minister of Malta's apology, the Archbishop of the Catholic Church in Malta, Paul Cremona, apologized for the church's involvement in the scheme.

Forgotten Australians **(AU4)**

Government (federal)

Details of the apologies to Child Migrants and Forgotten Australians by the Prime Minister and Opposition Leader in 2009 are listed above in Case AU3.

Government (state and territory)

The Senate Report (2009, pp. 21–32) presents and considers state responses for the degree to which they constitute a 'meaningful apology'. Most state responses were given some years before the Commonwealth government's apology.

Queensland

On 25 August 1999, several months after the tabling of the Forde Report (1999), a joint apology was issued by the government, church officials, and religious-affiliated organizations. The text is at <http://www.communities.qld.gov.au /resources/communityservices/community/forgotten-australians/queensland-apology.pdf>.

Western Australia

On 7 April 2005, a parliamentary statement of apology was issued by the Western Australian Government that 'apologises to all those people who were harmed as children while in institutional care and expresses deep regret at the hurt and distress this caused'.

Tasmania
On 17 May 2005, Premier Paul Lennon moved that 'this House acknowledges and accepts that many children in the care of the state were abused ... and apologises to the victims ...'

Victoria
On 9 August 2006, Premier Steve Bracks made a statement in Parliament, welcoming the Senate Report (2004) on Forgotten Australians because 'it offers an opportunity to make a public statement of apology about some of the past practices in the provision of out-of-home care services in Victoria'.

South Australia
On 17 June 2008, Premier Michael Rann moved that 'this Parliament recognises the abuses of some of those who grew up in state care and the impact ... and by this apology, we express regret for the pain that has been suffered by so many ...' Following the apology was a ceremony at Old Parliament House, where government and church representatives (Catholic, Lutheran, and Uniting) signed 'a formal apology parchment'. In attendance were '100 people who [had been] abused in state care; [they] received a plant ... and were later sent laminated copies of the apology parchment' (Senate Report, 2009, pp. 26–7). Survivor Deirdre Michell, who attended the ceremony, reflected on the meaning of receiving the plant (a small potted gardenia). She 'would have liked to find out if there was a symbolic relevance to this gift' (Michell, 2010, p. 164).

New South Wales
On 19 September 2009, Premier Nathan Rees gave a 'statement of acknowledgment' at a Healing Service and Memorial Unveiling in Sydney's Royal Botanic Gardens (see Appendix 5). In addition, non-government care providers (churches and religious-affiliated organizations) gave a 'statement of acknowledgment'. Some years before, on 23 June 2005, an apology-like response was made by the New South Wales Minister for Community Services; however, because it 'took the form of an answer to a question without notice in the NSW Legislative Assembly' it was criticized for insufficient planning, implementation, and lack of a ceremony (Senate Report, 2009, pp. 21–3).

Australian Capital Territory
On 17 November 2009, Chief Minister Jon Stanhope welcomed the federal apology that had been given the day before, and he expressed 'regret and sadness at the treatment and ... ongoing distress ... of Forgotten Australians and Child Migrants'.

Church

The Senate Report (2009, p. 32) lists church groups and religious-affiliated organizations, who had made 'formal statements of apology and regret acknowledging abuse of children while under their care'; see also Dow and Philips (2009). I could not source the response type (that is, 'unreserved apology' or 'regret') in all cases. The responses are as follows.

Anglican Church

- September 2004, 'unreserved apology' by the Synod of the Anglican Diocese of Canberra and Goulbourn.
- 6 October 2004, 'sincere apology' by the General Synod of the Anglican Church and its agencies.
- 25 October 2004, 'sincere apology' by the Sydney Synod of the Anglican Church and its care institutions.

Catholic Church

- December 1996, 'regret' by Australian Catholic Bishops and Leaders of Religious Institutes, as part of the *Toward Healing* process (renewed on 14 December 2004).
- 19 July 2008, 'general apology' by Pope Benedict to victims of sexual abuse by Catholic clergy in Australia.

Uniting Church in Australia (as of 1977, includes former Methodist, Presbyterian, and Congregational Churches):

- 27 September 2004, 'apologise unreservedly' by the Uniting Church in Australia and all of its agencies, including UnitingCare and Wesley Missions; separate apologies or responses were given by the Synods in all the states and territories, except the Northern Territory.

Religious-affiliated organizations and charities

- in 1997, 'public apology' and 2004 'unreservedly apologises' to survivors from the United Protestant Association of New South Wales.
- August 2003, 'formal apology' issued by the Salvation Army on the ABC's *Four Corners* television program, and in 2004, to residents of its Riverside home in Queensland.
- February 2004, 'unreserved apology' by Barnados.

Tasmanian Institutions **(AU5)**

Government (state and federal) and church

On 17 May 2005, Premier Paul Lennon moved to apologize to victims in state care (*Forgotten Australians*). The federal, and where relevant, church apologies extend to children in Tasmanian institutions (*Stolen Generations, Child Migrants,* and *Forgotten Australians*).

South Australian Institutions **(AU6)**

Government (state and federal) and church

On 17 June 2008, Premier Michael Rann moved to apologize to those who had been abused or witnessed abuse in state care (*Forgotten Australians*). The federal, and where relevant, church apologies extend to children in South Australian institutions (*Stolen Generations, Child Migrants,* and *Forgotten Australians*).

Tasmanian Stolen Generations **(AU7)**

Government (state and federal) and church

On 13 August 1997, Premier Tony Ruddle moved a motion of apology (*Stolen Generations*). The federal, and where relevant, church apologies extend to Stolen Generations members in Tasmanian institutions. However, the focus of this case was on redressing the policy of separating Indigenous children from families, not the abuse experienced in those institutions.

Redress WA **(AU8)**

Government (state and federal) and church

The federal, and where relevant, church apologies extend to children in Western Australian institutions (*Stolen Generations, Child Migrants,* and *Forgotten Australians*).

Appendix 5: Memorials and Commemorative Activities

Appendix 5 presents memorials (plaques, plinths, sculptures, statues, installations, garden designs) and commemorative activities associated with each case. For those cases where no entry is given (*George Epoch, St John's and St Joseph's, Grandview, Nova Scotia Institutions, Ontario Schools for the Deaf, New Brunswick Schools, Duplessis Orphans),* none could be found. For memorials, multiple entries are ordered countrywide, then by province/state and territory (listed alphabetically). In all cases, memorials are listed first. Commemorative activities are shown only for *Indian Residential Schools, Stolen Generations, Child Migrants,* and *Forgotten Australians* (the latter two are both listed under *Forgotten Australians*). Memorials for *Tasmanian Institutions, South Australian Institutions, Tasmanian Stolen Generations,* and *Redress WA* are listed in *Stolen Generations, Child Migrants, and Forgotten Australians* cases. All quoted inscriptions preserve the original text.

In Australia, an important source of information and visual imagery, which cuts across the cases, is the Find & Connect web resource, <http://www.findandconnect.gov.au>. The websites for Care Leavers Network of Australia (CLAN) and Alliance for Forgotten Australians (AFA) also contain information and photographs. As of June 2014, to access resources from the CLAN website, one needs to be a member; see <http://www.clan.org.au/about/offer/indexj.php>.

CANADA

Mount Cashel (CA1)

When: Estimated 1999

Where: St John's, corner of Torbay and Elizabeth Avenues

What: Small memorial park. After Mount Cashel was torn down in 1992, the developer wanted to build a supermarket complex, residential housing, and a small memorial park on the large property (8 hectares or 20 acres). This took some time because residents initially resisted development of the site. Approval was given in 1998; and by late 1998, the supermarket was opened, and the housing development was underway. The small park sits near the housing development, with access by a white gravel path from a sidewalk. It has two white pillars, some benches, and trees. It can be seen at <https://maps.google.com.au/maps ?hl=en&q=supermarket+built+on+mount+cashel+site+in+canada&ie=UTF-8&ei=llUdUuu7LcKSkwWc3YDYBA&ved=0CAgQ_AUoAg>. Although the two pillars seem small, they were two of the four original cement stanchions that stood at the entrance to Mount Cashel.

Jericho Hill School **(CA7)**

When: 9 August 2005 (Healing Day)

Where: Burnaby, Victory Hill Residential Program, 4334 Victory Street

What: Plaque honouring Jericho Hill students who experienced severe sexual abuse. The plaque was unveiled on Healing Day, which was planned by the Jericho Hill School Class Action Negotiating Committee, and to which all former students were invited. Speeches were given by members of the Negotiating Committee, and there was informal time to socialize (Anne Sheane, lawyer for the plaintiffs, personal communication, 9 January 2014). The plaque was one of 11 elements in the 2004 class action settlement; it was not part of the province's *Jericho Hill*-JICP.

Alberta Sterilization **(CA9)**

I have included the following item, although the two plaques have since been removed (Jon Faulds, personal communication, 16 July 2013).

When: 2011

Where: Edmonton, Louise McKinney Park

What: As part of a 'participational performance walk' called 'Perambulate: Louise McKinney Park', the artist Kay Burns placed an engraved brass plaque with the words 'Leilani Muir Footbridge', at each end of the bridge. Background and photo are at <http://leilanimuir.ca/266>, posted 8 January 2012.

Indian Residential Schools **(CA11)**

This case has many memorials and commemorative activities. Listed first is the major $20 million commemoration initiative, which was one element in the Indian Residential School Settlement Agreement.

In January 2011, the Canadian Truth and Reconciliation Commission (TRC) and Aboriginal Affairs and Northern Development Canada (AANDC) jointly launched the initiative. The TRC received and reviewed proposals and made recommendations to the AANDC, who approved and funded the projects. As of July 2013, all funds were allocated to 145 projects. The aims of the commemorative initiative are to

> assist in honouring and validating the healing and reconciliation of former students and their families…; provide an opportunity for former students and their families to support one another…; contribute to a sense of identity, unity, and belonging…; promote Aboriginal languages, cultures, and traditional and spiritual values;… memorialize in a tangible and permanent way the residential school experience <http://www.aadnc-aandc.gc.ca/eng/1100100015635/1100100015636>.

The 145 projects are impressive and imaginative, with a wide range of activities and outcomes. Some are national in scope, and others centre on a particular locale or community. Readers are encouraged to visit the websites (below) to read about each project's aim and plan. The projects have three types of activities or outcomes, and these can be combined in one project. Here are the types of activities and the number of projects that include it as an element (total will add to greater than 145):

- Monuments, plaques, commemorative gardens, and other permanent structures (82 projects).
- Ceremonies, gatherings, potlatch, and other community activities (87 projects).
- Books, films, artistic performances, photographic displays, oral history recordings, and language workshops (87 projects).

Projects funded in 2011–12 are described at <http://www.aadnc-aandc.gc.ca/eng/1370974213551/1370974338097>; those funded in 2012–13 are described at <http://www.aadnc-aandc.gc.ca/eng/1370974253896/1370974471675>.

In addition, a permanent structure was funded separately by the Government of Canada, that is, it was not one of the 145 Commemoration projects.

When: 26 November 2012

Where: Ottawa, House of Commons, above the west door of Centre block

What: Stained glass window designed by Métis artist Christi Belcourt. The window design commemorates the legacy of the Indian Residential Schools and the government's apology to former students and their families. The design was chosen by a selection committee that included former residential school students and leading Aboriginal art experts. More information is at <http://www.aadnc-aandc.gc.ca/eng/1354805080035/1354805131174>. Photograph available on the artist's website, <http://www.christibelcourt.com/>.

AUSTRALIA

Stolen Generations **(AU1)**

Memorials are in all states and territories except Victoria and Western Australia. Victoria is included, however, because there was a competition for a Stolen Generations memorial, which produced several designs. The memorials are listed alphabetically by state or territory name, and then by year, when there is more than one entry. National commemorative activities are shown, but the associated state activities are not.

Australian Capital Territory

When: 22 July 2002

Where: Canberra, Reconciliation Place (between the National Library and High Court)

What: The installation has 17 pieces of art, including sculptures, photos, and garden designs. Photographs and description are at <http://www.nationalcapital.gov.au/index.php?option=com_content&view=article&id=82&Itemid=300>.

New South Wales

When: 1999

Where: Sydenham, Sydenham Green, Reilly Lane

What: Aboriginal artist Joe Hirst created the installation of a stone and ceramic wall with stone water bowls. Information is at <http://monumentaustralia.org.au/themes /culture/indigenous/display/23125-stolen-generations-memorial>. Photograph is at <http://sydney-city.blogspot.com.au/2011 /12/sydenham-sculpture.html>.

When: 21 October 2001

Where: Nowra, site of former Bomaderry Children's Home, Beinda Street

What: Stolen Generation Memorial Garden Project, in conjunction with TAFE Illawarra, led by Nowra Aboriginal artist and community leader, Jason Groves. The site has gardens (with native plant species of significance to Aboriginal culture), a boardwalk, and a sandstone block with a dedication plaque in the centre of a circular garden bed. Photograph is at <http://www.environment.nsw.gov.au/heritageapp/HeritageItemImage.aspx?ID=5061330#ad-image-6>.

When: 2 October 2007

Where: The Australian Botanic Gardens, Mount Annan, a large area (416 hectares or 1,028 acres) with walking trails, educational information, restaurants, and gift shop. It is one of three large gardens maintained by the Royal Botanic Gardens and Domain Trust of New South Wales.

What: A monument set within the garden that includes a contemplative walking track. The sandstone sculpture, carved by Paakantyi artist Badger Bates, shows a mother holding a baby and a father with a small child. There is also a water feature that represents tears of those affected by the Stolen Generations. Sandstone boulders, located throughout the gardens, have plaques with inscribed quotes by Stolen Generations members. Photograph and description are at <http://www.rbgsyd.nsw.gov.au/annan /the_garden/buildings_and_art#sto>.

Northern Territory

When: 30 July 2005

Where: Darwin, George Brown Botanic Gardens, Gilruth Avenue

What: Stone monument with engraved plaques on the front and side. Front inscription begins, 'Heartbroken mother left with empty arms, hearts broken, mind with no claims. Children without an identity taken from their country…' The inscription excerpts from Prime Minister Paul Keating's 1992 Redfern speech on the right side. Photographs are at <http://www.ntsgac.org/index.php?page=photos>. Inscriptions are at <http://monumentaustralia.org.au/themes/culture/indigenous/display/80187-stolen-generations-memorial>.

South Australia

When: 31 May 1998 (The Fountain of Tears)

30 May 1999 (Grieving Mother)

Where: Adelaide metropolitan area, Colebrook Reconciliation Park, Eden Hills, Shepherds Hill Road (a park with a walkway, benches, and sculptures)

What: The Fountain of Tears is a sculpture of three faces, which sit in front of a taller granite structure with water flowing over the faces, surrounded by a circle of large boulders. It was created by Silvio Apponyi in collaboration with Indigenous artists. Front inscription begins, 'Let everyone who comes to this place know they are on Aboriginal land, the site of what was once Colebrook Training Home…'

What: Grieving mother, a life-sized bronze of a woman sitting on a boulder, created by Silvio Apponyi, assisted by Shereen Rankin and Yankunjatjara artists. Photos of the park, the sculptures, and inscriptions are at <http://www.flickr.com/photos/25792994@N04/5011664078/in/photostream/>. Information about Colebrook Park is at <http://www.mitchamcouncil.sa.gov.au/page.aspx?u=1249>.

Queensland

When: 1998

Where: Six sites in the Brisbane metropolitan area that were chosen for their historical significance to Aboriginal life, such as the openness of the landscape and availability of water; all were close to locations associated with child removal practices.

What: Identical circular plaques, with an inscription that reads, in part: 'They took the children away. Our souls will cry no more. For now we are going home…' The six sites are

- Brisbane CBD, King George Square, Adelaide Street (which contains an additional plaque inscribed with a section of the Federal Government's apology on 13 February 2008). Photograph is at <http://monumentaustralia.org.au/themes/culture/ indigenous/display/100427-stolen-generations-memorial>.
- Everton Park, Teralba Park, Osborne Road.
- Nundah, Kalinga Park, Kalinga Street. Photograph is at <http://monumentaustralia.org.au/themes/culture/indigenous/display/92196-bringing-them-home-plaque>.
- Sherwood, Sherwood Arboretum, Jolimont Road.
- West End, Orleigh Park, Riverside Drive.
- Wynnum Foreshore, the Esplanade, Breakwater Point.

Victoria

When: 2001

Where: Melbourne, Carlton Gardens

What: Projects designed, not built. The 'Stolen Generation Memorial Competition', initially conceived by Sue-Anne Ware and finalized in collaboration with others, sought designs that 'embraced the Anti-Memorial', that is those challenging 'ideas about memorials and linear, cyclical notions of time' and engaging 'in multiple readings of issues; politically, socially, and physically' (Ware, 2005, p. 35). The competition received over 140 entries, and the jury short listed 40; four were selected to be constructed at the Melbourne Museum in 2002. The projects were not physically realized for several reasons: a conservative national political climate (the Howard government had challenged the concept of a 'stolen generation'), concern by the Museum to commission art that appeared to be controversial, and a belief by the Museum's committee that only art by an Indigenous person or a member of the Stolen Generations should be eligible (Ware, 2005, p. 45). A fascinating account of the activities and outcomes of the competition is given in Ware (2005, pp. 33–47; see also Ware, 2004).

Stolen Generations **(AU1)**

When: Annually on 26 May

Where: Throughout Australia

What: On the first anniversary of the tabling of the *Bringing Them Home* report, 26 May 1998, the inaugural Sorry Day was held. Sorry Days have since been held across the nation every year on this day, initiated by the National Sorry Day Committee (NSDC). In addition, the NSDC created the *Journey of Healing* (26 May 1999) to bring Indigenous and non-Indigenous people together. On 13 February 2009, NSDC marked the first Anniversary of the Apology, holding celebratory events in this and subsequent years. Information on National Sorry Day activities is available at <http://www.nsdc.org.au/>.

Queensland Institutions **(AU2)**

In Queensland, memorials typically include Child Migrants and Forgotten Australians.

When: 5 August 2003

Where: Kabra, Meteor Park Road (near the Stanwell turnoff on the Capricorn Highway, at the start of the dirt road leading to St Joseph's Orphanage)

What: Bricks from the original entrance gates were used to make a smaller replica version of the entrance to St Joseph's Home in Neerkol. Photographs of the old buildings (set in from the highway) and the plaques (located on the highway) are at <http://www.sararosetta.com/2011/08/25/neerkol-orphanage-revisited/>. A photograph of the original entrance (since destroyed) is at <http://www.findandconnect.gov.au/ref/qld/biogs/QE00151b.htm>.

When: December, 2008

Where: Ipswich, University of Queensland, Ipswich Campus, 11 Salisbury Road

What: Sculpture of a book by Gavan Fenelon, with an inscription to commemorate former students of Karrala House in Ipswich. The inscription was developed in collaboration with the artist, former residents, and the Department of Communities, Child Safety, and Disabilities. There was no formal onsite dedication of the plaque at the request of Forgotten Australians, who expressed a preference for personal visits and acknowledgements to be made in the Lotus Place newsletters. Photograph is at <http://www.findandconnect.gov.au /ref/qld/objects/QD0000027.htm>.

When: 14 December 2011

Where: South Brisbane, Merivale Street Rail Bridge, 'Pylon Number 9'

What: Contemporary artwork created by Gavan Fenelon in consultation with young people who were placed in Queensland institutions. The base of the sculpture contains fragments of brick that were salvaged from the Sir Leslie Wilson facility when it was demolished. A plaque on the base is inscribed with words from the Forde Report (1999), along with quotes from a former staff member and youth detainee. Photographs of the sculpture (although not at the site of installation) and a discussion by the artist are at Micah Projects Inc. (2011, p. 5).

When: 2004 (unveiled), relocated in 2006

Where: Brisbane, Cathedral Square (Emma Miller Place, Albert and Roma Streets)

What: Called the Child Abuse Memorial, a bronze life-sized statue of a boy, with a suitcase. Inscription reads, in part, 'In memory of all the children who suffered and for those who did not survive abuse in Church and State Children's institutions and homes in Queensland...' Photograph and description are at <http://www.forgottenaustralians.org.au/monuments.html<>.

Child Migrants (AU3)

There are memorials in Australia and Malta. Memorials that honour both Child Migrants and Forgotten Australians are listed in Case AU4. Commemoration activities are shown in AU4.

South Australia

When: 23 February 2001

Where: Adelaide, Migration Museum, Kintore Street

What: Plaque commemorating the South Australian Government's recognition of child migration to the state. Inscription reads, in part, 'This plaque is dedicated to the innocent children sent to Australia from their homelands under the British Child Migration Schemes from the late 19th century to the mid 20th century...' Photograph is at <http://migration.historysa.com.au/collections/memorial-wall-plaques/british-child-migration-schemes-plaque>.

Tasmania

When: Estimated 1999 or 2000

Where: Glenorchy, chapel in John Bosco Boys' Town, a school run by the Salesians of Don Bosco

What: Plaque dedicated by former Child Migrants to their memory, which was 'an acknowledgment and recognition of the Child Migrants at Boys' Town, who through hardship and trying times were part of the history of the school' (former Child Migrant who spoke to the Senate inquiry in 2000, cited from Find & Connect web resource entry for Tasmania Boys' Town; see <http://www.findandconnect.gov.au /ref/tas/biogs/TE00042b.htm>).

Update: The plaque was destroyed in a fire in the chapel on 25 May 2003, but during October 2012 a new one was installed and re-dedicated to the first group to arrive at Boys' Town, as part of the 60th anniversary of the arrival of the first Child Migrants to the school. Find & Connect web resource has more information at <http://www.findandconnect.gov.au/ref/tas/biogs/TE00042b.htm>.

Western Australia

When: December 2005

Where: Perth, Fremantle Maritime Museum

What: Life-sized bronze statue of a young boy and girl, both with suitcases. The inscription reads, in part, 'This memorial is...dedicated to the British boys and girls who left their homeland to brave an unknown future in Western Australia. Hardships were endured and benefits were derived...' A second plaque is dedicated to Child Migrants from Malta. Photograph is at <http://otoweb.cloudapp.net/remembering/index.html>.

When: 13 August 2008

Where: Perth metropolitan area, Clontarf Aboriginal College (site of the former Clontarf Boys' Town), Waterford, 295 Manning Road

What: Plaque located at the front entrance of the main building. Inscription reads, in part, 'Clontarf Boys Memorial... Clontarf was home to many Australian and Child Migrant boys from the United Kingdom, Ireland, and Malta. The boys worked with the Christian Brothers and tradesmen to construct many of the buildings on this site... Their contributions should not be forgotten'. The plaque is part of the Clontarf History Project. Photographs and description are at <http://www.cbers.org/docs/Issue6_Network_newsletter_Dec_2008.pdf>.

In addition, a Clontarf Heritage Trail, created in consultation with the Clontarf 'Old Boys' is planned, with completion expected in 2014. Stone plinths will be placed at locations on the former Boys' Town grounds, including its bakery, workshop, piggery, and graveyard. When the project is completed, there will be a commemorative ceremony and regular 'walk and talk' tours of the grounds.

Malta

When: 2 March 2008

Where: Valletta Harbour

What: A memorial plaque and a sculpture in the shape of a child's paper boat, located in the quay where ships departed for Australia with Child Migrants. Photograph is at <http://www.timesofmalta.com/articles/view/20080302/local/child-migrants-monument-unveiled-at-valletta-waterfront.198737#.UsUZVLSZj09>.

Forgotten Australians **(AU4)**

New South Wales

When: 19 September 2009

Where: Sydney, Royal Botanical Gardens, Twin Ponds

What: A mid-height sandstone plinth, with an engraved plaque, which reads in part, 'in this place we remember the many thousands of NSW children who grew up in care in the decades leading up to the 1990s...' Photographs and description are at <http://www.forgottenaustralians.org.au/monuments.html>.

When: 11 Sept 2010

Where: Kiama, Peace Park, Manning Street

What: A plaque embedded in a boulder in Kiama's Peace Park. The plaque reads, in part, 'This plaque is dedicated to the "Remembered Australians", Children who grew up in orphanages, Children's Homes, foster care and the child migrants to our shores'. Photograph and description are at <http://monumentaustralia.org.au/display/101329-remembered-australians>.

South Australia

When: 17 June 2010

Where: North Adelaide, Peace Park, corner of Sir Edwin Smith Avenue and Brougham Place

What: Four huge stainless steel daisies, each in a different state of opening. The tallest daisy is over 6 metres (20 feet). An inscription reads, in part, 'In honour of children who suffered abuse in institutional and out of home care.... We celebrate our courage, strength and resilience. We are no longer forgotten ...' Photographs and description are at <http://www.forgottenaustralians.org.au/monuments.html>.

Tasmania

When: 26 November 2008 and 16 October 2010

Where: Hobart, Royal Tasmanian Botanic Gardens, Queens Domain

What: In 2008 a commemorative garden with a plaque was unveiled. In 2010 a wooden park bench with an engraved plaque, sponsored by the federal government, commemorated the first anniversary of the apology to the Forgotten Australians and former Child Migrants. Photographs and description are at <http://monumentaustralia.org.au/display/70358-forgotten-australians-rose-walk>.

Victoria

When: 25 October 2010

Where: Melbourne, Southbank Promenade

What: The memorial, created by Helen Bodycomb, is a rectangular stone block, approximately 3 by 2.5 metres and 400 mm high (10 by 8 feet and 1.3 feet high); the smooth top surface area is covered with painted wattle blossoms of different sizes. The design reflects 'the constellations above Victoria at 11am on 16 November 2009, when Prime Minister Kevin Rudd made his national apology to the Forgotten Australians.... [The] blossoms represent the one thousand most visible stars and planets, one for every one hundred children who were in Victorian state care ...' (text is drawn from <http://forgottenaustralians.org.au/monuments.html>, scroll to Victoria memorial, where there are photographs of the stone memorial and a plaque).

Western Australia

When: 10 December 2010

Where: Perth Cultural Centre, Jubilee Building, James Street

What: The memorial, created by Judith Forrest, in collaboration with academic Terri-Ann White, is for all those who experienced state care. It is 'modelled on a children's fortune teller game made of folding paper' into cushion folds. The folded corners contain phrases expressing the 'experiences and present situations' of Forgotten Australians. An inscription reads, in part, '...this memorial brings the "Forgotten Australians" out of the shadows and into the light. Their most enduring legacy will be that the people now and in the future will know their stories and build upon them a platform for better care...' Photographs and text are drawn from <http://forgottenaustralians.org.au/monuments.html>.

***Child Migrants* (AU3) and *Forgotten Australians* (AU4) combined**

When: Annually on 16 November

Where: Throughout Australia

Where: Find & Connect provides funding for jurisdictions to conduct events and activities specific to their area in connection with Child Migrants and Forgotten Australians. The events held in 2013 are described at <http://www.findandconnect.gov.au/news/2013/11/08/national-apology-anniversary-events>.

Appendix 6: Other Media

Appendix 6 presents a sampling of other media such as books and print media, audio-visual media, oral histories, and other memory projects associated with the cases. For those cases where no entry is given (*George Epoch, Nova Scotia Institutions, Ontario Schools for the Deaf, Jericho Hill, New Brunswick Institutions, Tasmanian Institutions, South Australian Institutions, Tasmanian Stolen Generations, Redress WA*), none could be found. This is not to say that none exists, but my search has not discovered them. However, country-wide cases (*Indian Residential Schools, Stolen Generations, Child Migrants,* and *Forgotten Australians*) contain experiences of those living in the states, provinces, or territories. I include items that demonstrate the variety of media available and provide other sources, in which lists of other media can be found.

CANADA

Mount Cashel **(CA1)**

Books and print media

Harris, M. (1990). *Unholy Orders: Tragedy at Mt Cashel* (Ontario: Viking Press).

O'Brien, D. (1991). *Suffer Little Children: An Autobiography of a Foster Child* (St John's: Breakwater Books).

Audio-visual media

The Boys of St Vincent (1992) and *The Boys of St. Vincent: 15 Years Later* (1993). Two-part docudrama series. Director John Smith, producer Sam Grana (Canada: National Film Board).

St John's and St Joseph's **(CA3)**

Books and print media

Henton, D. and D. McCann (1995). *Boys Don't Cry: The Struggle for Justice and Healing in Canada's Biggest Sex Abuse Scandal* (Ontario: McClelland & Stewart).

***Grandview* (CA4)**

Books and print media

Dubinsky, S. M. (2007). *A Qualitative Study of Grandview Training School and Grandview Survivor Healing Strategies*. Master of Social Work thesis (Saskatchewan: University of Regina).

Audio-visual media

The Girls of Grandview (2002). A play performed at Friendly Spike Theatre, Toronto. Written and directed by survivors and artists.

Until Someone Listens (1999). Documentary. Producer/director Laura Sky (Ontario: Skyworks Charitable Foundation and Commissioning Partner, Grandview Survivors Support Group).

***Alberta Sterilization* (CA9)**

Audio-visual media

Invisible Child: Leilani Muir and the Alberta Eugenics Board (2012). A play performed at Edmonton Fringe Festival. Director Vincent Forcier.

The Sterilisation of Leilani Muir (1996). Documentary. Director Glyni Whiting, producers Graydon McCrea and Jerry Krepakevich (Alberta: National Film Board of Canada).

Oral history project

Living Archives on Eugenics in Western Canada (2010–15). A Community University Research Alliance project by 30 research scholars and sterilization survivors and 12 community partners <http://eugenicsarchive.ca/>.

***Duplessis Orphans* (CA10)**

Books and print media

Dufour, R. (2002) *Naître rien: des orphelins de Duplessis, de la crèche à l'asile* (Québec: Éditions MultiMondes).

Gill, P. (1991). *Les enfants de Duplessis: l'histoire vraie d'Alice Quinton* (Montréal: Libre Expression).

Labrosse, J-G. (1964). *Ma chienne de vie: autobiographie d'un orphelin* (Montréal: Éditions du Jour).

Pagé, J. C. (1961). *Les fous crient au secours, témoignage d'un ex-patient de Saint-Jean-de-Dieu* (Montréal: Éditions du Jour).

Roy, B. (1994). *Mémoire d'asile: la tragédie des enfants de Duplessis* (Montréal: Boréal).

_____ (1998). *Les calepins de Julien* (Montréal: XYZ éditeur).

Audio-visual media

Bertrand, Jeanette, host of *Parler pour parler* (1989). Television program episode that has interviews with survivors (Québec: Radio Québec).

Les orphelins de Duplessis (1997). Television miniseries. Director Johanne Prégent (Québec: Radio Canada).

***Indian Residential Schools* (CA11)**

Books and print media

Graham, E. (ed.) (1997). *The Mush Hole: Life at Two Indian Residential Schools* (Ontario: Heffle Publishing).

Haig-Brown, C. (1988). *Resistance and Renewal: Surviving the Indian Residential School* (Vancouver: Tillacum Library).

Audio-visual media

Beyond the Shadows (1993). Documentary. Produced for the Cariboo Tribal Council by Peter and Sheera von Puttkamer (West Vancouver: Gryphon Productions).

Rhymes for Young Ghouls (2012). Drama. Directed and written by Jeff Barnaby, producers Aisling Chin-yee and John Christou (Montréal: Les Films Séville).

Unseen Tears (2009). Documentary. Filmmaker Ron Douglas (Erie and Niagara Counties: Native American Community Services).

Where the Spirit Lives (1989). Drama. Director Bruce Pittman, producers Heather Haldane and Eric Jordan (Canada: Amazing Spirit Productions Ltd.).

Oral history projects

Our Stories... Our Strength, Where are the Children? (Ottawa: Legacy of Hope Foundation). Exhibition of photographs and documents, which travelled throughout Canada, 2002–13; and audio- and video-recorded stories gathered from survivors during 2005–8. Stories are at <http://wherearethechildren.ca/stories/>.

Share Your Truth (Manitoba: Truth and Reconciliation Commission of Canada). Indian Residential School statement gathering was one mandate of the Truth and Reconciliation Commission of Canada. Approximately 6,200 personal statements were recorded during 2008 to 2013 and will be placed in the National Research Centre for Truth and Reconciliation, University of Manitoba, Winnipeg.

For more media items

Canadian Indian Residential School System entry in Wikipedia has comprehensive lists of films and novels; see <http://en.wikipedia.org/wiki/Canadian_Indian_residential_school_system>.

Law Commission of Canada (2000). *Restoring Dignity: Responding to Child Abuse in Canadian Institutions* (Ottawa: Minister of Public Works and Government Services). Many other media items are shown in the report's bibliography, appendix B.

Truth and Reconciliation Commission of Canada (2012). *They Came for the Children: Canada, Aboriginal Peoples, and Residential Schools* (Winnipeg: Truth and Reconciliation Commission of Canada). Many other media items are shown in the report's reference list.

AUSTRALIA

Stolen Generations **(AU1)**

Books and print media

Bird, C. (ed.) (1998). *The Stolen Children: Their Stories* (Melbourne: Random House). Collection of stories by and perspectives of Indigenous people that were in the *Bringing Them Home* report.

Haebich, A. and D. Mellor (eds) (2002). *Many Voices: Reflections on Experiences of Indigenous Child Removals* (Canberra: NLA Publishing). Book based on the *Bringing Them Home* oral history project.

Pilkington/Garimara, D./N. (1996). *Follow the Rabbit-Proof Fence* (Brisbane: University of Queensland Press).

Quall, L. (2002). *So Far from Home: Oral Histories of the Stolen Generation* (Katherine, NT: Diwurruwurru-jaru Aboriginal Corporation). Oral history in illustrated book form.

Randall, B. (2003). *Songman: the Story of an Aboriginal Elder of Uluru* (Sydney: ABC Books for the Australian Broadcasting Corporation).

Audio-visual media

Kanyini (2006). Documentary. Director Melanie Hogan, producers Bob Randall, Melanie Hogan, and Lynda House (NSW: Hopscotch Films).

Lousy Little Sixpence (1983). Documentary. Director Alec Morgan, producers Alec Morgan and Gerald Bostock (ACT: Ronin Films).

Stolen (1998). Playwright Jane Harrison. Fictional play. First performed at CUB Malthouse, Melbourne, and toured for 7 years.

Why Me? Five Stories of Removal from Family and Country (2007). Documentary. Director/producer Rick Cavaggion, producer Martin Gordon (ACT: Ronin Films).

Oral history projects

Bringing Them Home (Canberra: National Library of Australia). Stolen Generations oral history project gathered interviews during 1999 and 2002 with follow-up interviews in 2010. Audio recordings are available via a link at <https://www.nla.gov.au/oral-history/bringing-them-home-oral-history-project>.

The Voices, The Lives, The Testimonies of Australia's Stolen Generations (2009) (NSW: Stolen Generations Testimonies Foundation) <http://stolengenerationstestimonies.com/index.php>.

For more media items

Dow, C. (2008). Parliament of Australia background note; Sorry: the unfinished business of the Bringing Them Home report (Canberra: Parliament of Australia). Footnote 24 lists songs, books, and films produced before *Bringing Them Home* (1997) was published <http://www.aph.gov.au/About_Parliament/Parliamentary_Departments/Parliamentary_Library/pubs/BN/0708/BringingThemHomeReport>.

Queensland Institutions **(AU2)**

Books and print media

Care Leavers of Australia Network (2000). Memories ... Hopes ... and Dreams booklet to commemorate the first anniversary of the government's response to the recommendations in the Forde Report (1999).

Child Migrants **(AU3)**

Books and print media

Bean, P. and J. Melville (1989). *Lost Children of the Empire: The Untold Story of Britain's Child Migrants* (Sydney: Unwin Hyman).

Gill, A. (1997). *Orphans of the Empire* (Alexandria, NSW: Millennium Books).

Hill, D. (2008). *Forgotten Children: Fairbridge Farm School and Its Betrayal of Britain's Child Migrants to Australia* (Sydney: William Heinemann).

Humphreys, M. (1994). *Empty Cradles* (Sydney: Doubleday).

Moore, A. and J. Clarke (eds) (1990). *Growing up with Barnardo's* (Sydney: Hale & Iremonger).

Welsh, L. P. (1990). *Geordie: Orphan of the Empire* (Perth: P&B Press).

Audio-visual media

The Leaving of Liverpool (1992). Drama miniseries. Director Michael Jenkins, producer Steve Knapman (Australia and UK: ABC TV and BBC1).

The Long Journey Home (2009). Documentary. Director Emily Booker (Perth: ABC1).

Lost Children of the Empire (1989). Docudrama miniseries. Director/producer Joanna Mack (London: Granada Television).

On Their Own: Britain's Child Migrants (2011) (Sydney and Liverpool: Australian National Maritime Museum and National Museums Liverpool). Photography and film exhibition with three short films: *Children: Building Block of the Empire* and *Two Voyages: Part 1–Mary's Story 1878* and *Part 2–William's Story 1950.*

Oranges and Sunshine (2011). Historical drama based on Margaret Humphreys' book, *Empty Cradles*. Director Jim Loach, producers Camilla Bray, Iain Canning, Joan Schneider, and Emile Sherman (London: Sixteen Films).

Oral history project

You Can't Forget Things Like That (Canberra: National Library of Australia). Forgotten Australians and Child Migrants oral history project gathered interviews during 2009 to 2012.. Audio recordings are at <http://www.nla.gov.au/oral-history/forgotten-australians-and-former-child-migrants-oral-history-project>.

For more media items

Child Migrants Trust (CMT) lists a range of media on their News and Archives page at <http://www.childmigrantstrust.com/media-and-books/news-and-archives>.

***Forgotten Australians* (AU4)**

Books and print media

Alliance for Forgotten Australians (2008). *Forgotten Australians: Supporting Survivors of Childhood Institutional Care in Australia* (Canberra: Families Australia).

Fawdry, M. (2007). *The Little Mongrel: Free to a Good Home* (Tasmania: Self published).

Murray, S., J. Murphy, E. Branigan, and J. Malone (2009). *After the Orphanage: Life Beyond the Children's Home* (Sydney: UNSW Press).

Szablicki, R. (2007). *Orphanage Boy: Through the Eyes of Innocence* (NSW: New Holland Publishers Australia).

Walsh, K. and K. Olsson (2009) (eds). *Lives of Uncommon Children: Reflections of Forgotten Australians* (Brisbane: Micah Projects Inc.).

Audio-visual media

The Forgotten Australians (2010). Documentary. Writer/director Nicola Woolmington, producer Nell White (Melbourne: SBS Corporation).

Inside: Life in Children's Homes and Institutions (2013) (Canberra: National Museum of Australia). A permanent website that supports the National Museum's exhibition of stories, photos, artwork, poems, songs, articles, and comments is at <http://www.nma.gov.au/exhibitions/inside_life_in_ childrens_homes_and_institutions/home>.

Notes

1 Discovering Institutional Abuse

1. This summary draws from Harris (1990, pp. 260–3) and the Hughes Report (1991), which includes exhibits gathered during the inquiry and an *aide de memoire* by Hyslop, dated 17 February 1989, supplemented by Higgins (2012) and press reports.
2. Throughout this text, by children, I mean children and youth up to the age of 17 to 19 years, depending on the jurisdiction.
3. Prosecution and conviction of clergy had occurred throughout the 20th century, and even earlier in the 19th century; however, in the 1980s it was subject to intense media interest.
4. By 1990, four priests (including Hickey) had been convicted, one was acquitted, one received a stay of proceedings, and two were awaiting trial (Winter Commission, 1990, p. 1).
5. Except for a 4-month hiatus from December 1975 (when he left Mount Cashel after being beaten by a brother) to April 1976, when a judge ordered his return to Mount Cashel, Shane Earle was resident there from 1973 to 1986.
6. Earlier inquiries had been carried out in England and Wales in 1967 (Court Lees), 1985 (Leeways), and 1988 (Melanie Klein House); and Northern Ireland in 1986 (Kincora and other children's homes) (Corby et al., 2001, pp. 76–80).
7. Winter's report (1990) found that abuse had been known and reported to church authorities in the 1970s, and it recommended sweeping changes in responding to and preventing sexual abuse of children by clergy. The report's findings led to Archbishop Penney's resignation in February 1991.
8. The inquiry was televised from September to December 1989. According to Harris (1990, p. 303), 'the cable company providing gavel-to-gavel live coverage added a new channel…to replay each day's testimony in full every night…15 percent of the viewing audience in Newfoundland was tuning in…on a daily basis'.
9. Child rescue and child saving featured in the latter part of the 19th century and the first two decades of the 20th century in Australia, Canada, Great Britain, Ireland, and the United States, but 'child abuse' (physical or sexual) had not been named as social problems. Although child abuse was not the term used, parents had been convicted of cruelty to children before child abuse was 'discovered' in the 1960s (Parton, 1979, p. 435).
10. Precise years of social problem definition vary: the United States was somewhat earlier than other countries in the discovery and diffusion of child abuse as a social problem. For institutional abuse of children in England and Wales, Corby et al. (2001, p. 47) suggest that 'concerns…had taken hold by 1990'.
11. Some researchers continue to use this more inclusive definition (Penhale, 1999).

12. Of course, the literature on institutional abuse is not confined to children as victims or survivors, but also includes adults living in residential facilities (Stanley et al., 1999).
13. With the movement of families and children worldwide – displaced by civil war, state violence, and environmental disasters – total institutions for children are very much present today and taking new forms, such as immigration detention centres.
14. Children who have no fixed place to live except the streets would be even more vulnerable.
15. While sexual assault was not statute-barred, common assault was; thus, Hyslop had to prosecute the sexual assault allegations (Hughes, 1991, p. 182).

2 The Cases

1. In the 19 cases, institutional abuse arose from the practices or policies of governments (police, education, justice, welfare); church organizations and religious orders; charitable organizations; and medical authorities. Reponses were by government and/or church organizations. Institutional abuse may arise from other sources, and responses by other organizations are possible.
2. Five cases included both residential and out-of-home care (foster care) (see detail in Appendix 1).
3. Although a sixth Australian case (*Forgotten Australians*) initially included foster care, it was the subject of another report (Senate Report, 2005).
4. Sources vary in the numbers charged and convicted. My analysis is of alleged offending against boys at the Mount Cashel School, not by other priests in the St John's Archdiocese. I triangulated data from Bessner (1998), Shea (1999b), and Sylvia's Site (2014), supplemented by Alter (1999, p. 13) and the Canadian Legal Information Institute (CanLII) database.
5. In addition to the Mussell's report, I drew from a three-page memo by a person close to the Epoch case (Donald McLean, legal counsel for the Jesuit Brothers of Upper Canada, personal communication, 15 and 30 April 2013) to summarize this case.
6. The province took full control of the school in the late 1970s and renamed it the Kennedy Youth Detention Center; this institution for boys was closed in 1985.
7. Different years are given for the opening of St John's in Uxbridge; 1957 is sourced from an internal school document (reprinted in Hoffman, 1996, p. 44). The year of closure for St John's is unclear ('mid to late 1970s'); I chose 1977. The year for the closure of St Joseph's varies by source; I chose 1973, based on Hoffman (1996, p. 85).
8. Sources vary in the numbers charged and convicted. I triangulated data from Henton and McCann (1995), Hoffman (1996), and Shea (1999b), supplemented by the Canadian Legal Information Institute (CanLII) database.
9. According to Hoffman (1996), there were 250 members in 1992; but Henton and McCann (1995) say there were 282 members in 1992.
10. Galt changed its name to Cambridge in 1973.
11. In 1988, the boys were moved to the Nova Scotia Youth Centre in Waterville.

12. Kaufman (2002) repeats page numbers 332–42 in his chapter XVI. When I cite these pages, I am referring to the second time they appear in Kaufman's report.
13. Despite what was believed at the time, suspected claimant fraud was no higher than 5 per cent (based on my calculations of the numbers in Kaufman, 2002, p. 284). Of reports against 68 current employees, the IIU determined that two (3 per cent) were valid. By 2002, files for 11 former or current employees were submitted for prosecution (p. 288).
14. Throughout this book, I adopt Morley's (2001, p. 1, fn. 3) approach (and that of others) of capitalizing 'Deaf' in 'recognition ... that deafness is not a disability but rather that being Deaf means belonging to a distinct cultural group with its own language'. Such capitalization currently extends to DeafBlind, but not to blind or hard of hearing.
15. An earlier case was filed in 1988 by a former student against the Ministry of Education, alleging sexual assault 'on a continuing basis between 1975 and 1982' (British Columbia Ombudsman, 1993, p. 26). The case was settled for $50,000 in 1989 (Native Women's Association of Canada, 1992, p. 8).
16. Toft is a self-confessed prolific offender, having admitted to 200 sexual offence victims.
17. The RCMP lodged new offences against Toft, but these were stayed in October 1993. Three former employees, two of whom had worked in NBTS and one in the Boys' Industrial Home, were prosecuted. One was convicted and sentenced in 1992; a second, in 1995; and the third was acquitted. Charges were laid against a fourth employee in 2002, but the outcome is not known (Kaufman, 2002, p. 363).
18. Claims were still being processed after 2001. Information I sought from the New Brunswick Department of Public Safety showed that as of 2012, 98 of 443 claims were still outstanding. Kaufman (2002, p. 366) says that only claims made against five employees who had been charged with sexual offences 'were considered credible by the government'.
19. Arguably, *Alberta Sterilization* is a core-plus-two case because the *Act* discriminated against a group of people, those with mental disabilities, who were to be considered for sterilization. However, sterilization practices were aimed only at those in institutions.
20. Sources vary on the number approved and carried out. Caulfield and Robertson, 1996, p. 61) say 4,725 were approved, and 2,822 were carried out. I sourced the numbers from Grekul et al. (2004), whose empirical research on the Board's files is more detailed.
21. Grekul et al. (2004, p. 363) say that this was an amendment to the 1937 legislation, but Jon Faulds, a lawyer who represented many claimants, said the phrase was 'invented by the Board' without legislative support, a point noted in the *Muir* judgment (Faulds, personal communication, 16 July 2013).
22. This span of years is given by advocacy groups, but the government puts the start year at 1935; sources suggest that practices were concentrated in the 1940s and 1950s.
23. Like other cases in the sample, many children were not, strictly speaking, 'orphans'. They were placed in foundling homes and orphanages because their parents could not care for them, their mothers were not married, or they had physical or mental disabilities.

24. As of 30 September 2013, the total of 4,493 validated claimants exceeds these initial estimates.
25. Different dates are given for the year that COOID began (1991 and 1992); I sourced 1991 from the Comité Multipartite (2003).
26. The term 'Indian' is used in the literature, despite the fact that the three major Aboriginal groups in Canada – First Nations (formerly 'Indian'), Inuit (formerly 'Eskimo'), and Métis (those of mixed heritage) – were placed in the schools. However, the policy was aimed at 'status Indians'. In the 1980s and early 1990s, the term 'First Nations' was used to include all three groups, but a change in terminology occurred in the late 1990s.
27. The source of this phrase is unclear, but it is often attributed to George McDougall, originally from Scotland, who became a Methodist clergyman and missionary, spending most of his missionary life in the Canadian prairie provinces (Nix, 1972).
28. All citations to the RCAP final report are to Vol. 1, chapter 10, on the residential school system.
29. Sources vary in the numbers charged and convicted. I combined data in Bessner (1998) and Shea (1999b).
30. With respect to the RCMP's response to offending against children in residential schools, LeBeuf (2011, p. 4) reports there were '60 investigations... conducted by the RCMP between 1957 and 2005 in... British Columbia, Alberta, Saskatchewan, and Manitoba. There were 619 victims who appeared before the courts and over 40 perpetrators identified'.
31. The term was introduced by historian Peter Read (1981/2006).
32. Varied estimates are given of the number of Forgotten Australians, which may (or may not) include Stolen Generations members or Child Migrants. Because the estimated numbers in the two latter groups are relatively smaller (20,000 to 25,000 and 7,000, respectively), and the 500,000 figure is an acknowledged underestimate, I use 500,000 as the estimated number of Forgotten Australians. Based on the Senate Report (2004, appendix 5), the number includes those in out-of-home care.
33. The negotiator for Helpline, Douglas Roche, was also an advisor in creating the scheme for *George Epoch*.
34. There have been some successful outcomes for Stolen Generations members who have applied to Australian state criminal injuries schemes, when they can prove being physically or sexually harmed while in state care. Australian court decisions may also have reflected 'unconscious racism' in applying legal principles to the cases (Marchetti and Ransley, 2005, p. 538).

3 Institutions for Children and Memories of Institutional Life

1. I use care leavers, former residents, victims, and survivors throughout the text interchangeably.
2. NPM stands for Nationale Prevalentiestudie Mishandeling van Kinderen en Jeugdigen, for which the official English translation is National Prevalence Study of Maltreatment of Youth. Euser et al. (2013) do not show the four questions, but they appear to include one item for 'hands-off' offending (p. 225).

3. Euser et al. (2013) do not provide detail on gender differences in prevalence or whether or not this varies by the context of care. The Samson Commission summary (2012, p. 147) suggests that girls were victims twice as often as boys (26.4 per cent versus 12.6 per cent), but does not distinguish by residential and foster care context. Berger (1995, p. 13) reports ratios of victimization and offending in Jericho Hill School in 1994 as 2:1 girls (victimization) and 2:1 boys (offending).
4. Samson Commission (2012) is an English-language summary, but the detailed analysis is in Dutch. I thank two Dutch colleagues: Henk Elffers for helping me interpret the findings and Catrien Bijleveld for bringing this body of work to my attention.
5. Quinton is the subject of a biography by Pauline Gill (1991).
6. Fontaine was elected Grand Chief of the Assembly of Manitoba Chiefs in 1991, serving to 1997; he was elected National Chief of the Assembly of First Nations, serving from 1997–2000 and 2003–9; he played a significant role in developing the Indian Residential School Settlement Agreement.
7. Penglase distinguishes homes from Homes, the latter being institutionalized care environments for children, not real homes. Although I appreciate the distinction she draws, I do not capitalize Homes, except when quoting from her work.
8. Roy wrote several major works about the *Duplessis Orphans*, including *Mémoire d'asile: la tragédie des enfants de Duplessis* (1994) and *Les calepins de Julien* (1998).

4 Time and Knowledge

1. Pratt (2009) analyzed temporal change in the construction of child sexual abuse, including institutional abuse in Canada, but he examined the fluidity of child sexual abuse as applied to alleged offending, not victimization.
2. See Ferguson (2007) and McAlinden (2013) for developments in Ireland; and Sköld (2013) for Scandinavian and some European countries.
3. Bryce (1922) published an 18-page pamphlet, *The Story of a National Crime*, which exposed the failures of the Department of Indian Affairs to address the health of Aboriginal peoples in Canada.
4. The sex of the students is not reported by the source (TRC, 2012, p. 42).
5. He reviewed England and Wales, but did not include Northern Ireland and the Hughes (1986) report.
6. Although the source does not specify, the report was likely made to a departmental authority, not the police.
7. A dramatic example, but not from Australia or Canada, is the 1915 rebellion in the Bastøy Boys' Home, located on an island about an hour by ferry from Oslo. The boys set fire to the barn and attempted to escape. The Norwegian Government sent in a large contingent of 'soldiers, torpedo boats, aircraft, an armoured ship, and a submarine to catch them' (Norsk Folkemuseum, 2013). The film, *King of Devil's Island* (2010), dramatized events. The island now has a minimum security prison.
8. Criminal prosecutions of priests occurred in the United States in the 19th century, and civil litigation occurred decades before and during litigation

against Gauthe. However, his case became a major focus of national attention; and together with other cases in the United States, 'created the impression of a pervasive, nationwide problem' (Lytton, 2008, p. 11). Gauthe was first subject to civil litigation in 1984; he was criminally prosecuted and convicted in 1985.

9. Throughout the Hughes (1986) report, reference is made to 'homosexual abuse' and 'homosexual offences', but in the last section, 'sexual abuse of children' is introduced as a term.
10. Webster (2005) and Smith (2010) suggest that there were exaggerated claims in North Wales, the Channel Island of Jersey, and Scotland.
11. All cases have a core response of addressing the failure of authorities to protect and care for children. However, 12 are considered 'core' cases in that this is the only basis for the response; five are 'core-plus' cases, and two are redress scheme only cases that address abuse (or policies) in the core and core-plus cases.
12. According to a story by Greg Quill in the *Toronto Star* (8 December 1993), a 24-hour counselling service phone number, which was advertized at the beginning and end of the program, was 'swamped around the clock with calls from ... middle-aged men remembering similar events in their own lives 20 or 30 years ago'; 'more than 1,000 calls' were logged. Under court order, the airing of the television show was delayed one year in Ontario and most of Québec, while the trials of defendants in *St John's and St Joseph's* were underway.
13. It can be difficult to specify one factor that sparked an official response because there may be several. The key factors I identified were victims' complaints to authorities, media stories, victim group advocacy with media support, the press of civil litigation against government and/or church authorities, and preceding inquiries.
14. Tusyn brought a law suit against the government in 2003, but a news source (Macgregor, 2011) is not clear on whether the suit was lodged before or after the airing of the television program. Tusyn, who died in 2009, is remembered as 'fighting tirelessly for abuse victims' (Paine, 2009).
15. In July 2014, the Office of the Director of Public Prosecutions advised the Attorney General that there was 'no reasonable prospects of success' in prosecuting any former cabinet ministers who may have been involved in the decision to shred the documents, and thus, it was not in the public interest to pursue prosecution. The Attorney General 'does not intend' to pursue the matter further (Moore, 2014) .
16. In documents presented to the court, Leilani's name was originally spelled Lellani.
17. Space does not permit a justification for all 19 cases here, but I can provide a detailed analysis on request.
18. When the case focused solely on sexual abuse as *George Epoch, Jericho Hill, New Brunswick Institutions*, and *South Australian Institutions* did, the 'year of first complaint' was the year that sexual abuse was reported to authorities.
19. Criminal complaints had been made earlier (in the late 19th century in Canada, and the 1920s and 1930s in Australia), as had challenges to policy (late 1890s in Canada and 1910 in Australia).

20. In the 20th century, criminal prosecution and conviction for sexual offences by school staff against students began in 1988; some of these cases led to significant civil litigation. Established in 1991, the RCAP's scope was broader than the Indian residential school system.
21. The list of primary documents is available upon request.

5 Redress Structure and Process

1. In one case (*Tasmanian Institutions*), sources suggest that after Walter Tusyn's death, family members continued with his civil claim, but I do not know its current status. The two others are the Australian redress scheme only cases.
2. The seven cases are *Mount Cashel, George Epoch, Jericho Hill* (class action component), *Alberta Sterilization, Queensland Institutions, Child Migrants*, and *South Australian Institutions*.
3. The first civil case was received by the Canadian Government in 1988. As of 17 July 1996, 17,097 claimants had initiated abuse claims, and 4,134 had been resolved (Russell affidavit, 2006, p.16). When Frank Iacobucci was appointed in May 2005 as Federal Representative to negotiate a settlement, there were 'more than 13,500 individual claims filed and approximately 11 class actions seeking damages' (Iacobucci affidavit, 2006, p. 4).
4. According to the Senate Report (2004 p. 4), 'without doubt this inquiry has generated the largest volume of highly personal, emotive and significant evidence of any Senate inquiry'.
5. In the context of institutional abuse, *redress* is commonly used; however, in the context of international crime and violations of human rights, *reparations* is more common (Torpey, 2006), but so too is redress (McCarthy, 2012). I have not seen a definitional comparison of the two, and suspect that the choice of term arises from historical usage, coupled with a writer's academic discipline or field of research.
6. All the stipulated (that is, non-negotiated schemes) in my sample were government-stipulated; thus, I use this term. However, other organizational entities can and do stipulate the terms of redress schemes.
7. With a government response in mind, Winter (2009, p. 51) argues that 'the *ex gratia* content of state redress creates a straightforward mismatch with corrective justice' by not accepting liability for injury and by denying rights to full compensation. He suggests that the state should explain the 'financial argument for the payment's *ex gratia* character', but because it does not, it appears as a 'defective form of redress' (p. 53). I address these points in Chapters 7 and 8.
8. One sees victims' justice *needs* more often used in the literature (see Koss 2006; van der Merwe 2009) than justice interests. However, *needs* connotes a psychological requirement, whereas *interests* connotes a victim's standing as a citizen in a justice activity, a connotation I prefer.
9. The Toronto Christian Brothers were initially part of the negotiations, but they withdrew from the agreement.
10. For the Victims of Crime Fund, claimants are asked to provide information on when an offence was reported to the police; what if any information is known about the perpetrator, including ownership of assets, and 'special

damages' and loss of earnings. For the Abuse in State Care Fund, claimants are not asked about perpetrators or reports to the police, but rather the names of relatives and carers at the time of abuse, all places and times in state care, and the character and effect of sexual abuse experienced.

11. The total cost differs from what is reported in Kaufman (2002), but it was provided to me by the Nova Scotia Department of Justice with a Freedom of Information request, 7 October 2013.
12. One potential exception is the Independent Assessment Process [IAP] in the Indian Residential School Settlement Agreement, for which the assessment process is aligned more with standard civil damages, like the Irish Residential Redress Board scheme. However, I am not aware of a public document that justifies the logic of the IAP itself, including the basis for the $275,000 maxima (excluding additional consideration for proven loss of income).
13. *Grandview*'s matrix had three tiers of abuse: cruel and prolonged 'mistreatment' ($3,000 to $20,000); isolated act of sexual assault (penetrative) with threats of abuse or physical abuse involving hospitalization ($20,000 to $40,000); and repeated sexual assault and physical beatings and threats ($40,000 to $60,000). The levels of impact range from shorter- to longer-term detrimental impact (see Kaufman, 2002, pp. 338–9; this is the second time these pages appear in Kaufman's chapter XVI).
14. For Canada, Berger (1995) considers a one-off payment of $21,000 in 1988 for Japanese Canadians who had been interned during World War II. Relevant examples for Australia are $25,000 payments made from 2001 to 2007 to Australian veterans of World War II (or their partners), who were held as a prisoner of war by the Japanese, interned by the North Korean military forces, or prisoners of war in Europe.
15. Other problems can emerge, including which types of care arrangements or school settings are considered eligible (for example, foster care and day schools) and what records claimants are expected to provide to demonstrate eligibility.
16. Invest taps redress scheme 'investment' in claimants (excluding financial payments). It is the sum of two variables: the assessment process had an oral hearing (1=yes; 0=no) and counselling was provided as a benefit or service (1=yes; 0=no). If a scheme had more benefits or services ('a package'), 1 point was added; if it had a significant package of benefits and services, 2 points were added. A score of 0 or 1 is 'low invest'; 2 to 4 is 'high invest'.
17. Hearings in *Ontario Schools for the Deaf* and *Jericho Hill Class Action* (levels 2 and 3) had an interpreter present, who was fluent in American Sign Language (ASL) or in another dialect, if required (the latter was relevant only to *Jericho Hill Class Action*).
18. In exceptional circumstances, a $50,000 cap.
19. Allocations were made to two groups: (1) members of the Stolen Generations and (2) family members of deceased members of the Stolen Generations. Each family member received $5,000 (or family group to a maximum of $20,000). After this was distributed, the remainder was divided equally to members of the Stolen Generations.
20. When the scheme was announced, the cap was $80,000.
21. Scheme planners used terms such as different 'phases' or 'groups', and I adopt their language. For *Duplessis Orphans*, scheme planners differentiated

the 2001 and 2007 programs; these were based on different money logics, and thus, time 1 and time 2 are the accurate terms.

22. For Queensland's level 1 payment, a claimant was asked to 'declare' that s/he experienced abuse or neglect as a child in care, but did not have 'to provide a detailed account of experiences or a lengthy submission' (Queensland Communities, 2008, pp. 7–8).
23. However, review by an external assessor occurred in *Redress WA* when proposed payments were in the two higher bands.
24. Seven of 13 Canadian money outcomes gave reasons as a standard practice, but one of seven Australian money outcomes did.
25. Different terms are used in the literature: deed of release, deed of waiver and release, deed of settlement and release, indemnity, or simply, release. I use release for simplicity and because it is the most accurate, in a legal sense, in this context.
26. In the initial scheme for *Redress WA*, signing a release was required; however, this changed in 2010 (Western Australia Minister for Communities, 2010).
27. This is exemplified in the Compensation Advisory Committee's (2002) report, outlining the basis for the Irish Residential Institutions Redress Board, which used a more generous civil damages framework.
28. If a scheme had more than one round or phase over time, I added the total number of claimants, as in *Duplessis Orphans* and *Tasmanian Institutions*; for the three schemes with different levels, I used the overall number who were eligible or applied to the first level, as in *Jericho Hill Class Action*, *Indian Residential Schools*, and *Queensland Institutions*. This avoided double counting the total number of claimants in a redress scheme.
29. With a low number of cases for analysis, this and other analyses must be viewed as exploratory. For some analyses I created dichotomous variables and carried out 2 x 2 cross-tabulations; for others, I used bivariate correlations. When the phi (or correlation) coefficient was +.30 or –.30 or greater, I decided that there was an association worth remarking upon. The phi coefficient for the relationship between invest (high-low coded 1,0) and number of claimants (high-low, coded 1,0) was –.34 (N of 15 cases).
30. I carried out a correlation analysis for the validation rate (not dichotomized) and invest (high-low, coded 1,0), number of claimants (high-low, coded 1,0) and assessor type (external-internal, coded 1,0). There was an association between the validation rate and invest (.31), but not for number of claimants (–.04). The association between the validation rate and assessor type (.22) fell short of the .30 threshold (N=18 cases).

6 Redress Outcomes

1. For *Grandview*, Kaufman (2002, p. 339) reports that in addition to deciding a financial payment, an adjudicator could 'direct the government to pay service providers additional sums up to $10,000 to cover exceptional medical or dental costs related to the consequences of abuse or mistreatment' not covered by insurance. This does not appear to be part of the financial payment or a benefit, nor have I seen any published information on these outcomes.

2. Shea's (1999a, p. 33) analysis is of 134 women as of October 1999; however, the final number of validated claimants was substantially larger.
3. For *Indian Residential Schools*, legal fees were paid for those applying to the Independent Assessment Process (IAP), but not the Common Experience Payment (CEP). The two redress scheme only cases (*Tasmanian Stolen Generations* and *Redress WA*), did not require a release form and would not have needed to fund legal costs.
4. In addition to complete reports of process and outcome in two cases, five cases have reports or relevant information that is partly complete. *Tasmanian Institutions* has an excellent report on process in phase 1 (Tasmanian Ombudsman, 2004), with a shorter report in phase 2 (Tasmanian Ombudsman, 2006); but as yet, there is no final report on the four phases of the scheme. Reports on *Grandview* (Leach, 1997) and *Nova Scotia Institutions* (Kaufman, 2002) focus on process more than financial and benefit outcomes. Leach (1998) provides some (sketchy) outcome information for *St John's and St Joseph's* and *Grandview*, although the report contains an in-depth analysis of redress scheme planning and implementation. Henton and McCann (1995) provide insight on the creation and early days of implementing the *St John's and St Joseph's* scheme. The Comité Multipartite (2003) provides an analysis of processes and outcomes in decisions made in *Duplessis Orphans* (time 1), but the report is written in French, and thus less accessible to an Anglophone audience.
5. This amount is structured into the award and paid by the government; however, a lawyer is permitted to charge up to 30 per cent in legal fees.
6. Morley (2001, p. 1) reports 'an average of $35,000'. However, the report says that $13,090,000 was paid to 359 validated claimants; thus, I computed the average as $36,462.
7. Legal fees were likely to be about 30 per cent in this case, based on other Canadian cases where legal fees and expenses are discussed. Assuming 30 per cent, the average amount received by each plaintiff was $183,140.
8. See Appendix 1, column 8. The numbers reported in the press often double count individuals who sued again, or they may include others who were not Mount Cashel residents. I have sourced the number from a lawyer close to the case (Geoff Budden, personal communication, 23 December 2013).
9. The second settlement had 83 individuals and totalled $15.5 million; 28 of the 83 had already received a payment from the 1996 settlement, which was factored into the amount they received from the 2004 settlement to avoid double recovery (see *Re: Christian Brothers of Ireland in Canada* in Cases and legislation).
10. According to a news release (Alberta Government, 1999), the total amount paid by June 1999 was $60 million; if we subtract $47.8 million (Limited Trustee) and $3.8 million (40 additional cases), that leaves $8.4 million for 91 cases.
11. According to Jon Faulds, 'lawyers representing the claimants publicly rejected the Settlement Panel process when it was first announced because they had not been consulted, and they felt it represented an effort by the government to settle claims for less money than they would have otherwise attracted in court' (Faulds, personal communication, 16 July 2013).

12. There may be other civil settlements or *ex gratia* payments by church or charitable organizations, but data are not publicly available. My focus is on the larger group settlements.
13. Separate apologies were given by government officials to *Jericho Hill* survivors, who were part of the JICP and the Class Action; in both cases, different government officials expressed 'sincere regret' (1995 for the JICP and 2004 for the Class Action).
14. Most civil claims were lodged before the redress scheme was announced; thus, it was the only option available for 2 years.

7 Redress and Victims' Justice Interests

1. Unfortunately, no information is provided on what the appropriate denominator should be; nor can this be inferred from the number of hearings or interviews conducted.
2. Some schemes took a different approach. In *Tasmanian Institutions*, phases 1 and 2, the claimant made phone contact and then was interviewed by the Office of Ombudsman; there was no application form to complete. This changed in phases 3 and 4, when claimants completed an application form before the interview. In *Jericho Hill*-JICP, claimants had an intake interview with a compensation consultant (fluent in American Sign Language), who determined eligibility and explained the process. At a second interview of 4 to 40 hours in duration, claimants described their experiences of abuse to the consultants (Morley 2001, pp. 20–1).
3. The initial deadline of 2 January 1996 was extended to October 1997. *Grandview*'s first group had 257 claimants, who applied by the deadline; its second group of 72 applied after that.
4. For *St John's and St Joseph's*, an application to an Opportunity Fund was required for groups 1 and 2, but not post-group 2, for whom $3,000 was automatically allocated to eligible claimants. Leach (1998) argues that this approach is preferable to asking claimants to apply, often repeatedly, for different benefits.
5. For *Grandview*, there is no reported validation rate in any source, although Kaufman (2002, p. 347) says that 'most were validated'. I am assuming that *Grandview*'s validation rate was the same as *St John's and St Joseph's*.
6. One could say that this antimony is at the heart of tort; however, the calculation of damages for injury in successful civil litigation is more open-ended than it is in most (but not all) redress schemes.
7. Another 47 per cent were 'somewhat satisfied', which is a qualified positive.
8. For the others, 53 per cent were mixed (gave positive and negative responses), and 16 per cent were fully negative.
9. In this part of the article, Feldthusen et al. (2000, pp. 97–100) did not always distinguish between *Grandview* and non-*Grandview* claimants. However, I selected those quotes that were of time spent in an institution, which meant that they were former Grandview residents.
10. In the Senate Report (2004), by comparison, the recommendation was for the federal 'government to establish a national reparations fund for victims of institutional and out-of-home care abuse' (p. 226).

11. A case that comes up many times by Australian advocacy group members is the settlement amount for the wrongful imprisonment (and abuse) of Cornelia Rau. A permanent Australian resident, Rau was treated as an illegal immigrant and placed in various detention centres over a period of 10 months (Mark, 2007). The Commonwealth settled for $2.6 million in 2008 (*Sydney Morning Herald*, 2008).

References

Aboriginal Adjudicator (1998). *Aboriginal Adjudicator's Report on the Process of the Grandview Agreement*, 24 March.

AHRC *see* Australian Human Rights Centre.

Alberta, Government of (1998a). News release, Government announces settlements for 500 sexual sterilization claims, 5 June.

_____ (1998b). News release, Settlement Panel for sterilization claims announced, 21 October.

_____ (1999). News release, Stratton Agreement concludes sterilization negotiations; and Expression of Regret, 2 November.

Alliance for Forgotten Australians (2011). Monuments. Viewed December 2013. <http://www.forgottenaustralians.org.au/monuments.html>.

Alter, S. (1999). *Apologising for Serious Wrongdoing: Social, Psychological, and Legal Considerations*, Final Report (Ottawa: Law Commission of Canada).

Anderberg, K. (2009). American child institution history. Viewed 22 June 2013. <http://web.resist.ca/~kirstena/machallinstitutionhistory.html>.

Angelides, S. (2005). The emergence of the paedophile in the late twentieth century. *Australian Historical Studies*, 36(126), 272–95.

Auckland University of Technology Centre of Restorative Justice (2010). Submission to the Ministry of Justice on the 'Victims of Crime' Consultation Document. Viewed 27 January 2013. <http://www.restorativejustice.org/RJOB/Submission%20on%20 Victims%20Rights.pdf>.

Australian Government (2005). Response to the Committee's Reports: *Forgotten Australians: A Report on Australians Who Experienced Institutional or Out-of-Home Care as Children* and *Protecting Vulnerable Children: A National Challenge, Second Report on the Inquiry into Children in Institutional or Out-of-Home Care* (Canberra: Australian Government Publishing Service).

Australian Human Rights Commission (1999). *Aboriginal and Torres Strait Islander 1998 Social Justice Report*. Viewed December 2013. <https://www.humanrights.gov.au/publications/social-justice-report-1998>.

Australian Senate (2000). *Healing: A Legacy of Generations: The Report of the Inquiry into the Federal Government's Implementation of Recommendations Made by the Human Rights and Equal Opportunity Commission in Bringing Them Home*, Legal and Constitutional References Committee (Canberra: Commonwealth of Australia).

_____ (2001). *Lost Innocents: Righting the Record, Report on Child Migration*, Community Affairs References Committee (Canberra: Commonwealth of Australia).

_____ (2004). *Forgotten Australians: A Report on Australians Who Experienced Institutional or Out-of-Home Care as Children*, Community Affairs References Committee (Canberra: Commonwealth of Australia).

_____ (2005). *Protecting Vulnerable Children: A National Challenge, Second Report on the Inquiry into Children in Institutional or Out-of-Home Care*, Community Affairs References Committee (Canberra: Commonwealth of Australia).

_____ (2009). *Lost Innocents and Forgotten Australians Revisited: Report on the Progress with the Implementation of the Recommendations of the Lost Innocents and Forgotten Australians Reports,* Community Affairs References Committee (Canberra: Commonwealth of Australia).

_____ (2010). *Review of Government Compensation Payments,* Legal and Constitutional References Committee (Canberra: Senate Printing Unit).

Badgley, R. (1984). *Report of the Committee on Sexual Offences against Children and Youths* (Ottawa: Government Publications).

Balboni, J. and D. Bishop (2010). Transformative justice: survivor perspectives on clergy sexual abuse litigation. *Contemporary Justice Review,* 13(2), 133–45.

Barter, C., E. Renold, D. Berridge, and P. Cawson (2004). *Peer Violence in Children's Residential Care* (New York: Palgrave Macmillan).

Barth, R. P. (2002). *Institutions vs. Foster homes: The Empirical Basis for a Century of Action* (North Carolina: Jordan Institute for Families).

Battersby, L., L. Greaves, and R. Hunt (2008). Legal redress and institutional sexual abuse: a study of the experiences of Deaf and hard of hearing survivors. *Florida Coastal Law Review,* 10, 67–118.

Bédard, D. (1962). *Rapport de la Commission d'étude des hôpitaux psychiatriques* (Québec: Ministère de la Santé).

Berger, T. (1995). *Report of the Special Counsel Regarding Claims Arising out of Sexual Abuse at Jericho Hill School* (Vancouver: Ministry of the Attorney General).

Berridge, D. (2005). Child protection: research and researchers. In N. Axford, V. Berry, M. Little, and L. Morpeth (eds), *Forty Years of Research, Policy and Practice in Children's Services* (Chichester: Wiley), pp. 108–18.

Bessner, R. (1998). *Institutional Child Abuse in Canada* (Ottawa: Law Commission of Canada).

Best, J. (1990). *Threatened Children: Rhetoric and Concern about Child-Victims* (Chicago: University of Chicago Press).

British Columbia Ombudsman (D. McCallam) (1993). *Abuse of Deaf Students at Jericho Hill School,* Public Report No. 32 (Victoria: Ombudsman of British Columbia).

Broken Rites Australia (2013). Broken Rites supported these victims at a Queensland orphanage. Viewed December 2013. <http://brokenrites.org.au/drupal/node/34>.

Browne, K. (2009). *The Risk of Harm to Young Children in Institutional Care* (London: Save the Children).

Bryce, P. H. (1907). *Report on the Indian Schools of Manitoba and the North-West Territories* (Ottawa: Government Printing Bureau).

_____ (1909). Addendum to *Report on the Indian Schools of Manitoba and the North-West Territories* (Ottawa: Government Printing Bureau).

_____ (1922). *The Story of a National Crime* (Ottawa: James Hope & Sons Ltd.). Viewed December 2013. <http://www.archive.org/stream/storyofnationalc00bry cuoft/storyofnationalc00brycuoft_djvu.txt>.

Butler, B. (2004). *Protecting Children: An Inquiry into Abuse of Children in Foster Care* (Brisbane: Crime and Misconduct Commission).

Canadian Conference of Catholic Bishops (2013). Apology on Residential Schools by the Catholic Church. Viewed 27 December 2013. <http://www.cccb.ca/site/eng/media-room/files/2630-apology-on-residential-schools-by-the-catholic-church>.

Cassidy, J. (2006). The Stolen Generations – Canada and Australia: the legacy of assimilation. *Deakin Law Review,* 11(1), 131–77.

Caulfield, T. and G. Robertson (1996). Eugenic policies in Alberta: from the systematic to the systemic. *Alberta Law Review,* 35(1), 59–79.

CBC Digital Archives (2001). Duplessis Orphans: apology and amends. Television program episode of Canada Now with guests Bernard Landry and Bruno Roy, broadcast 3 July. Viewed December 2013. <http://www.cbc.ca/archives/categories/society/youth/the-duplessis-orphans/apology-and-amends.html>.

CBERS *see* Christian Brothers Ex-Residents and Students Services.

CCCB *see* Canadian Conference of Catholic Bishops.

Child Migrants Trust (2013). International Association page. Viewed December 2013. <http://www.childmigrantstrust.com/intl-association>.

Children's Commission of Queensland (1997). *Paedophilia in Queensland,* 5 August (Brisbane: Queensland Government).

Christian Brothers Ex-Residents and Students Services (P. White and D. Rosser) (2009). Letter to the editor. *The West Australian,* 4 August, p. 18.

CLAN *see* Care Leavers of Australia Network.

Closing the Gap Clearinghouse (2013). Strategies and practices for promoting the social and emotional wellbeing of Aboriginal and Torres Strait Islander people. Resource sheet no. 19. Viewed December 2013. <www.aihw.gov.au/closingthegap>.

Cohen, S. (1972). *Folk Devils and Moral Panics* (Oxford: Blackwell Publishing).

Cold Lake First Nations (2013). History of Indian Residential Schools. Viewed 23 December 2013. <http://www.clfns.com/community/index.php?option=com_content&view=arti cle&id=102&Itemid=129>.

Coldrey, B. M. (1993). *The Scheme: The Christian Brothers and Childcare in Western Australia* (Western Australia: Argyle-Pacific Publishing).

Comité des Orphelin(e)s de Duplessis Victimes d'Abus (2012). *La voix des sans-voix* (The voice of the voiceless), CI-018MA, C.G-Code de procédure civile (Montréal: National Assembly).

Comité Multipartite (2003). *Programme national de réconciliation avec les orphelins et orphelines de Duplessis: Rapport présenté à Madame la Ministre des Relations avec les citoyens et de l'Immigration* (Montréal: Ministère des Relations avec les Citoyens et de l'Immigration).

Commissie-Samson (2012). *Omringd door zorg, toch niet veilig: Seksueelmisbruik van door de overheid uit huis geplaatste kinderen, 1945 tot heden,* chapter 10 Summary, English Translation. Viewed July 2013. <https://www.onderzoek-seksueelkindermisbruik.nl/actueel/summary-rapport-commissie-samson-beschikbaar.aspx?cp=109&cs=578>.

Commission to Inquire into Child Abuse (2009). *Final Report.* Viewed December 2013. <http://www.childabusecommission.com/rpt/pdfs/>.

Commission for Public Complaints Against the Royal Canadian Mounted Police (2007). *Kingsclear Investigation Report: Public Interest Investigation into RCMP Investigations of the New Brunswick Training School* (Ottawa: Commission for Public Complaints against the RCMP).

Compensation Advisory Committee (2002). *Toward Redress and Recovery,* report in accordance with section 14 of the Irish Residential Institutions Redress Bill 2001 (Dublin: Minister for Education and Science).

COOID *see* Comité des Orphelins et Orphelines institutionnalisés de Duplessis.

Corby, B., A. Doig, and V. Roberts (2001). *Public Inquiries into Abuse of Children in Residential Care* (London: Jessica Kingsley Publishers).

COVA *see* Comité des Orphelin(e)s de Duplessis Victimes d'Abus.

CPC *see* Commission for Public Complaints Against the Royal Canadian Mounted Police.

Criminal Justice Commission (1998). *Inquiry into Allegations of Misconduct in the Investigation of Paedophilia in Queensland: Kimmins Report* (Brisbane: Queensland Government).

Csáky, C. (2009). *Keeping Children out of Harmful Institutions: why we should be investing in family based care* (London: Save the Children's Fund).

Curtis, M. (1946). *Report of the Care of Children Committee: Training in Childcare* (London: His Majesty's Stationery Office).

Dalton, T. (2009). Home truths. *Q Weekend*. Viewed July 2014. Available at <http://www.bishop-accountability.org/news2009/11_12/2009_11_15_CLAN_HomeTruths.htm>.

Daly, K. (2014). Reconceptualizing sexual victimization and justice. In I. VanFraechem, A. Pemberton, and F. Ndahinda (eds), *Justice for Victims: Perspectives on Rights, Transition and Reconciliation* (London: Routledge), pp. 378–96.

Daly, K. and G. Proietti-Scifoni (2011). Reparation and restoration. In M. Tonry (ed.) *Oxford Handbook of Crime and Criminal Justice* (New York: Oxford University Press), pp. 207–53.

Davin, N. F. (1879). *Report on Industrial Schools for Indians and Half-Breeds*. Viewed December 2013. <https://archive.org/details/cihm_03651>.

Davis, J. E. (2005). *Accounts of Innocence: Sexual Abuse, Trauma, and the Self* (Chicago: University of Chicago Press).

De Francis, V. (1969). *Protecting the Child Victim of Sex Crimes Committed by Adults* (Denver: American Humane Association).

Death, J. (2013). 'They did not believe me': adult survivors' perspectives of child sexual abuse by personnel in Christian institutions (Crime and Justice Research Centre: Queensland University of Technology).

Dion Stout, M. and R. Harp (2007). *Lump Sum Compensation Payments Research Project: The Circle Rechecks Itself* (Ottawa: Aboriginal Healing Foundation).

Dorman, N. and F. O'Cleirigh (2013). Police re-open child sex abuse investigation at boys home in Belfast. *Mirror Online*, 23 March. Viewed 30 May 2013. <http://www.mirror.co.uk/news/uk-news/police-re-open-child-sex-abuse-1781425>.

Dow, C. (2008). Parliament of Australia background note, Sorry: the unfinished business of the *Bringing Them Home* report (Canberra: Parliament of Australia). Viewed 27 December 2013. <http://www.aph.gov.au/About_Parliament/Parliamentary_Departments/Parliamentary_Library/pubs/BN/0708/BringingThemHomeReport>.

Dow, C. and J. Phillips (2009). Parliament of Australia background note, 'Forgotten Australians' and 'Lost Innocents': child migrants and children in institutional care in Australia (Canberra: Parliament of Australia). Viewed 28 December 2013. <http://www.aph.gov.au/About_Parliament /Parliamentary_Departments/Parliamentary_Library/pubs/BN/0910/ChildMigrants>.

Dozier, M., C. H. Zeanah, A. R. Wallin, and C. Shauffer (2012). Institutional care for young children: review of literature and policy implications. *Social Issues and Policy Review*, 6(1), 1–25.

Dubinsky, S. M. (2007). *A Qualitative Study of Grandview Training School and Grandview Survivor Healing Strategies*. Master of Social Work thesis (Saskatchewan: University of Regina).

Euser, S., A. Lenneke, A. Tharner, M. van Ijzendoorn, and M. Bakersmans-Kranenburg (2013). The prevalence of child sexual abuse in out-of-home care: a comparison between abuse in residential and in foster care. *Child Maltreatment*, 18(4), 221–31.

Farrington, K. (1992). The modern prison as total institution? Public perception versus objective reality. *Crime & Delinquency*, 38, 6–26.

Feldthusen, B., O. Hankivsky, and L. Greaves (2000). Therapeutic consequences of civil actions for damages and compensation claims by victims of sexual abuse. *Canadian Journal of Women and Law*, 12, 66–116.

Ferguson, H. (2007). Abused and looked after children as 'moral dirt': child abuse and institutional care in historical perspective. *Journal of Social Policy*, 36(1), 123–39.

Find & Connect (2014). Home page. Viewed July 2014. <http://www.findand connect.gov.au/>.

Fontaine, P. (1990a). Shocking testimony of sexual abuse. Television program broadcast 30 October. Viewed December 2013. <http://www.cbc.ca/archives/categories/politics/parties-leaders/phil-fontaine-native-diplomat-and-deal-maker/shocking-testimony-of-sexual-abuse.html>.

_____ (1990b). Abused to abuser. Radio program aired 5 November. Viewed December 2013. <http://www.cbc.ca/archives/categories/politics/parties-leaders/phil-fontaine-native-diplomat-and-dealmaker/abused-to-abuser.html>.

Forde Foundation (2008). *The Forde Foundation Review Summary* (South Brisbane: Board of Advice, The Forde Foundation).

Forde, L. (1999). *Report of the Commission of Inquiry into Abuse of Children in Queensland Institutions* (Brisbane: Queensland Government).

Forde Report or Forde inquiry *see* Forde, L. (1999).

Gallagher, B. (2000). The extent and nature of known cases of institutional child sexual abuse. *British Journal of Social Work*, 30, 795–817.

Garrett, J. (1979). Institutional maltreatment of children: an emerging public issue. *Residential & Community Child Care Administration*, 1(1), 57–68.

Gidney, Norman (2004). Ex-Jericho students settle for $12 million. *Victoria Times-Colonist*, 3 April. Viewed 11 May 2013. Republished at <http://www.blindcanadians.ca /publications/cbm/18/ex-jericho-students-settle-12-million>.

Gil, D. (1970). *Violence against Children: Physical Child Abuse in the United States* (Cambridge: Harvard University Press).

_____ (1975). Unravelling child abuse. *American Journal of Orthopsychiatry*, 45, 346–56.

Gil, E. and K. Baxter (1979). Abuse of children in institutions. *Child Abuse and Neglect*, 3, 693–98.

Gill, A. (1997). *Orphans of the Empire* (New South Wales: Millennium Books).

Gill, P. (1991). *Les enfants de Duplessis: l'histoire vraie d'Alice Quinton* (Montréal: Libre Expression).

Girard, D. (1998). Abuse victim ends silent suffering. *Toronto Star*,15 July.

Goffman, E. (1961). *Asylums* (Harmondsworth: Penguin).

Gordon, L. (1988). The politics of child sexual abuse: notes from American history. *Feminist Review*, 28 (Spring), 56–64.

Grandview Adjudicators (1998). *Report of the Grandview Adjudicators*, 13 May.

Graycar, R. and J. Wangmann (2007). Redress packages for institutional child abuse: exploring the Grandview Agreement as a case study in 'alternative' dispute resolution. Legal Studies Research Paper No. 07/50 (Sydney: The University of Sydney Law School).

Grekul, J., H. Krahn, and D. Odynak (2004). Sterilizing the 'feeble-minded': eugenics in Alberta, Canada, 1929–1972. *Journal of Historical Sociology*, 7(4), 358–84.

Hacking, I. (1998). *Mad Travelers* (Charlottesville: University Press of Virginia).

Haebich, A. (2000). *Broken Circles: Fragmenting Indigenous Families 1800–2000* (Fremantle: Fremantle Arts Centre Press).

Harris, M. (1990). *Unholy Orders: Tragedy at Mt Cashel* (Ontario: Viking Press).

Henton, D. and D. McCann (1995). *Boys Don't Cry: The Struggle for Justice and Healing in Canada's Biggest Sex Abuse Scandal* (Ontario: McClelland & Stewart).

Henton, D. (2004). McGuinty to apologise to victims of sex abuse. *London Free Press*, 2 June. Viewed December 2013. <http://www.bishop-accountability.org/news2004_01_06/2004_06_02_Henton_McGuintyTo.htm>.

Herbert, S. (1991). *Report of the Review of Student Care at the Provincial Schools for the Deaf and Blind and Demonstration Schools* (Toronto: Ontario Ministry of Education).

Herman, J. (2005). Justice from the victim's perspective. *Violence Against Women*, 11(5), 571–602.

Higgins, J. (2012). Mount Cashel Orphanage abuse scandal timeline. Viewed December 2013. <http://www.heritage.nf.ca/law/wells_gov_mt_cashel_timeline.html>.

Hil, R. and E. Branigan (eds) (2011). *Surviving Care: Achieving Justice and Healing for the Forgotten Australians* (Robina: Bond University).

Hoffman, B. C. (1996). *The Search for Healing, Reconciliation and the Promise of Prevention: The Recorder's Report Concerning Physical and Sexual Abuse at St. Joseph's and St. John's Training Schools for Boys* (Ontario: Reconciliation Process Implementation Committee).

HREOC *see* Human Rights and Equal Opportunity Commission.

Hughes, S. H. S. (1991). *Royal Commission of Inquiry into the Response of the Newfoundland Criminal Justice System to Complaints* (Vols 1–2) (St. John's, Newfoundland: Office of the Queen's Printer).

Hughes, W.H. (with W. J. Patterson and H. Whalley) (1986). *Report of the Committee of Inquiry into Children's Homes and Hostels* (Belfast: Her Majesty's Stationery Office).

Human Rights and Equal Opportunity Commission (1997). *Bringing Them Home: National Inquiry into the Separation of Aboriginal and Torres Strait Islander Children from their Families* (Sydney: Human Rights and Equal Opportunity Commission).

Iacobucci, Hon. F. (2006) Affidavit, Indian Residential Schools Settlement Agreement (IRSSA), Joint Motion Record, Vol IV. Viewed December 2013. <http://www.classactionservices.ca/irs/PDFs/JointMotionRecordVOL4.pdf>.

IHRD *see* Institute for Human Resource Development.

Indian Residential Schools Settlement Agreement (2006). (Ontario: Office of Indian Residential Schools Resolution Canada).

Institute for Human Resource Development (1998). *Final Report: Review of the Needs of Victims of Institutional Abuse* (Ottawa: Law Commission of Canada).

IRSSA *see* Indian Residential Schools Settlement Agreement.

Ison, J. (2012). The Newcastle Industrial School and Reformatory for Girls 1867–1871, home page. Viewed December 2013. <http://nis.wikidot.com/>.

Jacobs, L. (2007). Reconciling tort and administrative concepts of justice: the case of historical wrongs. *University of New Brunswick Law Journal* (Special symposium issue, Public Wrongs, Private Duties: Re-thinking Public Authority Liability in Canada), 57, 134–61.

Jenkins, P. (1998). *Moral Panic: Changing Concepts of the Child Molester in Modern America* (New Haven: Yale University Press).

JICP *see* Morley, J. (2001).

Johnstone, J. (2011). Consultation on the development of an RJ Toolkit for survivors of historical institutional abuse (Newcastle, UK: Newcastle University Law School). Viewed April 2014. <http://www.survivorscotland.org.uk/news-and-events/item/consultation-on-the-development-of-a-rj-toolkit-for-survivors-of-historical-institutional-abuse/>.

Jung, C. (2011). Canada and the legacy of the Indian Residential Schools: transitional justice for Indigenous people in a non-transitional society. In P. Arthur (ed.), *Identities in Transition: Challenges for Transitional Justice in Divided Societies* (Cambridge University Press), pp. 217–50.

Kaufman, F. (2002). *Searching for Justice: An Independent Review of Nova Scotia's Response to Reports of Institutional Abuse* (Vols 1–2) (Halifax, Nova Scotia: Department of Justice).

Keenan, M. (2012). *Child Sexual Abuse and the Catholic Church* (New York: Oxford University Press).

Kempe, C. H., F. N. Silverman, B. F. Steele, W. Droegemueller, and H. K. Silver (1962). The battered child syndrome. *Journal of the American Medical Association*, 181, 17–24.

Kingsclear Investigation Report *see* Commission for Public Complaints Against the Royal Canadian Mounted Police (2007).

Koss, M. (2006). Restoring rape survivors: justice, advocacy, and a call to action. *Annals of the New York Academy of Sciences*, 1087, 206–34.

Kune, R. (2011). The Stolen Generations in court: explaining the lack of widespread successful litigation by members of the Stolen Generations. *The University of Tasmania Law Review*, 30(1), 32–52.

LaPrairie, C. and P. Stenning (2004). Politics by other means: the role of commissions of inquiry in establishing the truth about Aboriginal justice in Canada. In G. Gilligan and J. Pratt (eds), *Crime, Truth and Justice: Official Inquiry, Discourse, Knowledge* (Cullompton, England: Willan Publishing), pp. 138–60.

Law Commission of Canada (2000). *Restoring Dignity: Responding to Child Abuse in Canadian Institutions* (Ottawa: Minister of Public Works and Government Services).

Layton, R. (2003). *Our Best Investment; A State Plan to Protect and Advance the Interests of Children* (Adelaide: Government of South Australia).

LCC *see* Law Commission of Canada.

Le Beuf, M-E. (2011). *The Role of the Royal Canadian Mounted Police during the Indian Residential School System* (Ontario: Royal Canadian Mounted Police).

Viewed December 2013. <http://www.rcmp-grc.gc.ca/aboriginal-autochtone/irs-spi-eng.htm>.

Leach, D. (1997). *Evaluation of the Grandview Agreement Process: Final Report* (Toronto: Ministry of the Attorney General).

_____ (1998). *Wind Down Report: Lessons Drawn by the Abuse in Provincial Institutions Office about the Grandview and St John's and St Joseph's Agreement Process, Final Report* (Toronto: Ministry of the Attorney General).

Liddell, M. J. (1993). Child welfare and care in Australia: understanding the past to influence the future. In C.R. Goddard and R. Carew (eds), *Responding to Children: Child Welfare Practice* (Melbourne: Longman Cheshire), pp. 28–62.

Lytton, T. D. (2008). *Holding Bishops Accountable* (Cambridge: Harvard University Press).

MacGregor, I. (2011). Why Tasmania needs an independent inquiry into child sex abuse. *Whistleblowers Tasmania* (Tasmanian Times.com). Viewed December 2013. <http://www.tasmaniantimes.com/index.php?/weblog/article/why-tasmania-needs-an-independent-inquiry-into-child-sex-abuse-jimbolinzo/show_comments>.

Manne, R. (2001). *In Denial: The Stolen Generations and the Right* (Melbourne: Schwartz Publishing).

Marchetti, E. and J. Ransley (2005). Unconscious racism: scrutinizing judicial reasoning in Stolen Generation cases. *Social and Legal Studies*, 14(4), 533–52.

Mark, D. (2007). Rau compensation case begins. *AM* radio program aired 9 April. Viewed December 2013. <http://www.abc.net.au/am/content/2007/s1892631.htm>.

McAlinden, A-M. (2013). An inconvenient truth: barriers to truth recovery in the aftermath of institutional child abuse in Ireland. *Legal Studies,* 33(2), 189–214.

MCATSIA *see* Ministerial Council of Aboriginal and Torres Strait Islander Affairs.

McCarthy, C. (2012). Victim redress and international criminal justice: competing paradigms or compatible forms of justice? *Journal of International Criminal Justice*, 10, 351–72.

McKenna, P. (1980). Sex racket at children's home. *Irish Independent,* 24 January, p. 1. Viewed December 2013. <http://spotlightonabuse.wordpress.com/2014/01/13/sex-racket-at-childrens-home-24-01-80/>.

McRae, H., G. Nettheim, T. Anthony, L. Beacroft, S. Brennan, M. Davis, and T. Janke (2009). *Indigenous Legal Issues: Commentary and Materials,* 4th edition (Sydney: Thomson Reuters).

Micah Projects Inc. (2011). The Lily Pad Newsletter, Spring edition. Viewed December 2013. <http://www.micahprojects.org.au/resource_files/micah/IR_91_Lotus-Newsletter-v6-08112011.pdf>.

Michell, D. (2010). Apology excepted: a response to the South Australian Government apology. In R. Hil and E. Branigan (eds), *Surviving Care: Achieving Justice and Healing for the Forgotten Australians* (Robina: Bond University), pp. 151–71.

Miller, J. R. (1996). *Shingwauk's Vision: A History of Native Residential Schools* (Toronto: University of Toronto Press).

Miller, R. L. (1995). *Report of a Commission of Inquiry Established by Order-in-Council 92-1022* (Vols 1–2) (New Brunswick: Office of the Attorney General).

Milloy, J. S. (1999). *A National Crime: The Canadian Government and the Residential School System, 1879 to 1989* (Winnipeg: University of Manitoba Press).

Mills, C. W. (1959). *The Sociological Imagination* (New York: Oxford University Press).

Minister of Indian Affairs and Northern Development (1997). *Gathering Strength: Canada's Aboriginal Action Plan* (Ottawa: Minister of Public Works and Government Services).

Ministère de l'Emploi et de la Solidarité sociale (MESS) (2007). Application for Financial Assistance, National Reconciliation Program for Duplessis Orphans Who Were Residents of Certain Institutions. Viewed December 2013. <http://www.mess.gouv.qc.ca/solidarite-sociale/programmes-mesures/duplessis/index_en.asp>.

Ministerial Council of Aboriginal and Torres Strait Islander Affairs (2003). *Evaluation of Responses to Bringing Them Home Report: Final Report* (Surrey Hills: New South Wales Department of Aboriginal Affairs).

Moore, T. (2014). No Heiner trial for Goss ministers: Bleijie. *Brisbane Times* (online), 2 July. <http://www.brisbanetimes.com.au/queensland/no-heiner-trial-for-goss-ministers-bleijie-20140702-zstrm.html#ixzz36qnhvLHQ>.

Morley, J. (2001). *The Jericho Individual Compensation Program (JICP): A Unique Response to Institutional Sexual Abuse, Final Report of the Compensation Panel Chair* (British Columbia: Attorney General and Minister for Treaty Negotiations).

Moss, J. (1953). *Child Migration to Australia* (London: Her Majesty's Stationery Office).

Mullighan, E. P. (2008a). *Children in State Care Commission of Inquiry: Allegations of Sexual Abuse and Death from Criminal Conduct* (Adelaide: Office of the Commissioner).

Mullighan, E. P. (2008b). *Children on Anangu Pitjantjatjara Yankunytjatjara (APY) Lands Commission of Inquiry: Report into Sexual Abuse* (Adelaide: Office of the Commissioner).

Murray, A. and M. Rock (2003). Child migration schemes to Australia: a dark and hidden chapter of Australia's history revealed. *Australian Journal of Social Issues*, 38(2), 149–67.

Mussell, M. (1995). *In the Spirit of Healing: Recorder's Report Written for the Survivors* (Ontario: Reconciliation Implementation Committee).

National Museum of Australia (2012). Audio transcript: Inside Children's Homes forum discussion with Dr Joanna Penglase. Viewed December 2013. <http://www.nma.gov.au/audio/transcripts/NMA_Inside_panel_20120214.html>.

National Sorry Day Committee (2013). The History of the NSDC. Viewed December 2013. <http://www.nsdc.org.au/about-us/the-history-of-nsdc>.

Native Women's Association of Canada (1992). Institutional abuse & public response, NWAC discussion paper (Ottawa: Native Women's Association of Canada).

New South Wales Public Charities Commission (1874). *Second and Final Report of the Commission Appointed to Inquire into and Report upon the Public Charities of the Colony*. Viewed August 2013. <http://search.records.nsw.gov.au/agencies /527;jsessionid=0A1745B7E14BA3CC11722D88C0DDDDDC>.

Nickerson, C. (2000). Québec's dark era: labeling orphans 'psychotic'. *Boston Globe*, 28 March, p. A01. Viewed December 2013. <http://rootsunknown.tripod.com/032800boston .html>.

Nix, J. E. (1972). McDougall, George Millward. Dictionary of Canadian Biography. Viewed December 2013. <http://www.biographi.ca/en/bio/mcdougall_george_millward_10E.html>.

Norsk Folkemuseum (2013). Bad Boy? Bastøy Boys' Home page. Viewed June 2013. <http://www.norskfolkemuseum.no/en/Exhibits/Previous-exhibits/Bad-boy-Bastoy-juvenile-correction-facility/>.

Nova Scotia Auditor General (1998). Report of the Auditor General 1998, chapter 13, section 13.34 (Halifax: Office of the Auditor General Nova Scotia). Viewed December 2013. <http://www.oagns.ca/index.php/publications?task=document.viewdoc&id=407>.

NWAC *see* Native Women's Association of Canada.

O'Brien, D. (1991). *Suffer Little Children: An Autobiography of a Foster Child* (St John's: Breakwater Books).

Pagé, J. C. (1961). *Les fous crient au secours, témoignage d'un ex-patient des Saint-Jean-de-Dieu* (Montréal: Éditions du Jour).

Paine, M. (2009). Child abuse fighter dies. *The Mercury*, 4 November. Viewed December 2013. <http://prelive.themercury.com.au/article/2009/11/04/107681_tasmania-news.html>.

Parragirls (2013). Parramatta Girls Home page, Parramatta Female Factory Precinct website. Viewed December 2013. <http://www.parragirls.org.au/parramatta-girls-home.php>.

Parton, N. (1979). The natural history of child abuse: a study in social problem definition. *British Journal of Social Work*, 9(4), 431–51.

Pemberton, A. and S. Reynaers (2011). The controversial nature of victim participation: therapeutic benefits in victim impact statements. In E. Erez, M. Kilching, and J. Wemmers (eds), *Therapeutic Jurisprudence and Victim Participation in Justice: International Perspectives* (Durham: Carolina Academic Press), pp. 229–48.

Penglase, J. (2005). *Orphans of the Living: Growing up in 'Care' in Twentieth-Century Australia* (Fremantle: Curtain University Books).

Penhale, B. (1999). Introduction. In N. Stanley, J. Manthorpe, and B. Penhale (eds), *Institutional Abuse: Perspectives Across the Life Course* (London: Routledge), pp. 1–15.

Perring, C. (1992). The experience and perspective of patients and care staff of the transition from hospital to community based care. In S. Ramon (ed.), *Psychiatric Hospital Closure: Myths and Realities* (London: Chapman Hall), pp. 122–68.

Perry, J. C., J. J. Sigal, S. Bouche, and N. Paré (2006). Seven institutionalized children and their adaptation in late adulthood: the children of Duplessis (Les enfants de Duplessis). *Psychiatry*, 69(4), 283–335.

PIAC *see* Public Interest Advocacy Centre.

Powers, J. L., A. Mooney, and M. Nunno (1990). Institutional abuse: a review of the literature. *Journal of Child and Youth Care*, 4(6), 81–95.

Pratt, J. (2009). From abusive families to internet predators? The rise, retraction and reconfiguration of sexual abuse as a social problem in Canada. *Current Sociology*, 57(1), 69–88.

Public Interest Advocacy Centre and Australian Human Rights Centre (2008). Supplementary submission to the Inquiry into the Stolen Generations Compensation Bill. Viewed December 2013. <http://www.piac.asn.au/publication/2008/06/080507-piacahrc-stolengens>.

Québec Ombudsman (1997). *The 'Children of Duplessis': A Time for Solidarity* (Sainte Foy: Le Protecteur du citoyen, Assemblée Nationale du Québec).

Queensland Communities, Department of (2008). Redress scheme application guidelines (Brisbane: Queensland).

Queensland Legislative Assembly (1996). Parliamentary Debates, 1 May, pp. 863–74.

Quill, G. (1993). Sexual abuse drama keeps phones ringing. *Toronto Star*, 8 December, p. D3.

Raidió Teilifís Éireann (2001). *Betrayal*, Prime Time, 28–29 November. Current affairs television program (Dublin, Ireland).

RCAP *see* Royal Commission on Aboriginal Peoples.

Read, P. (1981/2006). *The Stolen Generations: The Removal of Aboriginal Children in New South Wales 1883 to 1969* (Surrey Hills: New South Wales Department of Aboriginal Affairs).

Reimer, G., A. Bombay, L. Ellsworth, S. Fryer, and T. Logan (2010). *The Indian Residential Schools Settlement Agreement's Common Experience Payment and Healing: A Qualitative Study Exploring Impacts on Recipients*, Aboriginal Healing Foundation Research Series (Ottawa: Aboriginal Healing Foundation).

Rollinson, R. (2006). *Residential Child Care in England 1948–1975: A History and Report* (Bath: Bath Consultancy).

Ross, J. (1956). *Child Migration to Australia: Report of a Fact-Finding Mission* (London: Her Majesty's Stationery Office).

Royal Commission into Aboriginal Deaths in Custody (1991). *National Report* (Vols 1–5) (Canberra: Australian Government Publishing Service).

Royal Commission on Aboriginal Peoples (1996). *Report of the Royal Commission on Aboriginal Peoples* (Vols 1–5) (Ottawa: Canada Communication Group Publishing).

Russell, D. (2006). Affidavit sworn 25 July, Indian Residential Schools Settlement Agreement (IRSSA), Joint Motion Record, Vol IV. Viewed December 2013. <http://www.classactionservices.ca/irs/PDFs/JointMotionRecordVOL4.pdf>.

Ryan Report *see* Commission to Inquire into Child Abuse.

Sacro Restorative Justice Services for Adult Survivors Abused in Care as Children (2011). *Time to be Heard, Final Report of Pilot* (Edinburgh: The Scottish Association for the Care and Resettlement of Offenders [Sacro]). Viewed December 2013. <http://www.survivorscotland.org.uk/library/item/sacro-restorative-justice-services-for-adult-survivors-abused-in-care-as-children---time-to-be-heard-final-report-2/>.

Samson Commission *see* Commissie-Samson.

Samuels-Stewart, V. (1995). *In Our Care: Abuse and Young Offenders in Custody, An Audit of the Shelburne Youth Centre and the Nova Scotia Youth Centre – Waterville* (Halifax: Nova Scotia Department of Justice).

Scott, D. (1995). The social construction of child sexual abuse: debates about definitions and the politics of prevalence. *Psychiatry, Psychology and Law*, 2(2), 117–26.

Scott, M. B. and S. Lyman (1968). Accounts. *American Sociological Review*, 33(1), 46–62.

Scott, W. and S. Swain (2002). *Confronting Cruelty: Historical Perspectives on Child Abuse* (Melbourne: Melbourne University Press).

Senate Report or Senate inquiry *see* Australian Senate.

Shea, G. M. (1999a). *Redress Programs Relating to Institutional Child Abuse in Canada* (Ottawa: Law Commission of Canada).

Shea, G. M. (1999b). *Institutional Child Abuse in Canada: Criminal Cases* (Ottawa: Law Commission of Canada).

Shea, G. M. (1999c). *Institutional Child Abuse in Canada: Civil Cases* (Ottawa: Law Commission of Canada).

Sköld, J. (2013). Historical abuse – a contemporary issue: compiling inquiries into abuse and neglect of children in out-of-home care worldwide. *Journal of Scandinavian Studies in Criminology and Crime Prevention*, 14(1), 5–23.

Smith, M. (2010). Victim narratives of historical abuse in residential child care: do we really know what we think we know? *Qualitative Social Work*, 9(3), 303–20.

South Australia Attorney General's Department (2013). *Annual Report 2012–2013* (Adelaide: Government of South Australia).

South Australia House of Assembly (2003). Parliamentary Debates. 19 February, p. 2312.

_____ (2003). Parliamentary Debates. 22 October, p. 572.

South Australia Legislative Council (2004). Parliamentary Debates. 30 June, p. 1901.

Stanley, N., J. Manthorpe, and B. Penhale (eds) (1999). *Institutional Abuse: Perspectives Across the Life Course* (London: Routledge).

Stratton, S. G. (1995). *Report of an Independent Investigation in Respect of Incidents and Allegations of Sexual and Other Physical Abuse at Five Nova Scotia Residential Institutions* (Halifax: Nova Scotia Department of Justice).

Studsrød, I. (2012). Ulike modeller for gjenopprettende ordninger etter krenkelser, overgrep og omsorgssvikt under barnevernets omsorg (Different models for victim reparation schemes for violations, abuse and neglect under the care of child welfare services). *Sosiologi i dag*, Årgang, 42(3–4), 79–103.

Sullivan, D. and L. Tifft (2006). The healing dimension of restorative justice: a one-world body. In D. Sullivan and L. Tifft (eds), *Handbook of Restorative Justice* (New York: Routledge), pp. 1–16.

Sunga, S. (2002). The meaning of compensation in institutional abuse programs. *Journal of Law and Social Policy*, 17, 39–61.

Surviving the past (2013). Take part in criminal legal proceedings. Viewed December 2013. <http://www.survivingthepast.ca/gillsterinc/schools/44.2_Take_part_in_criminal_legal_proceedings.htm>.

Sweet, B. (2012). Picking up the pieces. *The Telegram* (St. John's), 20 July, p. A1.

Sweet, B. (2014). Compensation amount decided in last year's Mount Cashel settlement. *The Telegram* (St. John's), 20 February. Viewed March 2014. <http://www.thetelegram.com/News/Local/2014-02-20/article-3622373/Compensation-amount-decided-in-last-year%26rsquo%3Bs-Mount-Cashel-settlement/1>.

Sydney Morning Herald (2008). Rau wins $2.6m compensation. *Sydney Morning Herald*, 7 March. Viewed December 2013. <http://www.smh.com.au/news/national /rau-wins-26m-compo/2008/03/07/1204780046361.html>.

Sykes, G. and D. Matza (1957). Techniques of neutralization: a theory of delinquency. *American Sociological Review*, 22 (December), 664–70.

Sylvia's Site (2014). Mount Cashel Orphanage and the Christian Brothers. Viewed February 2014. <http://www.theinquiry.ca/wordpress/rc-scandal/mount-cashel/>.

Szablicki, R. (2010). A personal journey towards healing and redress. In R. Hil and E. Branigan (eds), *Surviving Care: Achieving Justice and Healing for the Forgotten Australians* (Robina: Bond University), pp. 65–77.

Tasmania Health and Human Services, Department of (2013). Abuse in State Care Support Service, Information for Applicants (Hobart: Tasmanian Government).

Tasmania Premier and Cabinet, Department of (2008). *Report of the Stolen Generations Assessor: Stolen Generations of Aboriginal Children Act 2006* (Hobart: Department of Premier and Cabinet).

Tasmanian Legislative Assembly (2006). Hansard, Tuesday 28 November, pp. 1–28.

Tasmanian Ombudsman (J. O'Grady) (2004). *Listen to the Children: Review of Claims of Abuse from Adults in State Care as Children* (Hobart: Office of the Ombudsman).

Tasmanian Ombudsman (R. Bingham) (2006). *Final Report – Phase 2: Review of Claims of Abuse from Adults in State Care as Children* (Hobart: Office of the Ombudsman).

Terry, K.J., M.L. Smith, K. Schuth, J. Kelly, B. Vollman, and C. Massey (2011). *Causes and Context of the Sexual Abuse Crisis in the Catholic Church* (Washington, DC: United States Conference of Catholic Bishops).

Tomison, A. M. (2001). A history of child protection: back to the future? *Family Matters*, 60, 46–57.

Toronto Star (1992). Sexual assaults alleged at school for Deaf. 3 March. Viewed December 2013. <http://pqasb.pqarchiver.com/thestar/doc/436599936 .html?FMT=&FMTS=&type=current&date=&author=&pub=&edition=&startpage=&desc=>.

Torpey, J. (2006). *Making Whole What Has Been Smashed: On Reparations Politics* (Cambridge: Harvard University Press).

TRC *see* Truth and Reconciliation Commission of Canada.

Truth and Reconciliation Commission of Canada (2012). *They Came for the Children: Canada, Aboriginal Peoples, and Residential Schools* (Winnipeg: Truth and Reconciliation Commission of Canada).

Tyler, T. (1990). *Why People Obey the Law: Procedural Justice, Legitimacy, and Compliance* (New Haven: Yale University Press).

Tyler, T. (1992). The psychological consequences of judicial procedures: implications for civil commitment hearings. *Southern Methodist University Law Review*, 46, 433–48.

Ulbrich, J. (1990). Archbishop offers resignation in sex abuse scandal, *The Free Lance Star*, 21 July, p. 13.

United States Senate (1979). *Hearings on Abuse and Neglect of Children in Institutions* (Washington, DC: Government Printing Office).

Until Someone Listens (1999). Documentary film. Producer/director Laura Sky (Ontario: Skyworks Charitable Foundation and Commissioning Partner, Grandview Survivors Support Group).

Van der Merwe, H. (2009). Delivering justice during transition: research challenges. In H. van der Merwe, V. Baxter, and A. Chapman (eds), *Assessing the Impact of Transitional Justice: Challenges for Empirical Research* (Washington, DC: United States Institute of Peace), pp. 115–42.

Van Krieken, R. (1991). *Children and the State: Social Control and the Formation of Australian Child Welfare* (Sydney: Allen and Unwin).

Van Ness, D. and K. Strong (2010). *Restoring Justice: An Introduction to Restorative Justice* (Cincinnati: Anderson Publishing).

Vienneau, R. (2008/translated 2012). *Collusion: The Dark History of the Duplessis Orphans*. Available in English as a Kindle e-book (Amazon Digital Services; Michel Anctil, editor; JKG Davidson, translator).

Walsh, K. (2010). From advocacy to policy. In R. Hil and E. Branigan (eds), *Surviving Care: Achieving Justice and Healing for Forgotten Australians* (Robina: Bond University Press), pp. 173–89.

Ware, S-A. (2004). Contemporary anti-memorials and national identity in the Victorian landscape. *Colonial Post,* Special Issue of *Journal of Australian Studies,* 81, 121–39; notes, 223–4.

Ware, S-A. (2005). *Anti-Memorials: Rethinking the Landscape of Memory*. PhD thesis (Melbourne: RMIT University).

Watson, I. (2011). Findings of a survey of Queensland Forgotten Australians, Vol. 2 (Brisbane: RPR Consulting).

Webster, R. (2005). *The Secret of Bryn Estyn* (Oxford: Orwell Press).

Weisblott, M. (2011). Oprah Winfrey's talk show affected Canadian scandal, literature and activism. *Canada News, Daily Brew*, 18 May. Viewed December 2013. <https://ca.news.yahoo.com/blogs/dailybrew/oprah-winfrey-talk-show-affected-canadian-scandal-literature-191231918.html>.

Wemmers, J. (2010). The meaning of justice for victims. In S. G. Shoham, P. Knepper, and M. Kett (eds), *International Handbook of Victimology* (Boca Raton: CRC Press), pp. 27–42.

Western Australia Communities, Department of (2009). Redress WA Newsletter No 2, November 2009. Government of Western Australia.

_____ (2011). Redress WA Guidelines, as amended 18 May. Government of Western Australia.

Western Australia Minister for Communities (2010). Media statement, Start of Redress WA *ex gratia* payment offers, 17 February. Government of Western Australia.

Winter, G. (1990). *The Report of the Archdiocesan Commission of Enquiry into the Sexual Abuse of Children by Members of the Clergy* (Vols 1–2) (Newfoundland: Archdiocese of St John's).

Winter, S. (2009). Australia's *ex gratia* redress. *Australian Indigenous Law Review,* 13(1), 49–61.

Wolfe, D. A., P.G. Jaffe, J.L. Jetté, and S.E. Poisson (2002). *Child Abuse in Community Institutions and Organizations: Improving Public and Professional Understanding* (Ottawa: Law Commission of Canada).

Wolmar, C. (2000). *Forgotten Children: The Secret Abuse Scandal in Children's Homes* (London: Vision Paperbacks).

Wood, J. R. T. (1997). *Royal Commission into the New South Wales Police Force, Final Report* (Sydney: The Government of the State of New South Wales).

The World Today (2012). ABC Radio program episode with reporter Rebecca Brice, 13 November. <http://www.abc.net.au/worldtoday/content/2012/s3631494.htm>.

Cases and Legislation

Muir v. Alberta (1996) 132 DLR (4th) 695
Re: Christian Brothers of Ireland in Canada (2004), 69 O.R. (3d) 507 (S.C.J.)
Trevorrow v South Australia (No 5) (2007) 98 SASR 136
Child Welfare Act 1960 (Tas)
Indian Act, SC 1894, c 32
Infants' Welfare Act 1935 (Tas)
Sexual Sterilization Act, SA 1928, c 37
Stolen Generation Compensation Bill 2008 (Cth)
Stolen Generations of Aboriginal Children Act 2006 (Tas)

Note: Citations reflect different formats used in Canadian and Australian jurisdictions.

Index

Printed and bound by CPI Group (UK) Ltd, Croydon, CR0 4YY